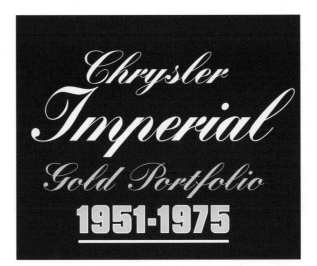

Compiled by R M Clarke

ISBN 1 85520 6625

BROOKLANDS BOOKS LTD.
P.O. BOX 146, COBHAM,
SURREY, KT11 1LG. UK
sales@brooklands-books.com

www.brooklands-books.com

A-CRIMGP

Printed in China

ACKNOWLEDGEMENTS

We published our first book on Imperials in the mid '90s and it subsequently went out of print last year. Because of the popularity of these luxurious cars we have doubled the page count in this new book and upgraded it to a Gold Portfolio and included, where possible, articles etc. in color.

Our books are printed in small numbers and now with over 400 titles are one of the main reference works for those that indulge in the hobby of automobile restoration. We exist because firstly there is a need by enthusiasts for this information and secondly because the publishers of the world's leading motoring journals generously support us by allowing us to include their copyright articles. We are indebted in this instance to the management of *Auto Topics, Autocar, Automobile Topics, Autosport, Car Facts, Car Life, Car Review, Cars, Classic American, Chrysler Division, Complete Road Test, Mechanix Illustrated, Motor Life, Motor Trend, Motor Trend Buyer's Guide, Motorcade, Road Test, Special Interest Autos, Speed Age, Wheels* and the *World Car Catalogue*.

We are also indebted to Tony Beadle, the motoring journalist, for his observations below and also for generously supplying our front cover photograph.

R. M. Clarke

Before Imperial was set up as a completely autonomous marque in 1955, the name had designated it as the most luxurious model of the Chrysler range for many years. In fact, the use of the Imperial name by Chrysler goes back to the very early days of the company, 1926 to be precise. As well as its reputation for superior comfort and elegant furnishings, the Imperial also had a history of performance. In 1929 for example, an Imperial roadster was chosen as the Pace Car for the Indianapolis 500.

In the immediate post-war years however, the Imperial was little more than a fancy Chrysler with lots of extras. It might have been slightly larger and a bit more luxurious, but the Imperial's styling was too similar to the less expensive Chrysler models to make it really distinctive. That changed when Chrysler Corporation split off Imperial as a separate division and attempted to create a totally different identity for those cars bearing the eagle crest.

In the beginning, it seemed to be working. The gorgeous 1955 and '56 models, with their unique free-standing taillights on top of gracefully sweeping rear fins, proved that stylish automobiles didn't need to be garish. The Imperial image received a tremendous boost from these designs and sales started to climb.

1957 was the best year ever for Imperial and it's not hard to see why. Even when surrounded by the glittering chrome and outlandish fins of other makes, the new Imperial definitely stood out from the rest. The annual sales figure of over 35,700 cars was more than triple that of the previous year and the marque's future looked assured. Unfortunately, a recession in the US economy throughout 1958 saw Imperial sales more than halve and, although they would recover somewhat, apart from an occasional peak, production averaged around 18,000 units for most of the remaining years.

The problem was that, despite some truly innovative styling, Imperial was never really able to shake off its close association with Chrysler - the two names were inextricably linked in the minds of the American car buying public. The energy crises of the early 1970s hit sales of all big luxury cars, but hit Imperial sales worst of all. Once production dipped below 10,000 units, the writing was on the wall. The last Imperial, a LeBaron four-door hardtop, rolled off the end of the assembly line at the Jefferson Avenue factory in Detroit on 12th June 1975.

Tony Beadle

CONTENTS

MINT
Imperial

Is this the only example of a '51 Imperial Convertible residing in Europe? Quite likely. No wonder we felt the need to head to Sweden to see this beauty for ourselves

WORDS & PHOTOGRAPHY: ERIK STIGSSON

WITH their monstrous tail fins and typically period styling, Chrysler's late Fifties models have always been popular wth enthusiasts in Sweden. Early Fifties cars from the same company however, have been largely forgotten over the years. Those Swedish enthusiasts, it appears, just don't know what they're missing.

Happily though, some rather impressive examples of Chryslers from the early part of the 1950s are now starting to appear in Sweden, one of the most fascinating being Peter Lindberg's 1951 Imperial. As soon as we caught sight of this classic from the Chrysler stable, we just knew it had the makings of a front cover car ...

It took a while for some of America's all-new post-war car designs to actually come about. Immediately after World War II, with demand for new cars running at phenomenal levels, most American companies concentrated on 'stop gap' pre-war designs, making only minor changes for the post-war market. Indeed, that's exactly what Chrysler did, its first totally new model line-up not appearing until 1949. Even then, the newcomers' appearance used a fairly discreet and sober style, Chrysler being known mainly for its quality and solidity rather than any kind of raciness.

The new Chrysler range for '49 may not have been totally revolutionary, but it still carried such modernities as a 25 per cent bigger windscreen and a massive new grille, making it obvious that, yes, these were completely new models.

Chrysler resisted any temptations it may have had to introduce a new engine though, instead keeping the reliable flathead 'eights' of earlier years, the largest version coming in 323cu.in. form for an output of 135 horsepower.

This policy of not updating the engine range though, turned out to be something of a mistake on Chrysler's part. Even the arrival of GM's OHV V8 for use by Oldsmobile and Cadillac did not seem to worry the powers-that-be; Chrysler assumed their customers would prefer good quality rather than outright performance. Unfortunately for Chrysler, such an assumption proved to be wrong. Once a faithful Chrysler buyer has test-driven a brand new Cadillac with its powerful 331cu.in. overhead-valve engine and 160 horsepower output, the temptation proved simply too big. Any previous faithfulness instantly disappeared and Cadillac's sales increased as a result.

Chrysler realised that something had to be done, and their engineers worked overtime to ensure an all-new Chrysler engine was on the drawing board within a comparatively short space of time. By the time the 1951 model range appeared, Chrysler was ready with its deadly weapon: the Hemi.

The Chrysler Corporation was justifiably proud of its completely new 331cu.in. Hemi V8. They had tested it thoroughly and knew that it was fit for the Chrysler-GM battle. It had enormous potential, with an output of 180bhp even in its first year; that was 45bhp more than the old flathead 'eight' and a full 20bhp more than Cadillac's own.

Suddenly, Chrysler's were among the fastest cars in America, particularly the new Saratoga model which was based on the smaller Windsor chassis but equipped with the new 331cu.in. Hemi engine; it was one of the new kings of the road. Sure, Chrysler had built fast cars during the Twenties, but the company had then focused on launching luxury, quality models instead. Suddenly though, thirty years on, Chrysler performance was back with a vengeance.

The new Hemi was not

MINT *Imperial*

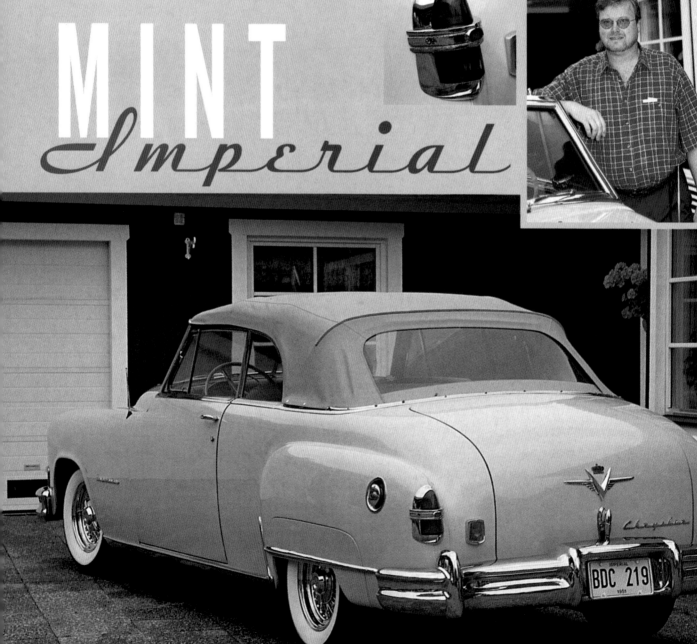

the only technical modernity of Chrysler's 1951 models. Other new additions included power steering, power windows and ventilated drum brakes. Naturally though, it was the high performance of the Hemi engine that grabbed the headlines.

The effort put into the Hemi by Chrysler engineers soon brought results. In 1951, Bill Sterling won the Stock Car class of the Mexican Road Race with an almost completely standard Saratoga. It was simply fantastic; Chrysler had not experienced success like that in a long, long time. But despite huge interest from the American public, the company decided not to keep too high a profile on the race tracks; it still wanted to be known first and foremost as a quality, luxury brand. The performance, it decided, should be something extra, not the main attraction.

Not until the new – and what would subsequently become the legendary – 300-series arrived in 1955 did Chrysler really go in for racing in a big way ... but that's another story. Since then, of course, the various incarnations of the 300-series have gained a major following worldwide, and it was a late Fifties' Chrysler 300 Convertible that Peter Lindberg and his friend, Christer Brunnstrom, were searching for back in '95 on a trip to California.

'Christer and I found an advert for a 1959 Chrysler 300 Convertible that was for sale, so off we went to have a look at it', recalls Swedish-based Peter.

The car was not in the kind of condition the guys had hoped for, but in the same garage they spotted a 1951 Imperial Convertible owned by the father of the chap who was selling the 300. Peter took a closer look at the Imperial and was immediately taken by her. He tried to persuade the owner to sell. He could then take it home to Sweden, safe in the knowledge that he'd never come across another one of its kind on the Swedish show scene.

Initially, the guy would not even consider parting with the Imperial. He had planned to attend to some minor details on it and then to start using it on the road once more. So Peter mounted a personal 'campaign of persuasion' and, after a while, the owner gave in and agreed to sell his beloved Imperial. It was Peter's lucky day.

The Imperial had already been extensively renovated some years earlier, although some relatively minor work needed to be taken care of before it could be called pristine once again, as Peter explains: 'Among the many things we ordered for the car was a new interior and a new top before it was shipped to Sweden. It made sense to have such work done before bringing the car home.'

Special Chrysler wire spoke wheels have also been added since Peter became proud owner of the Imperial. The superb 331cu.in. Hemi engine – still pumping out 180bhp – runs beautifully, while the 'Fluid Matic Drive' transmission is as good as the day it first engaged gear.

The overall feel of the Imperial now is of a car that has been extremely well cared for during its life, whilst benefitting from sympathetic restoration in later years. It still feels 'tight', a tribute to both these factors.

A 1951 Imperial Convertible may not be as dramatic looking as a late Fifties' machine, but it manages to combine elegance and style in a way that those later models do not, despite their bold and startling designs. Strange then, that the '51 Imperial represents a period of Chrysler's history that, up until now, has perhaps not been fully appreciated by our friends over in Sweden. After seeing Peter's superb example of an Imperial Convertible, we've a feeling this may well change in the future. **CA**

> **THE OVERALL FEEL OF THE IMPERIAL NOW IS OF A CAR THAT HAS BEEN EXTREMELY WELL CARED FOR DURING ITS LIFE, WHILST BENEFITTING FROM SYMPATHETIC RESTORATION IN LATER YEARS**

1951 CHRYSLER IMPERIAL

drive report

LOW-KEY HIGH PERFORMANCE

AFTER a decade of dormancy, the Imperial flowered again in 1951. Since 1926, Walter P. Chrysler had used the Imperial name on his company's proudest products, including some custom-bodied creations that rivaled Cadillac, Lincoln, and Packard for elegance. But by the time Mr. Chrysler died in 1940, a wave of post-Airflow conservatism had turned his flagship into the "Crown Imperial" — a stately but ungainly line of limousines on a long, long 145-inch wheelbase.

In 1941, Chrysler assembled just 894 "Crown Imperial Town Sedans" on the 127.5-inch New Yorker chassis — a tantalizingly brief glimpse into the future of the nameplate. But after that,

by John F. Katz
photos by Roy Query

Chrysler didn't offer another standard-wheelbase Imperial until it had debuted an all-new generation of automobiles in 1949.

The new look of those '49s had been conceived by clay model supervisor Charles G. Walker, but no one who saw them could doubt that Highland Park's stylists still answered to the engineers — and to President K.T. Keller, who

personally approved all body designs. And Keller's oft-quoted remark about people who still wore hats while driving pretty well summarized *his* styling philosophy (see sidebar, page 28). At least the new Chryslers traded the porcine roundness of the 1946-48 models for a crisper, more up-to-date appearance, with more glass and a more aggressive stance.

Most of the line appeared in February 1949, followed by the Crown Imperial in September. Again, this was a stretch-wheelbase version of the standard Chrysler, distinguished externally by unique rear fenders and taillamps and some unique trim. This time, however, Chrysler also offered an *Imperial* (no

"Crown") sedan, built on the new 131½-inch New Yorker chassis and featuring custom paint and interiors by former Chrysler design chief Ray Dietrich. Dietrich, then an independent coachbuilder in Grand Rapids, Michigan, turned out 50 of the hand-built cars — and later told historian Richard Langworth that he could have sold many more were it not for a continuing dispute with a local union.

The standard-wheelbase Imperial sedan joined Chrysler's production line-up in mid-1950, now sporting wrap-around rear glass and some interior touches from the Dietrich custom to set it apart from same-size New Yorkers. And while the corporation had sold 135 Imperials (sedans and limousines) in the abbreviated 1949 model year, now 11,064 rolled off the lines between May and January.

No doubt encouraged by this success, Chrysler expanded the Imperial range for 1951, supplementing the four-door sedan with a club coupe, a fashionable two-door hardtop, and — the subject of our driveReport — the first cataloged Imperial convertible since 1938 (see *SIA #132*).

Chrysler had begun the model year late again — on February 9, 1951 — but the new season had brought revised front sheet metal and a somewhat softer look for all of the corporation's products. Gone were the bluff, vertical faces of 1949-50; new engine hoods bulged less and sloped back from the top of the grille, while the grille opening itself angled downward slightly toward the pavement. The change benefited the Imperial especially, which now sported its own grille and a slotted bumper that further lightened its front end. Toward the rear, skirted fenders emphasized

Above: Typical of the quality touches found in Imperials of this era are the cloisonné enamel crowns on the big wheel covers. Left: Stainless steel splash shields accent rear fenders. Below: Heavy horizontal bands emphasize width of the Imp.

1951 IMPERIAL

Above: Big V proclaims hemi power lurking under the hood. *Below left:* Chrome trim continues deep into grille recesses. *Below right:* Taillamps are exclusive to the Imperials.

Chairman Keller Speaks on Styling

In *Chrysler & Imperial: The Postwar Years*, Richard Langworth reproduced a rather telling excerpt from then-Chrysler President Kaufman T. Keller's famous 1948 address at the Stanford University School of Business. "Automobiles," said Keller, "are looked at and admired. The buyer is proud of his car's symphony of line; its coloring and trim express his taste; he welcomes the applause of his friends and neighbors. But he bought the car to ride in, and for his wife and children and friends to ride in.... Many of

you Californians may have outgrown the habit, but there are parts of the country containing millions of people, where both the men and the ladies are in the habit of getting behind the wheel, or in the back seat, wearing hats."

Langworth has aptly compared the '49-54 Chryslers to the postwar Mercedes-Benz. In both cases, a genuine interest in practicality, comfort, and safety seemed to produce, quite naturally, automobiles of handsome proportions and understated elegance.

the Imperial's quiet elegance, complemented by a unique rear bumper and taillamps. If still not exciting, the Imperial at least looked solid, handsome, and tasteful.

More significantly, 1951 Chryslers and Imperials featured a long list of mechanical innovations, headed up by the new hemi-head "FirePower" V-8. Displacing the same 331 cubic inches as Cadillac's valves-in-a-line V-8, the Chrysler "Hemi" developed 20 more horsepower, for a total of 180 bhp at 4,000 rpm. It also made more horsepower per cubic inch than any other engine then mass-produced in the United States. And it ran on regular fuel — while the Caddy, and the new V-8 Oldsmobile as well, required premium.

At the same time, Chrysler unveiled its new "Fluid-Torque" transmission — another tentative step toward a fully automatic drive. Since 1939, some Chrysler models had offered "Fluid drive," which combined a simple hydraulic coupling with a conventional clutch, backed up by a four-speed synchronized transmission with a combination of electric, hydraulic, and manual controls. Renamed "Prestomatic" in 1949, this semi-automatic concoction appeared as standard equipment on all eight-cylinder Chryslers. The Fluid-Torque system of 1951 featured revised gearing and replaced the hydraulic coupling with a four-element torque converter for better acceleration with even less shifting. The old Prestomatic — now called Fluid-Matic — remained the standard set-up for Saratogas, New Yorkers, and Imperials; Fluid-Torque came standard on Crown Imperials and, as the model year progressed, became available on other V-8 models. Only the six-cylinder Windsor could be ordered with a conventional three-speed stick.

Also in '51, electric window lifts replaced the electro-hydraulic units used since before the war. New "Oriflow" shock absorbers provided more progressive damping, which improved handling on rough roads without sacrificing ride quality. Finally, Chrysler's "Hydraguide" power steering — an industry first — wasn't integrated with the steering gear as a modern system would be, but instead acted directly on the Pitman arm. Still, it permitted a 20 percent faster steering ratio on the road with less steering effort in the parking lot.

Chrysler called the new Imperial "the finest car and the greatest performing car built in America" — and with some

Why a Hemi?

Of the many factors that engineers must consider when designing a combustion chamber, two of the most important are the ratio of surface area to volume, and the distance the flame must travel from the spark plug to the most distant point in the chamber.

The first, the question of surface area vs. volume, impacts directly on the engine's thermal efficiency. Put simply, the larger the surface of the chamber, the more heat can leak out through the walls. And every bit of heat that leaks out through the walls leaves less energy in the chamber to force the piston down the cylinder.

Flame travel affects efficiency less directly. But the shorter the path, the sooner the flame gets there. And the sooner the flame gets there, the less time there is for shock waves to develop, or for glowing carbon deposits to light off their own competing flame fronts. So a shorter flame path provides resistance to "ping" or "knock," which in turn allows a higher compression ratio and/or a lower-octane fuel. And since higher compression directly improves thermal efficiency, an engine with a shorter flame path can potentially produce *more* power while using *less* fuel — and cheaper fuel at that. And that's about the closest thing to free lunch that you'll find, anywhere.

Based on these factors alone, the ideal combustion chamber would be a sphere, with the spark plug suspended at the center. The surface area-to-volume ratio would be as small as natural law allows. (This is why soap bubbles prefer a spherical form, incidentally.) So would the flame path. There just wouldn't be any place to put the piston.

But you can approximate this unobtainable ideal with a *hemi*-spherical chamber (think of a soap bubble floating in your bathtub) — a dome over the piston, with the spark plug inserted through the top of the dome. This provides about the smallest surface area and shortest flame path practically possible, and almost as a bonus, leaves ample room for relatively large valves, placed opposite each other for optimal breathing at high rpm.

Chrysler never claimed to have invented the hemi, and officially took credit only for "developing it and perfecting it...on a production-built automobile." In fact, the first imported automobile to win the Indianapolis 500 — Jules Goux's 1913 Peugeot — did so on hemi-power. Later, Harry Miller built American hemis for Indy, and Stutz and Duesenberg built hemi straight-eights for the street. But Chrysler gave the world its first mass-produced, hemi-head V-8.

The designers of racing engines had generally used dual overhead camshafts to operate the hemi-head's widely splayed valves. Chrysler Engine Development Chief W.E. Drinkard and Assistant Chief Engineer M.L. Charpentier experimented briefly with a twin-cam straight-six, but for the production V-8 they avoided multiple camshafts by installing a double row of rocker arms — shorter for the intake valves than for the exhausts — prodded by pushrods and a single camshaft in the block. They *did* borrow a bit of racing practice when they gave each valve *two* concentric, cadmium-plated valve springs. Since two springs of differing diameter won't resonate at the same speed, the Hemi could rev higher without risking valve float.

The engineers also designed in the highest valve lift — 0.378 inches for intake, 0.362 inches for exhaust — of any ohv engine in the US industry. Manifold design took full advantage of the hemi-head's breathing potential, and each of the carburetor's two venturis fed one bank of cylinders exclusively.

Chrysler's first experiments with alternative head designs began as early as 1937. Since 1943, Drinkard and Charpentier had also been developing a short-stroke V-8 block, first as a military project but then for postwar consumer production. And although they had conceived it as a separate project, it didn't take them long to decide to mate the hemi heads to this block. Because of the short stroke, Chrysler claimed, a piston in the Hemi would travel only 148,500 feet in 100 miles of driving — compared to 199,500 feet in the Chrysler straight-eight. And the bigger bore left even more room for big, free-breathing valves. Like the Cadillac and Oldsmobile V-8s that appeared in 1949, the Hemi featured a five-bearing crank with slipper pistons, and proved both lighter and more rigid than the generation of engines it would replace.

	'50 Chrysler L-8	'51 Chrysler V-8	'51 Cadillac V-8
Bore, in.	3¼	3¹³⁄₁₆	3¹³⁄₁₆
Stroke, in.	4⅞	3⅝	3⅝
Displacement	323.5 cu. in.	331.1 cu. in.	331.1 cu. in.
Compression	7.25:1	7.5:1	7.5:1
Torque @ rpm	270 @ 1,600	312 @ 2,000	312 @ 1,800
Bhp @ rpm	135 @ 3,200	180 @ 4,000	160 @ 3,800
Bhp/cu. in.	.417	.543	.483
Weight, lb.*	1,002	933	903
Pounds/bhp	7.42	5.18	5.64

* with flywheel, transmission, and all accessories

As much as possible, Chrysler exploited the natural symmetry of the hemi to simplify mass production. The right and left heads were interchangeable, and the intake manifold reversible front to back. Still, with its double rows of non-interchangeable rockers and pushrods, the Chrysler Hemi weighed more and cost more to manufacture than the more conservative and conventional V-8s offered by the competition. The lunch wasn't free after all.

In a paper presented to the Society of Automotive Engineers in 1951, Chrysler engine designer James C. Zeder (brother of pioneering Chrysler engineer Fred Zeder) actually pointed out the Hemi's potential for "preserving natural resources" — since it extracted more power from less, and less highly refined, gasoline. In those days, however, natural resources cost less than materials and manufacturing hours. In 1955, Chrysler debuted a companion line of "polyspherical" V-8s, whose staggered valves required only a single row of rockers. And by 1959, both these and the Hemis had given way to wedge-head, valve-in-line V-8s — just like the competition's. Of course, the Hemi returned in 426-cubic-inch form in the sixties — but only as a limited-run, ultimate-performance option.

But the mass-produced hemi head lived on in Italy, with twin-cam, four-cylinder examples introduced by Alfa Romeo in 1954 and by Fiat in 1967. Today, nearly every performance-oriented engine on the planet burns its fuel in a hemispherical combustion chamber. Even Chrysler's.

GROSS HORSEPOWER

HORSEPOWER vs. ENGINE SPEED-RPM

— CHRYSLER FIREPOWER ENGINE (331 CU. IN.)
-- COMPETITIVE 331 CU. IN. ENGINE
-·- 1950 SPITFIRE 8 CYL. ENGINE (324 CU. IN.)
-··- COMPETITIVE 304 CU. IN. ENGINE

GROSS TORQUE

TORQUE-LB.-FT. vs. ENGINE SPEED-RPM

— CHRYSLER FIREPOWER ENGINE (331 CU. IN.)
-- COMPETITIVE 331 CU. IN. ENGINE
-·- 1950 SPITFIRE 8 CYL. ENGINE (324 CU. IN.)
-··- COMPETITIVE 304 CU. IN. ENGINE

57.1 inches

131.5 inches

1951 Chrysler Imperial Convertible

Base price, conv.	$4,427
Standard equipment	Electric lifts for front windows, M-6 semi-automatic trans.; Leather upholstery, white sidewall tires
Options on dR car	Fluid-Torque drive; Hydraguide power steering*; eight-tube radio; heater; undercoating; spare tire
Price as tested	$4,700

* Different sources disagree about whether power steering was standard or optional on standard-wheelbase Imperials. It appears as an option on a sales document pertaining to this particular car. But owner Chip Loree told us he's *never* seen a '51 Imperial without it.

ENGINE
Type	V-8
Bore x stroke	3.81 inches x 3.63 inches
Displacement	331.1 cubic inches
Compression ratio	7.5:1
Horsepower @ rpm	180 @ 4,000
Torque @ rpm	312 lb. ft. @ 2,000
Taxable horsepower	46.5
Main bearings	5
Valve gear	Ohv
Valve lifters	Hydraulic
Lubrication system	Pressure to main, rod, and cam shaft bearings; metered pressure to tappets
Carburetor	Carter WCD-8305 2-bbl downdraft
Fuel system	mechanical pump
Cooling system	Pressure, centrifugal pump
Electrical system	6-volt, positive ground
Exhaust system	Single

TRANSMISSION
Type	"Fluid-Torque" 4-speed semi-automatic with torque converter
Ratios: 1st	3.28:1
2nd	2.04:1
3rd	1.61:1
Fourth	1.00:1
Reverse	3.69:1
Torque converter, max. ratio at stall	2.34:1

CLUTCH
Type	Borg and Beck 10.25-inch single dry disc

DIFFERENTIAL
Type	Hypoid
Ratio	3.54:1
Drive axles	Semi-floating

STEERING
Type	Gemmer worm & roller
Ratio	16.4:1
Turning diameter	N/A
Turns, lock to lock	3.5

BRAKES
Type	4-wheel hydraulic with vacuum servo; front, 12x2-inch drum with dual cylinders; rear, 12x2-inch drum
Total swept area	201.1 square inches
Parking brake	Mechanical, "Easi-Lock" 7-inch drum on transmission output shaft

CONSTRUCTION
Type	Box section frame with central X-member; separate body
Body type	Welded steel stampings
Body style	2-door, 6-seat convertible coupe

SUSPENSION
Front	Independent, upper and lower control arms, coil springs, anti-roll bar
Rear	Live axle with tapered leaf springs
Shock absorbers	Chrysler Oriflow, straddle-mounted in rear
Wheels	15 x 6, Safety-Rim stamped steel
Tires	8.20 x 15 four-ply Goodyear Super Cushion

WEIGHTS AND MEASURES
Wheelbase	131.5 inches
Overall length	212.6 inches
Overall width	75.8 inches
Overall height	65.2 inches
Front track	57.1 inches
Rear track	58.3 inches
Min. road clearance	N/A
Shipping weight	4,570 pounds

INTERIOR MEASUREMENTS
Leg room	42.3 inches front, 30.8 inches rear
Head room	38.2 inches front, 36.4 inches rear
Seat height	7.3 inches front, 9.7 inches rear
Trunk capacity	8 cubic feet

CAPACITIES
Crankcase	5 quarts
Cooling system	25 quarts (with heater)
Fuel tank	20 gallons
Transmission	10.5 quarts
Rear axle	3.5 pints

CALCULATED DATA
Horsepower per c.i.d.	.54
Weight per hp	25.4 pounds
Weight per c.i.d.	13.8
P.S.I. (brakes)	22.7
Production	650

This page: *Imperial's flanks are characterized by very restrained use of brightwork.* **Facing page, top:** *When pushed, there's scads of understeer.* **Below left:** *Rear passenger room is quite adequate.* **Below right:** *Rear passengers get their own lighter along with ashtray.*

1951 IMPERIAL

justification. Suddenly, Highland Park was selling modern luxury cars with V-8 engines, power steering, power windows, and a nearly automatic transmission. And the Imperial convertible led the lineup with — after the stretch-wheelbase Crown Imperial limo — the highest base price and lowest production of any Chrysler product.

Unfortunately, the material shortages caused by the Korean War caught up with Chrysler the following year. The 1952 models, introduced in December 1951, differed from their immediate predecessors only in minor details — except that a number of low-volume nameplate-and-body-style combinations had disappeared from the lineup. Among them was the magnificent Imperial convertible.

There wouldn't be another open-top Imperial until 1957. But that's another story, for another time.

Driving Impressions

Eugene Mehrhof had sold Chryslers in Bloomfield, New Jersey, for nearly as long as Walter P. made Chryslers to sell. And he always saved the best trade-ins for his family. So when great-nephew Chip Loree first learned to drive in 1968, he inherited one of these hand-picked cream puffs from his grandmother.

"My first car ended up being a '52 Saratoga," Chip told us, "which was the first hemi engine in the small body." The car's performance astounded Chip's college-age contemporaries, most of whom were equally surprised to learn that Chrysler had built a hemi-head *anything* before the 426-cubic-inch monsters of 1964.

"Of course, I migrated to Imperials when I became a collector," Chip continued. "But I've had a lot of cars — all Chrysler products." His collection currently encompasses three '51 Imperial convertibles and a '53 Imperial hardtop.

Chip bought our driveReport car in Indianapolis in 1987, from another collector who had dismantled it and then lost interest in the project. Three years of restoration brought it back to the pristine state you see here.

Slipping in behind the wheel is as effortless as Mr. Keller intended it to be. A complete set of gauges surrounds the great, semi-circular speedometer; unfortunately, the elegant gold-on-gray color scheme hampers readability somewhat. And the accessory controls, while well-differentiated for the era, require some reaching. The seat is a big, overstuffed sofa, comfortable enough, but bolt upright and lacking any contour whatsoever.

Betting on the Saratoga

The Imperial wasn't the only Chrysler nameplate to enjoy a renaissance in 1951. Since 1946, the Saratoga had been Chrysler's most basic eight-cylinder model, built on a New Yorker wheelbase but trimmed more like the cheaper Windsor. In straight-eight days, the Saratoga *needed* the longer wheelbase so the engine would fit. But in July 1951, taking advantage of the compact dimensions of the new V-8, Chrysler shrank the Saratoga down to the 125½-inch wheelbase of the six-cylinder Windsor.

This may sound at first like a demotion in status, but with the same horsepower as a New Yorker and some 250 fewer pounds of frame and sheet metal to accelerate, the Saratoga quickly emerged as Chrysler's star performer. Driven by Bill Sterling in the 1951 Carrera Panamericana, a Saratoga finished first in the big-displacement class and third overall, just eight minutes behind Alberto Ascari's Ferrari.

Even *Road & Track* took notice. By side-stepping the clutch and manually shifting the semi-automatic transmission, *R&T* hustled a new Saratoga Club Coupe from 0 to 60 mph in ten seconds flat — quicker, the editors noted, than an XK-120 Jaguar. Letting the transmission drop into fourth at 65 mph, they crossed the quarter mile in 18.7 seconds and measured a two-way-average top speed of 104 mph. "*Road & Track*'s test crew seldom gets excited about American cars," wrote the jaded road-testers. "The Chrysler is an exception. While it has its faults, and some of them are serious, we feel that it is outstanding among local efforts.... The acceleration was startling.... When you touch that throttle, you know something mighty impressive is happening under the hood."

Engineering an Achievement

This intimidatingly elaborate chart first appeared in *Motor Trend* in February 1952, when the magazine bestowed its Engineering Achievement Award on Chrysler. Comparing 15 cars in 13 performance categories, a Chrysler New Yorker scored highest in seven, and tied for first with Cadillac in two others, to obtain the highest overall score by a comfortable margin.

Oddly, DeSoto, Plymouth, and Chevrolet do not appear on the chart; Editor Griffith Borgeson noted, but did not explain, their absence in the accompanying text. Perhaps those marques simply didn't make *MT*'s 1951 press-car schedule. Certainly, none of them could have rivaled the Chrysler's modern engine.

We should note that the New Yorker scored highest in ton-miles per gallon — an important measure of efficiency — only because *MT* had leveled the playing field by excluding any fuel economy figures obtained by using an overdrive gear. In OD, Borgeson noted, a Lincoln would have beaten the Chrysler (which didn't offer an overdrive option). The one category in which the Chrysler fell flat on its face — percent of brake horsepower at wheels — probably tells us more about the efficiency (or lack thereof) of the Fluid-Matic drive than anything else.

Still, the editor concluded, "Chrysler had built a car that combines safety, economy and outstanding performance. It is not perfect — yet it is closer to the goal than any other family automobile currently produced in America."

Average Braking Distance in feet	Average Fuel Consumption in mpg	Ton Miles Per Gallon	Average Acceleration in sec.	Accel. over stdg. 1/4 mile in secs.	Average top speed in mph	Maximum Road HP	% of bhp at wheels	Dollars per road HP	Lb. per road hp	Max. Torque in lb./ft.	Road HP per cu. in.	Max. BMEP in PSI	Total Points
Chrysler 90.2	Studebaker 21.41	Chrysler 39.9	Chrysler 10.63	Chrysler 19.32	Chrysler 102.27	Chrysler 104	Oldsmobile 68.1	Stude. 30.8	Chrysler 42.7	Cadillac Chrysler 312	Studebaker .448	Cadillac Chrysler 142.0	Chrysler 176
Nash Statesman 91.4	Kaiser 19.70	Cadillac 39.1	Hudson 12.52	Hudson 19.41	Hudson 97.09	Lincoln 95	Mercury 67.9	Lincoln 31.3	Hudson 43.1	-----	Chrysler .314	-----	Oldsmobile 153.5
Hudson 96.3	Nash Statesman 19.07	Lincoln 37.4	Oldsmobile 13.70	Lincoln 19.90	Lincoln 97.08	Cadillac Oldsmobile 92	Stude. 63.2	Oldsmobile 31.7	Stude. 43.2	Lincoln 275	Oldsmobile .303	Nash Ambass. 134.8	Studebaker 145
Ford 103.2	Ford 18.28	Oldsmobile 35.2	Cadillac 14.72	Studebaker 20.67	Cadillac 95.44	-----	Hudson 62.0	Hudson 32.08	Oldsmobile 43.7	Oldsmobile 263	Mercury .297	Oldsmobile 130.7	Hudson 135
Dodge 104.3	Chrysler 17.98	Stude. 35.1	Stude. 15.10	Oldsmobile 20.93	Packard 93.17	Hudson 90	Lincoln 61.6	Chrysler 34.0	Lincoln 46.0	Hudson 257	Hudson .292	Buick 129.0	Lincoln 131.5
Oldsmobile 110.5	Cadillac 17.70	Kaiser 33.3	Packard 15.15	Kaiser 20.99	Stude. 92.78	Packard 80	Packard 59.1	Ford 34.4	Cadillac 48.0	Packard 230	Lincoln .282	Dodge Stude. 127.5	Cadillac 130
Kaiser 110.8	Olds. 17.50	Pontiac 33.0	Buick 15.20	Packard 21.04	Oldsmobile 92.54	Mercury Stude. 76	Ford 59.0	Mercury 34.8	Mercury 49.5	Pontiac 220	Cadillac Packard .277	-----	Packard 96.5
Studebaker 111.2	Dodge Pontiac 17.20	Dodge 32.5	Ford 15.31	Ford 21.19	Mercury 91.18	-----	Pontiac 58.6	Pontiac 34.9	Packard 51.1	Buick 217	-----	Kaiser 126.7	Kaiser 91.5
Pontiac 115.1	-----	Buick 32.4	Kaiser 15.40	Cadillac 21.22	Pontiac 87.72	Buick 70	Buick 58.3	Buick 35.5	Kaiser 54.5	Nash Ambass. 210	Kaiser .273	Hudson 125.8	Mercury 90.5
Mercury 116.0	Lincoln 17.07	Nash Statesman 31.2	Lincoln 15.44	Mercury 21.74	Ford 87.25	Pontiac 68	Chrysler 57.9	Cadillac 39.4	Ford 55.9	Mercury 206	Buick .266	Pontiac 123.6	Ford 85
Packard 121.7	Nash Ambass. 16.30	Ford 30.2	Pontiac 16.40	Nash Ambass. 21.75	Nash Ambass. 86.95	Kaiser, Nash Amb. 62	Cadillac 57.4	Packard 39.8	Pontiac 56.4	Dodge, Stude/Kaiser 190	Nash Ambass. .265	Lincoln 123.2	Pontiac 84.5
Cadillac 124.4	Buick 16.20	Packard 30.1	Mercury 16.85	Buick 21.878	Kaiser 83.57	-----	Kaiser 54.0	Nash Ambass. 34.9	Buick 57.1	-----	Pontiac .254	Mercury 121.6	Buick 78.5
Buick Lincoln 128.1	Packard 14.69	Nash Ambass. 29.8	Nash Ambass. 17.96	Pontiac 22.03	Dodge 83.41	Ford 59	Nash Ambass. 53.9	Kaiser 35.9	Nash Ambass. 58.9	-----	Ford .247	Packard 120.4	Nash Ambass. 61.5
-----	Mercury 14.62	Mercury 27.5	Dodge 19.03	Dodge 23.68	Buick 82.98	Dodge 50	Dodge 48.5	Dodge 53.4	Dodge 75.6	Ford 181	Dodge .216	Nash Statesman 114.8	Dodge 57
Nash Ambass. 130.9	Hudson 14.07	Hudson 27.4	Nash Statesman 21.98	Nash Statesman 24.47	Nash Statesman 77.19	Nash Statesman 39.5	Nash Statesman 46.5	Nash Statesman 60.7	Nash Statesman 82.3	Nash Statesman 140	Nash Statesman .214	Ford 113.6	Nash 44

NOTES: All cars tested were four-door sedans. Series and types of transmissions were: Buick Special, Dynaflow; Cadillac 62, HydraMatic; Chrysler New Yorker, Prestomatic; Dodge Coronet Diplomat, Gyro-matic; Ford, Fordomatic; Hudson Hornet, HydraMatic; Kaiser Deluxe std. with overdrive; Lincoln 74, std. with overdrive; Mercury std. with overdrive; Nash Ambassador, HydraMatic; Nash Statesman, HydraMatic; Oldsmobile Super 88, HydraMatic; Packard 200, Ultramatic; Pontiac Eight, HydraMatic; Studebaker Commander, Automatic Drive.

AVERAGE BRAKING DISTANCE IN FT.: Averages of our published braking figures which themselves were averages of many stops from speeds of 30, 45, and 60 mph.

AVERAGE FUEL CONSUMPTION IN MPG: An average of scores of readings made with each car under operating conditions ranging from stop and start driving in heavy traffic to a steady 60 mph on the open highway. Mpg with OD not counted.

TON MILES PER GALLON: $\dfrac{\text{car weight in tons} \times \text{distance traveled in miles}}{\text{fuel consumed in gals.}}$

AVERAGE ACCELERATION: Average of all acceleration figures.

AVERAGE ACCELERATION FOR STANDING 1/4 MILE: Average of two-way runs from standing start over measured 1/4 mile.

AVERAGE TOP SPEED: Average of two-way flying runs over measured 1/4 mile.

MAXIMUM ROAD HP: Engine power output delivered at driving wheels on Clayton chassis dynamometer.

PERCENT OF HP AT DRIVING WHEELS: $\dfrac{\text{Rhp}}{\text{Bhp}} \times 100$

DOLLARS PER RHP: $\dfrac{\text{West Coast delivered price}}{\text{Rhp}}$

LB. PER RHP: $\dfrac{\text{Weight of test car in lbs.}}{\text{Rhp}}$

RHP PER CU. IN. OF ENGINE DISPLACEMENT; $\dfrac{\text{Rhp}}{\text{Cu. ins. displacement}}$

MAXIMUM TORQUE IN LB. FT.: From Automobile Manufacturers Assn. specifications

MAXIMUM BMEP: From Ethyl Corp. "Brief Passenger Car Data 1951."

Motor Trend made these comparisons in declaring the 1951 Chrysler "Car of the Year."

1951 IMPERIAL

Above left and center: There's more chrome on the dash alone than on most entire modern cars! *Right:* First edition of a legendary powerplant. *Below left:* Fine leather and wool dominate the interior. *Right:* Restrained use of chrome is also evident at rear.

Getting in the back seat with the top up isn't as easy, but the space is reasonably comfortable once you're there. Head room is particularly generous, though leg room is no more than adequate, and the bottom cushion itself is skimpy — a concession, no doubt, to the room taken up by the folded top.

The bulky top also limits visibility to the rear quarters, with a backlight barely bigger than a mail slot. But with a frame of sturdy sheet-metal channels, the top mechanism looks and feels very solid indeed. Just a twist of a knob in the center of the windshield smoothly unlatches the roof, then a flip of a switch mounted low on the left side of the dash neatly stashes it in a well behind the seats.

It does seem odd at first to settle in behind a clutch pedal *and* an automatic shift quadrant (reading R-L-N-D). But the clutch is only necessary when changing the position of the gear lever, and it forgives the most clumsy use imaginable. Only the slightest lurch will chastise the driver who simply dumps the pedal at idle, without feeding any gas at all. And you can stop without touching the clutch at all — another odd sensation indeed. Chip explained that most contemporary Chrysler jockeys simply started the car, clutched into Drive, and then drove as if the transmission were fully automatic. One does have to remember to lift off the gas around 20-25, which allows the transmission to shift itself audibly but gently from third to fourth.

In fact, the Imperial accelerates smartly from rest, and once under way delivers an impression of tremendous flexibility and power reserve, emphasized by a quick response to the throttle. The hemi-head V-8 idles in silence, and even under way only a faint, distant hum filters into the cockpit from the engine bay. Every time I looked at the speedometer, I was surprised by how fast I was going. The Imperial just doesn't give any impression of speed — even with the top down. The windshield doesn't stand particularly tall — especially considering the high seating position — yet I noticed virtually no wind buffeting below 50 mph. At 60, the wind began to catch at my sleeves, but the sensation was hardly unpleasant. I didn't detect any chassis flex, either, and very little noise beyond the rush of the wind.

The Imperial rides firmly, yet smoothly, with no abrupt jolts but no wasted motion either. The steering is fast, easy, and utterly numb, and the wheel itself is much bigger than it needs to be. Cornering limits arrive quickly and without much warning. There just isn't a lot of difference between a cornering speed at which the Chrysler is perfectly content and one at which it's trying to leave the road nose first, while carving furrows in the pavement with its outboard rocker panel. Overall, the chassis just doesn't match the modern feel of the engine. On the other hand, the Imperial's brakes deserve credit for their effectiveness as well as their firm feedback. And in all fairness to this fine old lady, US luxury cars remained overpowered and under-sprung for at least another quarter-century.

Just for comparison, we briefly sampled another of Chip's '51 Imperial convertibles, a Haze Blue example with only 28,800 original miles. The big difference was the blue car's Fluid-Matic transmission (a rare choice on Imperials), which lacks the Fluid-Torque unit's torque converter. Despite a numerically higher axle ratio, the Fluid-Matic Imperial felt flat-footed and lifeless after driving our featured Fluid-Torque car. With the Fluid-Matic, the Low range became genuinely useful for quick getaways — especially in one spot, where we had to accelerate, from rest, *uphill* across an intersection. On the positive side, I noticed just a trace of throaty V-8 rumble from the original exhaust, which seemed to be missing from the restored car.

Either way, the Imperial strikes us as regal ride for sedately cruising country roads, or for barreling along straight stretches of highway, the wind in your hair, a V-8 under your toes — and a structure as solid as any four-door sedan's. ❏

Acknowledgements and Bibliography
Griffith Borgeson, "Motor Trend Engineering Achievement Award," Motor Trend, *February 1952; George Dammann,* 70 Years of Chrysler; *Jeffrey I. Godshall, "Imperial: Chrysler's Flagship,"* Automobile Quarterly, *Vol. 21, No. 2; John A. Gunnell (Editor),* Standard Catalog of American Cars 1946-1975; *Beverly Rae Kimes and Henry Austin Clark, Jr.,* Standard Catalog of American Cars 1805-1942; *Richard M. Langworth,* Chrysler & Imperial: The Postwar Years; *and "Of Tail Fins and V-8's,"* Automobile Quarterly, *Vol. 13, No. 3; John G. Tennyson, "Postwar Chrysler Imperials: Rarest of the Luxury Ragtops,"* Special Interest Autos #85; *and "Reminiscences of Imperial,"* Car Collector, *March 1985; Walt Woron, "Chrysler Saratoga,"* Motor Trend, *October 1952; "The New Chrysler 180 HP Engine,"* Road & Track, *March 1951; "Misc. Ramblings,"* Road & Track, *February 1951 and April 1951; "Chrysler Saratoga Club Coupe,"* Road & Track, *November 1951; "Hemi in Full Flite,"* Special Interest Autos #14.
It would be difficult indeed to write anything about the Chryslers of this era without acknowledging the pioneering research of Richard Langworth and Jeff Godshall. Thanks also to Kim M. Miller of the AACA Library and Research Center, to Henry Siegle, and of course special thanks to Chip Loree.

The Motor Continental Road Test No. 9C/51

Make: Chrysler **Type:** Imperial

Makers: Chrysler Corporation, Detroit 31, Michigan, U.S.A.

Dimensions and Seating

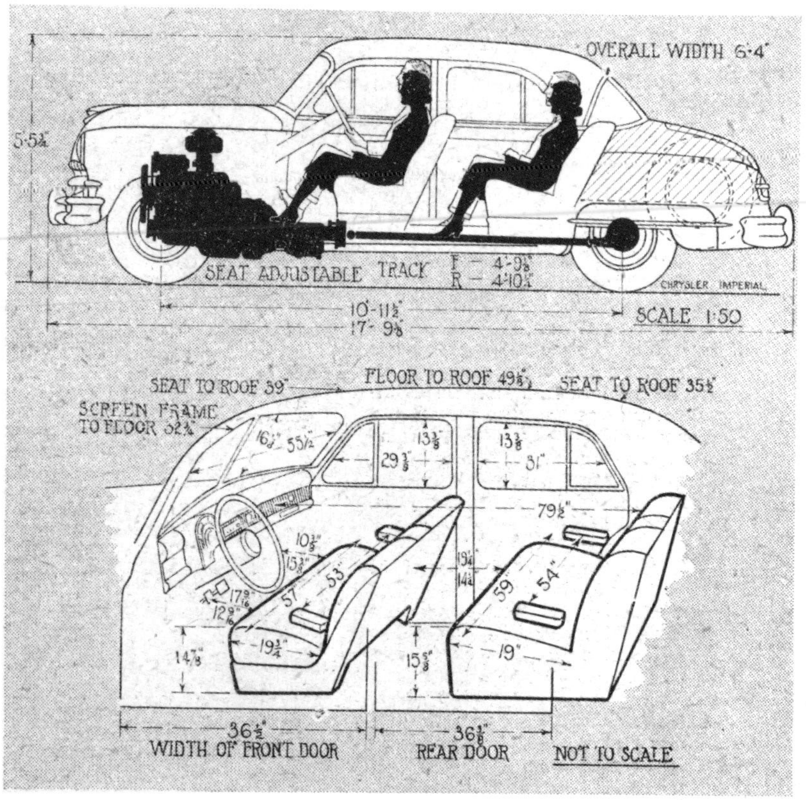
OVERALL WIDTH 6'4"
5'5¼"
SEAT ADJUSTABLE
TRACK F – 4'9⅝" R – 4'10¼"
CHRYSLER IMPERIAL
10'-11⅝"
17'-9⅜"
SCALE 1:50
SEAT TO ROOF 39"
FLOOR TO ROOF 49⅜"
SEAT TO ROOF 35½"
SCREEN FRAME TO FLOOR 32⅞"
WIDTH OF FRONT DOOR
REAR DOOR
NOT TO SCALE

In Brief

Price, car with radio and heater £1,275 (including U.S. Federal tax and delivery charge) £1 = $2.80.

Capacity . .. 5,440 c.c.
Unladen kerb weight 41¼ cwt.
Fuel consumption 14.4 m.p.g.
Maximum speed 101.2 m.p.h.
Maximum speed on 1 in 20 gradient 85 m.p.h.
Maximum top gear gradient .. .. 1 in 8.3
Acceleration
10-30 m.p.h. in top (see text)
0-50 m.p.h. through gears .. 11.8 secs.
Gearing: 22 m.p.h. in top at 1,000 r.p.m. 92.6 m.p.h. at 2,500 ft. per min. piston speed.

Specification

Engine

Cylinders	V8
Bore	97 mm.
Stroke	92 mm.
Cubic Capacity	5440 c.c.
Piston Area	91.3 sq. in.
Valves	Inclined o.h.v. (pushrods)
Compression ratio	7.5/1
Max. power	180 b.h.p.
at	4,000 r.p.m.
Piston speed at max. b.h.p.	2420 ft. per min.
Carburetter	Carter
Ignition	Auto-Lite
Sparking plugs	Auto-Lite AR 8
Fuel Pump	Mechanical
Oil filter	Full-flow

Transmission

Clutch	Chrysler torque converter
Top gear	3.54
3rd gear	6.20
2nd gear	8.36
1st gear	11.61
Propeller shaft	Open
Final drive	Hypoid bevel

Chassis

Brakes	Chrysler 2 LS
Brake-drum diameter	12 ins.
Friction lining area	201 sq. ins.
Suspension:	
Front	Wishbone and coil
Rear	Leaf
Shock absorbers:	
Front	Oriflow hydraulic
Rear	Oriflow hydraulic
Tyres	Goodyear 8.20 x 15

Steering

Steering gear	Gemmer Hydromechanical
Turns of steering wheel lock to lock	3½

Performance factors (at laden weight as tested)

Piston area, sq. ins. per ton	41
Brake lining area, sq. ins. per ton	90
Specific displacement, litres per ton/mile	3,320

Test Conditions

Moderate wind, showery, car tested at Montlhèry track on Super Carburant fuel.

Test Data

ACCELERATION TIMES on Two Upper Ratios

	Top	3rd.
10-30 m.p.h.	—	5.5 secs.
20-40 m.p.h.	8.0 secs.	5.4 secs.
30-50 m.p.h.	8.1 secs.	6.1 secs.
40-60 m.p.h.	9.7 secs.	6.4 secs.
50-70 m.p.h.	11.9 secs.	8.8 secs.
60-80 m.p.h	14.3 secs.	—
70-90 m.p.h.	21.0 secs.	—

ACCELERATION TIMES

	Through 3rd and 4th gears	Through 1st and 2nd gears
0-30 m.p.h.	6.0 secs.	4.0 secs.
0-40 m.p.h.	8.8 secs.	8.7 secs.
0-50 m.p.h.	11.8 secs.	12.6 secs.
0-60 m.p.h.	15.2 secs.	—
0-70 m.p.h.	25.0 secs.	—
0-80 m.p.h.	30.5 secs.	—
0-90 m.p.h.	43.1 secs.	—
Standing Quarter Mile	19.6 secs.	20.6 secs. (inc. 3rd)

FUEL CONSUMPTION

19 m.p.g. at constant 20 m.p.h.
19 m.p.g. at constant 30 m.p.h.
19 m.p.g. at constant 40 m.p.h.
17.5 m.p.g. at constant 50 m.p.h.
16 m.p.g. at constant 60 m.p.h.
14 m.p.g. at constant 70 m.p.h.
12 m.p.g. at constant 80 m.p.h.
Overall consumption for 190 miles, 13.2 gallons, equals 14.4 m.p.g.

MAXIMUM SPEEDS

Flying Quarter Mile

Mean of four opposite runs	101.2 m.p.h.
Best time equals	102.2 m.p.h.

Speed in Gears

Max. speed in 3rd gear	76 m.p.h.
Max speed in 2nd gear	50 m.p.h.

WEIGHT

Unladen kerb weight	41¼ cwt.
Front/rear weight distribution	56/44
Weight laden as tested	44¾ cwt.

INSTRUMENTS

Speedometer at 30 m.p.h.	3% fast
Speedometer at 60 m.p.h.	7% fast
Speedometer at 90 m.p.h.	10% fast
Distance recorder	3% fast

HILL CLIMBING (At steady speeds)

Max. top gear speed on 1 in 20	85 m.p.h.
Max. top gear speed on 1 in 15	77 m.p.h.
Max. top gear speed on 1 in 10	65 m.p.h.
Max. gradient on top gear	1 in 8.3 (Tapley 270 lb./ton)
Max. gradient on 3rd gear	1 in 5.3 (Tapley 420 lb./ton)
Max. gradient on 2nd gear	1 in 4.5 (Tapley 500 lb./ton)

BRAKES at 30 m.p.h. No test; see text.

Maintenance

Fuel tank: 20 gallons. **Sump:** 10 pints, S.A.E. 30 (plus 2 pints for Full-Flow oil filter) **Gearbox:** 3 pints, S.A.E. 10 W. **Rear axle:** 3½ pints, S.A.E. 90 E.P. **Steering gear:** S.A.E. 90 fluid gear lubricant. **Radiator:** 50 pints (3 drain taps, 2-engine block, 1 radiator). **Chassis lubrication:** By grease gun every 1,000 miles to 28 points. **Ignition timing:** T.D.C. **Spark plug gap:** 0.035 in. **Contact Breaker gap:** 0.018 in. **Valve timing:** I.O. 15 degrees B.T.D.C., I.C. 57 degrees A.B.D.C., E.O. 49 degrees B.B.D.C., E.C. 15 degrees A.T.D.C. **Tappet clearances:** Hydraulic tappets. **Front wheel toe-in:** 0 to $\frac{1}{16}$ in. (0 preferred). **Camber angle:** $-\frac{3}{8}$ degree to $+\frac{3}{8}$ degree (left side to be ¼ degree to ½ degree greater than right side within these limits). **Castor angle:** – 1 degree to – 3 degrees (– 2 degrees preferred). **Tyre pressures:** (cold) Front 24 lb., rear 24 lb. **Brake fluid:** MoPar. **Battery:** 6-volt, 135 amp.-hour, positive earth. **Lamp bulbs:** Head lamps Sealed Beam, Instruments 2 cp. bulbs (3); Map light 15 cp.; glove compartment 2 cp.; clock 2 cp.; luggage locker 15 cp.; reverse light 21 cp. (2); interior light 15 cp. (2); tail light 3 cp. (2); stop light 21 cp. (2). Ref. U.S./55/51.

THE CHRYSLER IMPERIAL

An Exceedingly Powerful, Fast, Family Car with Power-assisted Steering

WHEN the Chrysler car was first put on the market it embodied many advanced features of automobile engineering. These in 1924 included light alloy pistons, hydraulic brakes, high compression engine and an all-round performance substantially greater than other American cars of comparable size and price. Later they were amongst the first in the field of the modern gear shifting system, embodying fluid flywheel and choice of automatically engaged gears, but, nevertheless, in the past decade Chrysler cars have been noted more for their sound construction along conservative lines than for essays in the unconventional, or efforts at high performance. In the light of this background it is especially interesting to observe that their well-tried line of side valve straight-eight engines is now replaced by an advanced type of V.8, of

TYPICAL SPACE—In common with most U.S.A. models the Chrysler has an exceedingly capacious luggage boot which is shown open in this picture.

which a full description appeared in "The Motor" of February 28 last.

It is desirable now to recapitulate that, in addition to the change from in-line to Vee formation, the bore was so enlarged as to become greater than the stroke and the valves were placed not only in the head but also inclined therein with ports on opposite sides, operation being through the medium of a single centrally placed camshaft with pushrods and rockers of unequal length. These changes resulted in an engine output of no less than 180 h.p., making the Chrysler substantially the most powerful car in large-scale production today.

Although showing little change in external appearance compared with its predecessors, certain important chassis modifications were included simultaneously. The simple two-element fluid flywheel was replaced by a four-piece torque converter, so designed as to rather more than double the torque available at the rear wheels when any given ratio in the box was en-

gaged. In addition, the number of turns required on the steering wheel to pass from one full lock to the other was reduced from 5 to 3½ and hydraulic servo assistance was provided, this being the first time that power steering had been made available in a passenger car. Finally, on certain models the normal shoe brakes were replaced by disc brakes.

With this wealth of new technical features, we naturally looked forward greatly to an opportunity for road testing one of these cars, and this was afforded us through the courtesy of Mr. Briggs Cunningham, who placed at our disposition an Imperial saloon which had been used as a tender car for the Cunningham team at Le Mans. This particular model had

SIDEWAYS SUPPORT —The rear seat of the Imperial will comfortably carry three people and is therefore provided with this exceptionally wide centre arm-rest for use when only two are aboard.

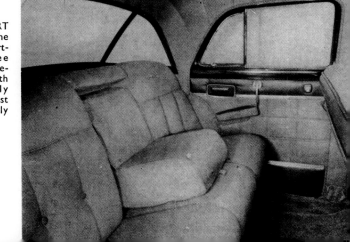

done 1,500 miles and was carefully greased and adjusted before being handed to us. It had not, however, received any factory attention since it had left the works and all the figures quoted may therefore be regarded as fully representative of an ordinary production model as supplied to the public, with no knowledge that special tests involving performance figures would be made. It should also be stated that the engine is designed to run on fuel having a higher octane rating even than the Super Carburant which is the best available in France, and also that, due to centrifugal forces, speeds attained at Montlhèry are rather less than those which can be put up on selected stretches of straight flat road. It is thus all the more remarkable that the car proved by a significant margin to be the fastest U.S.A. vehicle that we have had occasion to drive, and it would indeed cover a complete lap of Montlhèry in 56.5 secs., which is fractionally in excess of 100 m.p.h. At this speed the engine is running at 4,550 r.p.m., i.e. above the power curve peak, but at only 2,700 ft./min. piston speed. It is therefore scarcely surprising that there is no feeling of strain or effort even at these relatively high speeds, although there is, of course, a considerable measure of wind noise.

It will be observed from the data panel that the car will reach a genuine 90 m.p.h. (i.e. approximately a speedometer 100 m.p.h.) in 43 secs. from rest, and in little more than 18 secs. from a cruising 70 m.p.h., and this will bring home the fact that the new Chrysler really is among the fastest cars in the world today, so far as maximum speed is concerned.

NEATLY DONE—Both in layout and finish the Chrysler instruments present an attractive appearance. This picture also shows the parked position of the electrically driven windscreen wipers.

The acceleration figures on top gear are perhaps less outstanding, but one must bear in mind that the car weighed well over 2 tons in its tested condition, although, even so, a figure of 80 h.p./laden ton is one which can be exceeded by very few full saloon cars. All accelerating and hill climbing is carried out normally on one of two alternative ratios, but the torque on each of these can be increased by up to double the action of the torque converter. If from rest the throttle is fully depressed, the car will accelerate in the lower of the two normal ratios (actually third speed in the gear box), on which ratio a genuine 70 m.p.h. can be reached, if the driver wishes. At any speed above 15 m.p.h. direct top gear can be engaged by releasing the accelerator and waiting for two or three seconds whilst an automatic device makes the change. If the accelerator pedal be not quite fully depressed, the car will gain speed with very reasonable rapidity on the fairly high top gear, but as there is an automatic change-down at about 15 m.p.h., it is not possible to obtain the normal quoted 10/30 m.p.h. acceleration in direct drive.

Semi-Automatic Gear Changing

The downward gear-change from direct to third gear can be made in alternative ways. There is an automatic and immediate response to opening the throttle below 60 m.p.h. to the fullest possible extent, and if this be done at, say, 40 m.p.h. there is an immediate surge forward of noticeable magnitude. A somewhat smoother and less dramatic change can be made by holding the throttle in the half-open position and pressing a button on the end of the steering column gear lever. This brings third gear into play and the transmission will remain in this ratio unless the throttle is shut for the required period of time. As, with the torque converter adding its effect, the car will climb a 1 in 5.3 gradient on third gear, there is no normal occasion on which any use of the hand or foot will be needed in the gear-changing process. For emergencies, however, a pair of two low ratios is provided with automatic change up or down between them exactly as in the fashion above described. These may be conveniently regarded as first and second gears and to change either up or down from second to third involves the use of a friction clutch connected to a conventional clutch pedal and a movement of the steering column gear lever by hand.

If all four gears are used on a standing start acceleration, it is only the time from rest to 30 m.p.h. which is substantially improved. The standing ¼-mile time is not affected. Hence only extremely severe conditions, or any case where severe loss of engine power had arisen, could require the use of the lower ratios, which for all normal purposes can be neglected.

Unless the driver is in a particular hurry, the Chrysler may be thought of as a single-gear car and one which will also put up remarkably high average speeds due to the excellent acceleration particularly in the upper part of the speed band. On Continental roads 50 miles in the hour could be recorded with ease, and 60 miles without difficulty in favourable conditions, figures all the more remarkable in view of the large size of the car and the fact that the steering and suspension are designed far more with United States than Continental standards in mind.

This brings one immediately to the issue of power steering, for the results obtained in this matter can only be assessed in relation to American conditions and driving requirements, amongst which finger-light parking ranks extremely high. The large size and high weight of American cars, and their frequent use in towns, presents a basic problem to which the only solution has been progressively to lower the steering gear ratio to over five turns to one, despite the obvious disadvantages of this practice. Servo power has been employed on the Chrysler mainly to secure very light operation with "only" 3½ turns from lock to lock, and not with a view to improving the high-speed handling.

The result is at first acquaintance somewhat disconcerting. There is ample caster return, but at any speed the car can be steered by the little finger alone pressing against the spoke of the perimeter of the wheel, for the servo action contributes four-fifths of the effort needed. In consequence, one has steering which has, so to speak, a position but no magnitude, and the male European driver might even prefer the same linkage without the servo, a condition which may be simulated by coasting downhill with the engine switched off. For all drivers in city use, and for an overwhelming majority in general conditions, this power steering is, however, a notable step forward and the Chrysler must in the large high-performance class, be reckoned as the smoothest and the lightest-to-drive-car in the world.

The car tested did not have the disc brakes and figures on the normal braking system could not be obtained owing to a cloudburst which flooded the track immediately before the usual tests were about to be made. For general service on the Continent they appeared adequate with perhaps rather higher pedal pressure than is usual on some U.S. cars, which was surprising as Chrysler are amongst the few U.S.A. cars to have two leading shoes in the front drums and a vacuum servo.

The suspension, although soft by European standards, is well damped by the latest type of Oriflow telescopic shock absorbers, and mastered even the bad bumps of Montlhéry without difficulty. There is notable roll on corners, but the correct technique on U.S.A. vehicles is to take curves gently and to rely on high acceleration to secure the required average speed.

Passengers are well insulated from the effect of roll by the exceptionally wide centre armrests in both sets of seats, which are upholstered in a good quality cloth.

Good Equipment

The interior of the car commands high marks for lay-out and equipment. Electric operation with two-speed drive for the windscreen wipers makes a very great advance on the normal American system, and each window is moved by its individual motor with a switch in each door and a battery of over-riding switches on the driver's door. This is an extremely convenient arrangement, but by contrast there are no door pockets and a very inadequately sized glove locker on the facia panel. The centre of this is occupied by the radio, heater and de-mister apparatus, the instruments being grouped immediately in front of the driver.

The rarely needed gear-change lever is mounted on the steering column but the measures against the accidental engagement of reverse gear are somewhat overdone and lead to delay when parking. To the left-hand side of the steering column is a smaller lever operating the flashing-light indicators which has a self-cancelling apparatus which works on most occasions. Powerful horns are operated by a ring surmounting the three-spoke wheel, and some reference to the finish of these and other metal parts should be made.

This brush chrome finish gives the impression of stainless steel (which is in fact used for some parts) and makes one feel that the Chrysler Imperial is a thoroughly well-engineered motor car. It has undoubtedly abundant power and performance with extreme ease of driving and reasonable fuel economy.

Reference to the table of fuel consumption in relation to speed will show that the overall figure is somewhat lower than one might expect from the steady speed results. This seems to be an inherent disability of torque converter drive which over the whole range is not so efficient as a gear drive—in other words, the utmost simplicity of control is bought by a loss of two or three m.p.g. For this class of car this is no great price to pay, and although it is not in every way suitable for European, and still less for British, road conditions, this latest V.8 Chrysler can be reckoned as one of the finest examples of the modern American car.

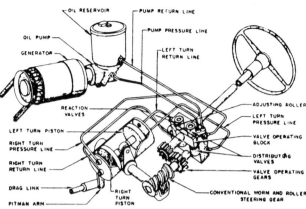

A POWER-STEERED CAR

ELECTRICALLY-OPERATED windows, lashings of cigarette lighters, flashing lights, windscreen washers, gleaming chrome-plate and push-button radios — at last we were ensconced in the midst of Detroit luxury!

We had heard many conflicting reports on the characteristics of power steering and fluid drive, but this was our first opportunity to sample them for ourselves. We went into the experiment with open minds, and came out of it impressed by the smoothness of acceleration and ease of driving.

The car was a privately-owned 1952 Chrysler Imperial, borrowed for the test by Chrysler Corporation's New South Wales distributors, York Motors Pty. Ltd. It had a California hard-top body and a Chrysler V8 engine developing 180 b.h.p. at 4,000 r.p.m.

The driver who had brought out the car sat beside us as we eased ourselves behind the steering wheel.

"Turn the ignition key and press the accelerator pedal," he said.

We did, and the big car slid smoothly out from the kerb and picked up speed without any further ado. There was a clutch pedal alongside the accelerator, but there was no need to use it, or to worry about any manual gear change; the fluid drive did this automatically. When we wanted a little extra pull from the engine to overtake another car or climb a stiff hill, all we had to do was give the accelerator a smart tap and let it come up again; the car automatically shifted into the lower

of the two forward gears, accelerating powerfully.

Steering was absolutely effortless —so much so that there was no feeling of steering in the normal sense of the word—the wheel turned at the slightest pressure, and we found that, even when parked at the kerb, it was possible to turn the wheel from lock to lock with one finger on a spoke of the steering wheel; to do this, of course, you had to have the engine running, as the steering mechanism gets its power assistance from the engine.

We noticed a small gearshift lever set behind the steering wheel, with positions for reverse, neutral, forward drive, and extra-low gear. This shift was not used at all in normal driving, however. The clutch pedal and gear shift are used only when:

● Selecting forward drive to start off after a long period of parking, when the car is usually left in neutral.

● Selecting reverse gear for backing.

● Selecting extra-low gear for an extremely steep upgrade or to get out of a bog.

(Continued on page 24)

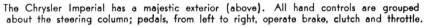

The Chrysler Imperial has a majestic exterior (above). All hand controls are grouped about the steering column; pedals, from left to right, operate brake, clutch and throttle.

The 6-passenger Custom Imperial used in the road test.

Road Testing Chrysler's

PHOTOS BY DICK ADAMS

Chrysler finally has joined the fully automatic parade . . .with a transmission which combines the smoothness of cream with the scat of a scalded tomcat.

SINCE the 1934-37 period and the fiasco of the super-streamlined Airstream-Airflow models, Chrysler's styling department has been as conservative as a pre-Eisenhower Republican.

The '53 body is no exception and, although some of the box-like corners have given way to gentle curves, the current Chrysler isn't the Marilyn Monroe of the automotive world.

What it lacks in road sex is more than made up in the engineering department. The overhead valve V8 introduced in 1951 sparked the current horsepower race and remains a masterpiece of design. Although rated at a conservative 180 HP since its debut, it is believed to have more potential horses in its innards than any other V8 on the market. The soon to be released '54 models will probably put out 235 HP without straining a head bolt.

And now, 13 years after the competition decided a clutch pedal was superfluous, Chrysler has introduced a fully automatic transmission — one of the smoothest ever dropped into a drive train. An automatically shifted planetary gearset teamed with a torque converter, it has been named PowerFlite.

It was introduced late this summer with remarkably little fanfare, perhaps because it was available only as standard equipment on the Imperial models. Chrysler's most expensive line. This undoubtedly

Instruments are grouped around steering post.

Tufted door covering is luxurious.

Power Flite ▪ ▪ ▪ ▪ ▪ ▪

was due to the fact that only one plant, Indianapolis, was engaged in its manufacture. In 1954 it will continue as standard equipment on the Imperials and be on the optional list for all other series including the sixes. In addition, it will be offered as extra cost equipment on the De Soto and Dodge.

PowerFlite gives Chrysler buyers the largest selection of transmissions of any car in the industry—standard. standard-overdrive, and two other semi-automatic fluid clutch gearboxes being available.

In developing PowerFlite and abandoning the clutch pedal, Chrysler has improved on existing designs insofar as parts and weight are concerned. They use only 185 major parts compared to 218 to 295 in competing boxes and, although some of the other self-shifters have as many as 33 sliding valves, Chrysler has found it possible to do the job with nine. The liberal use of aluminum and magnesium, sacrificing nothing to strength, has held weight to 214 pounds — four to 100 pounds lighter than other automatic transmissions.

Much has been written about torque converters and automatic transmissions, much of it beyond the comprehension of the layman for this is one gismo that baffles even a first-class mechanic unless he has taken special training in the diagnosis and repair of its illnesses. It is sufficient

to say that PowerFlite's torque converter is similar to others in that it includes an impeller, a turbine and two stators, or fluted wheels, mounted between the impeller and turbine. These stators help the impeller to accelerate the oil in the converter, providing the driving force to the turbine.

Actually, Chrysler pointed the way for the development of the torque converter, having introduced the fluid flywheel with its Fluid Drive unit in 1939. In this system, as in torque converters, there is no direct mechanical linkage of engine and driveshaft, oil or a hydraulic fluid serving that purpose. In PowerFlite, the torque converter transmission holds 12 quarts of fluid which is circulated through a water-cooled heat exchanger behind the left side of the fan. Changing of the transmission oil is recommended every 20,000 miles.

The planetary gearset behind the torque converter, so named because of its resemblance to the solar system, has three 'planet' or pinion gears enclosed in a ring gear and revolving around a 'sun' gear. The planet gears are in constant engagement with both ring and sun gear. A system of clutches—hydraulically operated in this case—makes it possible to hold and drive various members of this assembly, transferring engine power to the rear wheels through Low, direct drive or reverse.

So smooth the shift point is almost impossible to detect, PowerFlite's torque converter ratio of 2.6 to 1 plus the gear ratio of 1.72 to 1 gives the highest overall starting torque multiplication in Drive range of any transmission. This transmission was in the 6-passenger custom Imperial furnished for road test by Charles E. Sumrall, Chrysler regional manager in the Washington area. Although this automobile weighs more than 5,000 pounds it was repeatedly accelerated from 0 to 60 MPH in 12.6 seconds using Low and Drive range. If this transmission was available for the New Yorker which weighs almost 1,000 pounds less, acceleration time would probably be lopped a second and a half. Zero to 80 MPH requires only 21.5 seconds.

The 'gated' shifting arrangement allows the driver to move the selector lever into the desired range without taking his eyes from the road. Under normal operating conditions there are only two points into which the gears can be shifted—a push upward puts the transmission into neutral and downward into Drive. Lifted and pushed upward, the lever shifts the transmission into reverse. When the lever is pulled all the way down, the transmission is in Low. This can be accomplished anytime when the speed is below 65 MPH and actually won't cause damage if the shift is made above that speed. Although

Fenders are almost level with hood.

Rear window is of wrap-around design.

Low range is of some assistance in fast starts its primary value comes into play in descending steep hills when it provides considerable engine braking.

Low is not a gear especially designed for heavy pulling as is the case in many other automatics, Instead, this position locks out the upshift and you can wind the car in this gear until the engine runs out of oomph. The SPEED AGE test crew hadn't found the end when the speedo needle was crossing the 80 MPH mark but the road was dwindling rapidly.

Below 55 MPH, this gear takes over the burden when the driver punches the throttle into kickdown position. Unlike the upshift, this does not have a velvet quality; you know the engine and drive train are really at work. The 55 MPH limit on the kickdown seems a bit low but Chrysler apparently believes their V8 is a big enough animal to handle demands for emergency acceleration above that speed. Frankly, there were a few times—and the test crew drove this automobile more than 2,000 miles—when the absence of kick-

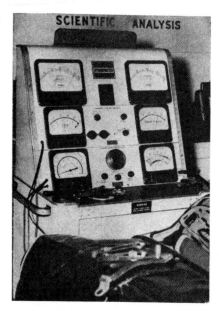

Imperial on the dynamometer

down up to 80 MPH was felt to be sorely lacking. The Imperial can climb from 60 to 80 MPH in less than eight seconds; with a kickdown such as in the Hydra-Matic, this could probably be pared one or two seconds—enough to mean the difference between living and dying if trapped on the wrong side of the highway in passing.

PowerFlite's ability to multiply engine torque ceases above 50 MPH and it acts as a fluid coupling. This 'coupling' of impeller and turbine can occur at speeds as low as 35 MPH although between that point and 50 its multiplication factor can be called into play by jumping on the throttle. And, unlike some other transmissions, PowerFlite's upshift comes at varying speeds. It occurs between 18 and 65 MPH, depending upon throttle opening. With steady pressure on the gas pedal, the changeover from the 1.72 to 1 to 1 to 1 ratio is so imperceptible as to be unnoticeable. The transmission can be made to shift, however, by relaxing throttle pressure above 18 MPH. In slowing, the downshift takes place when car speed drops below 11 MPH.

Chrysler advertising brochures say of the Imperial: "As it will be built in limited numbers only, it is obviously not a price-built car, but one of priceless quality, built with infinite precision, consummate skill and admirable patience."

The advertising copywriter who penned these words wrote with restraint. From the chair-high seats and tufted door upholstery to the hassocks for rear seat passengers, this is the last word in comfort. When the folding armrests in the center of front and rear seat are pulled down, the Imperial is transformed into a living room on wheels. Large ash receptacles matched by lighters are fitted in each of the armrests on the rear doors and chrome assist grips are anchored to the back of the front seat. Notchback doors at the rear, and extremely wide ones at the front, make entrance and exit easy. The enamel job, inside and out, is so well done it appears to have been rolled into the metal at the steel mill.

Chrysler standardized on an instrument panel a few years ago and its design is

undeniably excellent. The cluster is around the steering column with all gauges easily visible. A lip hoods the dials and, except when the rheostat controlling dashlight intensity is full on, there is no light reflection in the windshield during night driving. Radio and heater controls and ashtray are in the center of the dashboard, within reach of the driver. The arrangement would be perfect if the glove compartment had been moved into the center from the extreme right. Light-absorbent material covers the dash panel deck behind the single-piece, curved windshield, eliminating reflection. Below this, and extending across the front compartment, is a crash pad which apparently is stuffed with foam rubber. Some other, more absorbent material would have been a wiser choice to lessen injury in event of a collision.

When you slide behind the wheel after Chrysler's 180 horses have been let out of the stable, the first impression is that a mechanic failed to attach all the appurtenances normal to a steering gear. The Imperial is easier to steer than Junior's kiddie car.

This is full-time power steering, contrasted to those systems where a certain amount of pressure is necessary before the assist mechanism takes over. Resting your little finger on the Imperial wheel is sufficient to change the direction of this better than 18-foot land yacht; this, in conjunction with an increased ratio which calls for three and a half turns lock to lock, can lead to some embarrassing situations unless the first few corners are approached with caution.

For the person accustomed to 'feeling' the road, this is the same as 'hands off' driving until one learns to judge the car's position and speed. The latter is important for the quietness of the powerplant and smoothness of the ride are deceptive . . . 60 MPH in the Imperial feels like 40 in many other transportation pieces.

The Gemmer power steering mechanism itself is an exceptionally clean installation. By substituting aluminum for cast iron, Chrysler reduced the weight of the '53 unit 25% over last year's. Bolting the pump directly behind the generator

22

and driving it by the armature shaft eliminates extra pulleys, shafts and brackets and goes a long way toward keeping the engine compartment uncluttered. It does, however, run up the bill in event of an accident resulting in damage to either the generator or steering. Complete replacement costs better than $100 and this does not include the valving on the steering column.

Coupled with the steering are servo brakes—perhaps the best in the industry. When you can haul down two and a half tons in less than 180 feet from a mile a minute speed, that's stopping. As was true last year when SPEED AGE's staff tested the Chrysler Saratoga, the '53 brakes are so accurate and positive as to represent a threat to the safety of the passenger in the front seat if applied without warning.

Pedal pressure required is negligible, due to the vacuum assist mechanism located under the floor at a point beneath the driver's seat. This is tucked away sufficiently that it won't be damaged in driving over deeply rutted roads yet is still accessible for repair. In operation as long as the engine is running, the result is a brake pedal as sensitive as a boil. With the power off, the driver still has brakes although more pressure is required on the pedal.

The phenomenal capacity of the Imperial's brakes to take punishment was emphasized with repeated panic stops from 50 MPH. It wasn't until after 17 such lining scorchers that three of the four shoes called it quits. Recovery was complete after a 2-minute breather. This is far more abuse than the average automobile is called upon to take either in traffic or mountain driving.

Braking area on the Imperial is 201 square inches, the same as on other models in the Chrysler line—with the exception of the Crown Imperial which employs disc brakes and has an effective area of 260 square inches. All Chrysler models have two cylinders on each front wheel, aiding materially in fast stops.

The emergency brake, in this case, is well named. Attached to the drive shaft, behind the transmission, it is of the internal expanding type. It is one of the few such brakes which has a lasting and positive action. Retaining this feature permitted Chrysler to eliminate a 'Park' pawl from its transmission, also saving weight.

The power features do not end here however. As with many cars in its price class, Chrysler also has a power seat— this one driven electrically. A button on the side of the seat and within easy reach of the driver moves the cushion and seat back through a distance of five inches, automatically elevating the cushion as it moves forward.

Windows, also, are electrically operated; each has its control button and a master control for all four is provided for the driver. With radio, heater, defroster, wipers, lighters and fog lamps plugged into the circuit, Chrysler engineers might have done their customers a favor had they installed the 12-volt system used in the Crown series rather than the somewhat old-fashioned 6-volt supply which is standard.

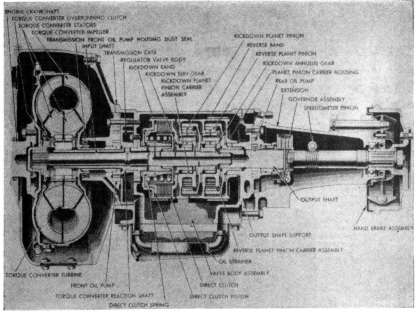

Cutaway drawing of Power Flite transmission.

With a wheelbase of 133½ inches, the Imperial is no rollerskate. But, since considerable flexibility is necessary with such a span between the axles, the chassis is formed by double channel box rails reinforced with cross members. Suspension is orthodox with coil springs in front and semi-elliptics, splayed for additional stability at the rear. Oriflow shock absorbers are used all around. Weight distribution puts 54% on the front and 46% on the rear—very favorable by modern standards.

The ride is better than comfortable; it's luxurious at any speed sustained in a straight line. Last year's terrific declination on braking has been overcome and the Imperial rides practically flat when the brakes are applied. There is, however, considerable body heel — even on moderate turns. Following a late model car equipped with Air Lifts through the numerous curves on Route 222 between Lancaster, Pa., and Route 40 at Perryville, Md., SPEED AGE test drivers discovered the Imperial's absolute safe limit was 55 to 60 MPH although the leading automobile was handling easily at speeds 10 to 15 MPH faster. Admittedly, the speeds on this run were far above those recommended for amateurs; but Air Lifts would do much to eliminate the possibility of the unsuspecting succumbing to the potential high speed of this automobile and ending up as a statistic in a coroner's notebook.

In the flat-out department, the Imperial comes close to being a record-breaker. With a running start of two miles, the average of six runs in opposite directions through a timing trap was 104.9 MPH. Control at this speed was perfect; there was little wind-wander and the automobile had the feeling of being glued to the road.

Economy undoubtedly isn't important to the buyer who can lay out more than $4,500 for his transportation and the Imperial with its weight and big tire cross section won't win any fuel sweepstakes. Although few will be content to

so curb the Imperial—fuel consumption comes out to 18 MPG at 30 to 40 MPH. Increasing throttle pressure to 50 MPH, the V8 drinks at a rate of a gallon every 15 miles and that thirst increases at 60 MPH to 13 MPG. In city traffic, with its stop-and-go driving and long periods of idling, the best average was 12 MPG. With Gulf No Nox used throughout the test period, the average of 2,070 miles, including all special testing, was 13.4 MPG.

Chrysler's 331 cubic-inch V8 has been around long enough that it is often taken for granted by the buying public. Rated officially at 180 HP, a more accurate figure is probably 187 since the published rating was obtained with all accessories—representing a considerable drain —in operation.

Before taking the Imperial on the street, the SPEED AGE staff had the engine tuned to factory specifications on the Clayton chassis dynamometer at H. B. Leery's, Chrysler dealers in Washington. When the mechanics were finished, this engine was delivering 88 HP to the rear wheels at 2400 RPM. The published rating of 180 HP is reached at 4000 RPM.

Accessibility is one of the most striking features about the Chrysler engine for, with the possible exception of the distributor, there is no portion of the powerplant that cannot be reached. Specially designed tools may be necessary for some repair jobs but this is true of most late-model cars. The distributor is best worked on by removing it to a test bench, for adjusting these dual point systems is virtually impossible with the distributor in the block.

With an engine that has more in reserve than the average driver can handle with safety and a new transmission which —with a more favorable weight load— can provide the scat of a scalded tomcat, Chrysler has two sides of the sales triangle. The third is body design and 1954 models are due.

Statistical data on page 24

23

CHRYSLER IMPERIAL

ROAD TEST REPORT AND STATISTICAL DATA

(Continued from page 19)

Engine Specifications

Cylinders	8
Arrangement	V
Valve arrangement	OH
Bore (inches)	3 13/16
Stroke (inches)	3⅝
Displacement (cubic inches)	331.1
Compression ratio	7.5 to 1
Taxable horsepower	46.51
Brake horsepower	180
Max. torque (foot pounds at rpm)	312 @ 2000
Oil capacity (quarts)	5
Fuel capacity (gallons)	20
Water capacity (quarts)	
Without heater	25
With heater	26

Transmission
Powerflite

Torque converter ratio	2.6:1
Gear ratio	1.72:1
Overall torque multiplication	4.47:1

Interior Specifications

Width of front seat at shoulder (inches)	56⅝
Width of rear seat at shoulder (inches)	53¾
Depth of front seat (inches)	14⅞
Depth of rear seat (inches)	14¾
Headroom, front (inches)	36¼
Headroom, rear (inches)	35¼
Legroom, front (inches)	44¼
Legroom, rear (inches)	43¾

Chassis

Frame:

Type	welded, double channel, box
Wheelbase (inches)	133½
Overall length (inches)	219
Overall width (inches)	76¾
Overall height (inches)	63
Road clearance (inches)	7½

Tread:

Front (inches)	57 3/16
Rear (inches)	60⅜
Weight (pounds)	5,060
Percent on front	54
Percent on rear	46

Suspension:

Front	coil springs
Rear	semi-elliptics

Rear axle:

Type	semi-floating
Gearing	Hypoid
Ratio	3.54 to 1

Tires:

Size	8.20 x 15
Pressure (pounds)	24 front
	24 rear

Brakes:

Drum diameter (inches)	12
Effective area (square inches)	201
Type	hydraulic, internal expanding

Steering:

Type	Gemmer, power
Ratio	16.2 to 1
Turning diameter (feet)	44⅔

Performance Data
Acceleration

Drive range:

0-30 mph	5.5 seconds
0-40 mph	7.2 seconds
0-50 mph	9.5 seconds
0-60 mph	13.5 seconds
0-70 mph	17.8 seconds
0-80 mph	22.4 seconds

Low and drive range:

0-60 mph	12.6 seconds
0-80 mph	21.5 seconds

Drive:

30-60 mph	8.5 seconds ▲
50-60 mph	4.6 seconds ▲
60-80 mph (drive range only)	7.8 seconds

Top speed:

▲ Kickdown

Average of six runs in opposite directions, timed ... 104.9 mph

Braking:

Complete stop, 30 mph	56 feet
60 mph	178 feet

Speedometer Error:

Indicated	Actual
30 mph	30 mph
40 mph	40 mph
50 mph	49 mph
60 mph	57 mph
70 mph	66 mph
80 mph	75 mph
90 mph	84 mph

Fuel Consumption:

30 mph	18 mpg
40 mph	18 mpg
50 mph	15 mpg
60 mph	13 mpg
Traffic	12 mpg

Average for 2,070 miles . 13.4 mpg
Fuel used: Gulf premium

Chrysler Prices

DELIVERED AT WASHINGTON, D.C. INCLUDING FEDERAL TAX

Windsor—6-cylinder:

Club coupe	$2,717.85
6-passenger sedan	$2,740.35
8-passenger sedan	$3,692.10
Town and Country	$3,544.85

Windsor Deluxe:

6-passenger sedan	$2,840.00
Newport	$3,146.25
Convertible coupe	$3,370.75

New Yorker—V8

Club coupe	$3,289.50
Newport	$3,659.00
6-passenger sedan	$3,319.50
8-passenger sedan	$4,515.00
Town and Country	$4,074.75

New Yorker Deluxe—V8

Club coupe	$3,435.50
6-passenger sedan	$3,466.50
Newport	$3,829.75
Convertible coupe	$4,125.00

Custom Imperial—V8

6-passenger sedan	$4,401.50
Town limousine	$4,942.00
Newport	$4,704.25

Crown Imperial—V8

Limousine—8-passenger	$7,191.75
8-passenger sedan	$7,065.50

Accessory Prices
Windsor

Fluid-Torque Drive	$106.40*
Power steering	$177.35**
Radio	$101.00**
Heater	$ 78.25**
Solex glass	$ 21.50**
Wire wheels	$290.25**
Electric window lifts	$139.75***

*$139.75 on New Yorker series.
**Also for New Yorker and Imperial models.
***Also for New Yorker; standard equipment on Imperials. ☆ ☆

● Selecting neutral to park the car for a long period.

All one does to stop the car is remove the foot from the accelerator and press the brake pedal.

The value of power steering was particularly noticeable when parking in a confined space; with no effort required to turn the wheels, we found the task easier than with many much smaller cars.

With all this mechanical assistance, practically no skill is required to drive the car; anyone could learn to manipulate the extremely simple controls after a few minutes' tuition, and then it would only be a question of developing the necessary skill in manoeuvring. The clutch-accelerator-gearshift relationship, which is the main stumbling-block to most learners, plays almost no part in the car's operation.

We found the Chrysler a powerful performer on hills; the one or two climbs which required the use of low gear were taken with ease, the car shifting automatically into high as soon as it had built up enough speed. The extra-low gear will take it over anything climbable.

The smoothness of acceleration was remarkable throughout the test drive; at no time did we feel any harshness when ratios were changed, nor did we hear the slightest mechanical noise to indicate that this was being done.

Chrysler engineers originally developed and put into commercial production the power-steering mechanism, to which they have given the name of Hydraguide. Power assistance comes from a hydraulic-mechanical unit coupled to the engine, which recudes manual effort by 90 per cent. When fitting it to the 1952 models they reduced the number of steering wheel turns from lock to lock from 5½ to 3½. A diagram at the top of page 224 shows how the power-steering unit operates.

The automatic gear changes are effected by a fluid-torque drive mechanism, which combines the smoothness and torque multiplication of the torque converter with all the desirable features of a two-range, four - speed, hydraulically - operated geared transmission. This gives the car a smooth, quick getaway; as speed increases, the driver may choose, by accelerator action alone, between direct drive plus the converter effect —or a combination of the geared ratio and the converter ratio for extra performance.

Other refinements include self-returning electric windshield wipers, splashproof ignition, and safety-rim wheels which prevent a tyre stripping off after a blowout. This last improvement is a Chrysler patent, fitted as standard to all cars made by the Chrysler Corporation.

the Custom Imperial Sedan

In the Imperial for 1954, Chrysler stylists and designers have combined smart styling and conservative beauty to create a car that has a distinguished appearance, quite in keeping with the distinguished performance for which the Imperial is already so well and so widely known and respected. ■ With the distinctive new grille and bumper design; the long, graceful, perfectly blended lines, from front to rear; the wide, one-piece curved windshield; the Clearbac wrap-around rear window; and the exclusive Diving Eagle and the Chrysler winged-V on the hood, there is little likelihood anyone would mistake the Imperial, by Chrysler, for *any other car.*

The 1954 Imperial by Chrysler

the Custom Imperial Sedan

The interiors of the New Imperial have breath-taking elegance, living-room comfort and spaciousness, and every conceivable feature for the comfort, convenience, and safety of the driver and passengers. The finest materials are hand-tailored by expert craftsmen, and everything is in impeccable good taste. The seats are chair-height for your comfort. Center arm-rests in both front and rear compartments make the long trips comfortable, pleasurable. And the doors, in both front and rear, are exceptionally wide, and they open fully, so that you can get in and out of the car easily, gracefully.

the Imperial Newport

The Imperial Newport, an original body style created by Chrysler Engineers especially for those who wanted the open-car freedom of the Convertible Coupe, with the safety of the steel top and protection from the sun and wind. It is a beautiful car—a smart looking car—and, when you combine this style and individuality with the *incomparable performance* of the 235-horsepower FirePower Engine, the PowerFlite Fully-Automatic Transmission, Power Brakes, and Power Steering, it is easy to understand why the Imperial Newport, by Chrysler, is regarded as the most desirable motor car produced in America today.

The 1954 Imperial by Chrysler

the Custom Imperial Newport

Illustrated on the right is one of many beautiful combinations available on the Custom Imperial Newport, which permit you to tailor the interior to your taste, to harmonize with the many exterior colors from which you can make your selection. This combination is genuine Leather and Nylon fabric, in rich Two-Tone Blues. The large windows, in both the doors and the rear quarter panels, are electrically operated. The front seat, also, can be adjusted electrically, forward and backward, to the best position for any driver. As the seat moves forward, it raises so as to give you greater visibility and driving comfort.

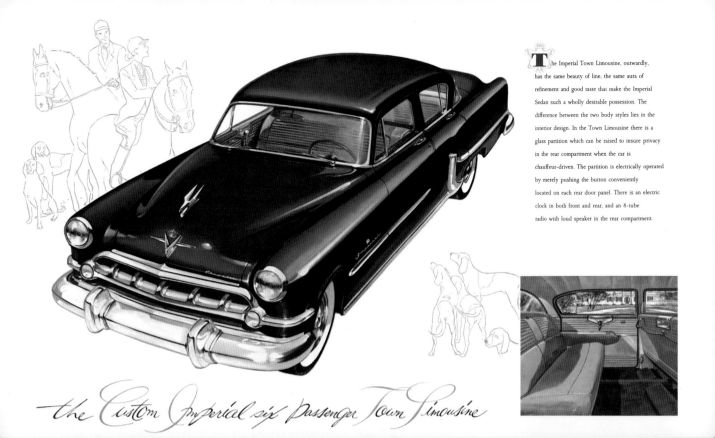

The Imperial Town Limousine, outwardly, has the same beauty of line, the same aura of refinement and good taste that make the Imperial Sedan such a wholly desirable possession. The difference between the two body styles lies in the interior design. In the Town Limousine there is a glass partition which can be raised to insure privacy in the rear compartment when the car is chauffeur-driven. The partition is electrically operated by merely pushing the button conveniently located on each rear door panel. There is an electric clock in both front and rear, and an 8-tube radio with loud speaker in the rear compartment.

the Custom Imperial six passenger Town Limousine

the Crown Imperial limousine

It cannot be denied that Imperial by Chrysler is conceived, styled and priced for those of affluence and influence; you have but to read a roster of today's Imperial owners to see numbered there many of the most prominent men and women of our time. Similar in styling to the Crown Imperial Sedan, the stunning Limousine differs principally by virtue of the electrically-operated glass partition that divides the chauffeur's compartment, which is beautifully upholstered in fine grain leather, from the rear seat passengers.

Mention America's prestige marques and most of us think of
Cadillac and Lincoln; but Chrysler's luxury division, Imperial, came
up with some stunning cars too, like this 1955 Imperial

Imperial
Highway

Words: **Sarah Bradley** Photography: **Anders Odeholm**

In the booming post-war years of Fifties America, almost anybody could enjoy the 'ultimate motoring experience'. All the auto manufacturers were offering bigger, better and flashier machines, from the budget names through to the big-money marques. Whatever the price bracket, glitz and gadgets were the order of the day. Keeping up with the Joneses by driving the newest, fastest, most futuristic car in the neighbourhood was the major preoccupation of a nation keen to display its new-found affluence.

But when it comes to cash, they say that people who have the most feel the least need to flaunt it. Those with established wealth and good breeding – and the inherent impeccable taste these things usually bring – traditionally prefer restrained elegance to blatant exhibitionism. And so it was that the most prestigious makers of the time often delivered automobiles that, while huge, sumptuous and cosseting to the extreme, were subtle, almost conservative, in their styling.

As Chrysler's most eminent model line since way back in 1926, Imperial had always been a prime example of how true class rises above the trends and fads of the day – and never more so than in the early Fifties. While lower-priced machines from other manufacturers embraced budding tailfins and ever-more chrome embellishments, Imperials boasted an altogether cleaner, more sensible design. Their looks remained unashamedly similar to those of their pre-war forerunners, and so they were to stay until the marque underwent a significant shake-up in the middle of the decade.

Design supremo Virgil Exner was hugely influential in the changing face of American automobiles, and he was at his most powerful in the mid-Fifties. It was then that, at a reputed cost of around $250million, he introduced the innovative and thoroughly modern 'Forward Look' to the Chrysler Corporation stable of Plymouth, Dodge, DeSoto and top-line Chrysler itself. This was also the time it was finally decided that Imperial was to go it alone as a separate division. The launch of the 1955 model on November 17th, 1954, consolidated the bid for exclusivity in the luxury-car field. It was hoped that at last the image of simply being a 'fancy Chrysler' – smart, but no more than a variation of a mass-produced machine – would be left behind.

Although the all-new Imperial used the same intrinsic body as Chrysler, much of its bodywork was unique. It also had a four-inch longer wheelbase (130 inches to the other's 126 inches). Two closed models were available in the standard range but there was no convertible, although it is said a running prototype was built. Indeed, Imperial had stopped producing rag tops in 1951, and customers looking for open-air thrills would have to wait until the next incarnation of the marque arrived in 1957. Along with 1955's four-door sedan and Newport two-door hardtop (pictured here), there were the long-wheelbase, eight-passenger Crown Imperial sedan and limo. These shared the same styling as the shorter cars but boasted a different roof and rear screen.

The new Imperial was at its most spectacular when viewed from the front, thanks to its divided 'eggcrate' grille and stylised eagle insignia. A restrained bumper sported integral indicators, while the headlamps wore peaked chrome bezels. Moving along the flanks, rounded, chrome-rimmed wheelarches and a belt-line moulding which ran nearly the entire length of the car were virtually the only decoration on the integrated fenders and conservative bodylines.

Rocker panel trim also reached through to the rear, where it widened just behind the back wheels to blend with the wraparound bumper. Novel free-standing 'gunsight' tail lights located on top of the fenders were borrowed from the 1951 K-310, Exner's first showcar for Chrysler. Incidentally, the chrome mounting beneath the right-hand-side unit flipped up to reveal the gas filler cap.

Inside was as luxurious as you would expect, with deeply padded bench seats and a covered dashboard. Power steering and power brakes were standard, with electric windows and air-conditioning among the options. Two large chrome-rimmed instruments relayed speed and other vital mechanical information to the driver, and the three-speed Powerflite automatic transmission was operated via an unusual dash-mounted gearstick.

The 'box was teamed with a 331cu.in. Firepower hemi V8, first introduced in 1951 and named for its hemispherical combustion chambers. By 1955 this produced 250bhp at 4600rpm and could propel the car to around 115mph. A much-

'Despite stiff competition from Cadillac, Lincoln and Packard, Imperial's traditional luxury competitors, the marque's sales for 1955 nearly doubled over the previous year's thanks to the huge image boost'

modified version of this basic engine also lay under the hood of the year's most awesome new performance machine, Chrysler's 130mph, 300bhp, C-300 two-door sport coupe. This very special model, which used the New Yorker hardtop body, also borrowed the Imperial's split grille and floating tail lights.

Despite stiff competition from Cadillac, Lincoln and Packard, Imperial's traditional luxury competitors, the marque's sales for 1955 nearly doubled over the previous year's thanks to the huge image boost. In all, just short of 11,500 units were produced. Of these, the breakdown was 7840 for the $4483 four-door sedan, 3418 for the $4720 two-door hardtop, 45 for the $7603 stretched sedan and 127 for the $7737 limo.

Apart from a slightly longer, 133-inch wheelbase, changes for the 1956 model year were mainly limited to minor trim revisions and mechanical upgrades. Again, Imperial managed to resist the temptation to fit over-blown tailfins. However, subdued versions were evident, sprouting from mid-body and sweeping up to create taller rear fenders, which were once again topped off by floating tail lamps. As if to counter this cursory nod to the styling crazes of the era, the new back bumper arrangement was simpler and less distinctive than the previous year's. The hemi V8 was bored out to

Imperial Highway

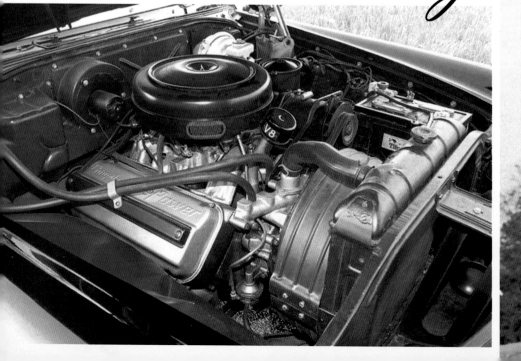

354cu.in. and now produced 280bhp at 4600rpm.

A new model was introduced into the standard-wheelbase range, the $5225 four-door hardtop. Both this and the $5094 two-door hardtop were now referred to as Southamptons. The $4832 four-door sedan remained the most popular purchase, accounting for 6821 sales – nearly two-thirds of the overall figure – by the year's end. The long-wheelbase Crown Imperials stayed the same as for the previous year, although once again there were minor styling changes. Of most interest inside all the cars was the introduction of a mechanical push-button gear selector for the ultimate in relaxed cruising.

Sales for the calendar year were 12,130, while model year production totalled 10,685. It was a fine achievement for the marque, and further success was to come in 1957 when an all-new Imperial line-up was introduced with automobiles that, for the first time, shared no outer body panels with their Chrysler cousins. But these distinctive machines abandoned the 'less is more' doctrine. Instead of reserved refinement, the '57 range indulged in exactly the kind of styling excesses Imperial had scrupulously avoided for so long, boasting an elaborate, full-width grille, heavily peaked headlamps and monster tailfins. However controversial the move was considered by the marque's more conventional customers, it worked – temporarily. Sales soared to more than 37,500 units for 1957, the division's highest total yet and, as would eventually be shown, the best of all time. But ultimately Imperial discovered that prestige is a very different thing to exclusivity. It learned that if it coveted the latter, it would just have to yield to the limited demand that went with the territory. ★

FAR LEFT: 1955 IMPERIALS USED THE FIREPOWER VERSION OF CHRYSLER'S MIGHTY HEMI MOTOR. **BELOW:** BOMBSIGHT-TYPE TAILLIGHTS WERE A SHORT-LIVED MID-FIFTIES FASHION FAD

The Custom Imperial is slim, taut and commanding in appearance. It is powered by a 250-hp engine.

IMPERIAL

With the accent on beauty and quality, Chrysler presents the impressive Imperial to the fine-car field.

WITH the introduction of the new 1955 Imperial, Chrysler brings to the fine-car field a new car and a dramatic new concept in American automotive styling," said E. C. Quinn, president, Chrysler Division, Chrysler Corporation. "The Imperial is slim, taut and commanding in appearance and combines elegance and distinction with a feeling of agility that sets it apart. We feel that ownership of an Imperial will be the most rewarding period of any motorist's life."

Imperial Has Individual Design

The new Imperial's designers aimed at creating an impressive motor car, large and commanding yet with slim lines and classic proportions to keep it free from bulkiness. Its body is not shared with any other car in the Chrysler Corporation line and it is built on its own assembly line.

The long, low sloping Imperial hood suggests power and affords excellent driver visibility. The roof runs in a smooth, tapering line from the sun cap visor to the rear deck. Its slimness serves to concentrate the mass of the car low to the ground.

A character line, formed in the side metal and accented by a thrusting chromed lance-like molding, runs back from the headlight and into the rear fender, giving the Imperial a strong feeling of forward motion, emphasizing the car's length and lowness, and unifying the side treatment. Fenders have been clearly defined to avoid bulkiness and full wheel openings emphasize the functional beauty of the wheels.

The superscenic windshield is wrapped around both top and bottom, terminating in side pillars which are sloped rearward to convey the feeling of forward motion. It is topped by a sun cap visor which flairs into the roof line.

The Imperial's divided grille, with its simple box-check effect, conveys the feeling of slimness by reducing front end bulk. The tapering area of body metal that divides the two grille elements points up the simplicity of the dual openings and, by carrying the body color down to the bumper line, adds to the feeling of lowness.

The bumper, which wraps around and extends to the wheel openings, underlines the front end treatment. At its outer ends, large, nacelle-like bumper guards emerge from heavily chromed hoods set against the fenders. The size and outboard location of these guards serve to accent width, and the chromed hoods which flow over them integrate the bumpers with the body. Parking lamps are deeply inset inside the guards and are protected by crossed bars of chrome.

A large Imperial eagle spans the dividing strip between the grille elements and assures positive model identification.

Rear View Distinctive

The unity of design which characterizes the new Imperial is evident when the car is viewed from the rear. Bumper guards, repeating the front end motif, are inset into chromed hoods and blend with the side and rear fender treatment. Their extreme outboard location adds a strong accent to width. Slim backup lights are recessed into the tall bumper guards and below them twin tailpipes extend through the bumper.

Centers of interest in the rear end treatment are the gun sight taillights mounted on chrome saddles on top of the rear fenders. Unlike the taillights

32

found on any other cars, they add to the distinctive character of the new Imperial. Mounted high and wide, they accent, by contrast, the sweeping lines of the rear fenders and are important aids in parking. When the lights are on, the recessed button in the forward end of the taillight nacelle glows with a subdued amber light, thus defining rear fender location. The gas tank filler tube is concealed beneath a hinged cover which is actually the rear half of the right fender saddle.

Imperial cars are available in two lines for 1955—the Custom Imperial on a 130-inch wheelbase and the Crown Imperial on a 150-inch wheelbase. Custom Imperials are offered in six-passenger sedan and Newport hardtop coupe.

Crown Imperial eight-passenger sedan and limousine models are offered for 1955. Over twenty feet in overall length, these cars have the same proportioning of elements that is characteristic of the Custom Imperial models. Despite their length and impressive size, they retain slimness and a feeling of vitality. Major body trim items such as grille, side moldings, bumpers, and taillights are identical to those found on Custom Imperial models, assuring positive identification

1955 IMPERIAL SPECIFICATIONS

Engine

	Custom	Crown
Type	90-V	same
Bore and stroke (in.)	3.81 x 3.63	same
Displacement (cu. in.)	331	same
Compression ratio	8.5 to 1	same
Brake horsepower	250 at 4600 rpm	same
Taxable horsepower	46.5	same
Maximum torque (lb. ft. at rpm)	340 at 2800	same
Transmission	Standard	Standard
	Optional	Optional
	Automatic	Automatic

Interior Dimensions

Front shoulder room (in.)	58.3	same
Rear shoulder room (in.)	58.3	same
Front hip room (in.)	62.5	same
Rear hip room (in.)	62.0	same
Steering wheel center to body center	15.1	same

Tires

Standard	8.20 x 15-4	8.90 x 15-6
Optional	8.20 x 15-6	————

Capacities

Oil (quarts)	5	same
Water (quarts)	26	same
Without heater	25	
Gasoline (gallons)	20	same

General

Wheelbase	130.0	149.5
Overall length (in.)	223.0	242.5
Overall width (in.)	79.1	N/A
Overall height (in.)	61.2	N/A

between these lines.

Imperials feature 16 solid and 17 two-tone color combinations of exterior finishes, plus 21 cloth, leather and vinyl interior trim options.

Every engineering feature designed for luxury motoring is incorporated in the new Imperial. Heading the list are the improved 250-horsepower FirePower V-8 hemispherical head engine, fully-automatic PowerFlite transmission, with PowerFlite range selector on the dash,

full-time coaxial power steering, four-way power-operated front seat, double-width-pedal power brakes, a new heating and ventilating system, and a new high-capacity air conditioning unit.

Other features include power window lifts, search-tuning radio, luxury coil spring seats, rigid full-length box-section frame, new suspension and new steering linkage. Crown Imperials are equipped with disc brakes—the only disc brakes offered on an American automobile. •

The Custom Imperial 6-passenger sedan combines elegance and distinction with a feeling of agility. It is built on its own assembly line and is also available in the hardtop coupe shown opposite.

CHASSIS AND BODY

Wheelbase	130
Tread	61 front, 60-4/10 rear
Length overall	223
Width overall	79-1/10
Height overall	61-2/10
Ground clearance	6-2/10 (minimum)
Turning circle diameter	45 feet 2 inches
Steering wheel lock-to-lock	3-½ turns with power
Tire size	8.20 x 15 tubeless
Weight, shipping	4565 pounds
Overhang	37 front, 56 rear
Brake lining area	201 square inches
Weight to brake area ratio	22.71 pounds per square inch
Weight to power ratio	18.26 pounds per BHP

ENGINE and contributing equipment

Cylinders, block, valves	8, 90-degree V, OHV laterally inclined
Bore and stroke	3.81 x 3.63
Displacement	331 cubic inches
Compression ratio	8.5:1
Brake horsepower (maximum)	250 @ 4600 RPM
Torque	340 foot pounds @ 2800 RPM
Carburetor	Single, 4-barrel
Choke	Automatic
Fuel pump	Mechanical
Fuel recommended	Premium
Fuel tank capacity	20 gallons
Exhaust system	Dual, reverse-flow mufflers
Crankcase capacity	5 quarts (add 1 for filter)
Drive shaft type	Exposed
Rear axle type	Hypoid
Rear axle ratio	3.54:1
Transmission	Automatic only
Piston speed @ maximum RPM	2783.0 feet per minute
Electrical system	6 volts
Cooling system capacity	26 quarts (with heater)

Acceleration (from standing start)

	to 30 MPH true speed:	4.2 seconds
	to 45 MPH true speed:	7.4 seconds
	to 60 MPH true speed:	11.2 seconds

Highway acceleration (with step-down) from 50 to 80 MPH .... : 10.0 seconds

Weather during tests .... Sunny, dry and cold

19 ft. 6 in.

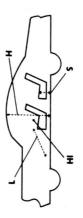

Hi	Hiproom	62-½ front, 62 rear
H	Headroom	35 front, 34-6/10 rear
S	Seat Height	13-3/10 front, 13-½ rear
L	Legroom	44-6/10 front, 48-4/10 rear

VISION over hood (driver 5' 10") .... 19 ft. 6 in. forward of bumper

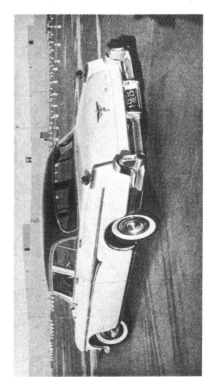

Imperial's front lines are much like Chrysler's, but with two horizontal bars in grille

Unusual tail-lights proved to be highly popular on experimental cars

THE IMPERIAL

The most elegant member of the Chrysler line shows a strong continental influence

Wheel discs on test car are cut out to provide more brake cooling

The Imperial is a completely new car that has the custom look and several features of styling drawn from the series of experimental cars that Chrysler has been showing around the country.

The Imperial I tested was the standard model with 130-inch wheelbase. The Crown Imperial has a mammoth 149½ inch wheelbase and will appeal chiefly to the carriage trade as a limousine that can carry eight persons.

Actually, there's a lot of similarity between the Chrysler New Yorker and this new prestige car, especially under the hood where the engine is identical, four-barrel carburetor, dual exhausts, and all. The chassis is longer, but otherwise de-

sign is about the same underneath the body with one exception: the much larger and heavier Crown Imperial has disc brakes, the first ones ever offered on an American car. You'll be seeing more disc brakes before many years—possibly in '56—for they cool better, have more effective braking area and fade less.

My test Imperial was a two-tone gray four-door sedan that had everything from power window lifts to power brakes. PowerFlite automatic transmission is standard on this car.

In spite of its size, the Imperial's styling gives the car a low, long, lean appearance without much suggestion of bulk. I did not have the feeling of driv-

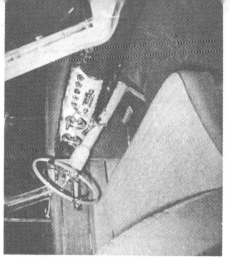

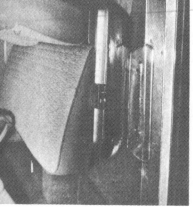

Four-way power seat is regulated by easily reached push-buttons on the driver's side

▲ Top of dash is padded, but extends to an edge sharp enough to be hazardous

▼ Custom Imperial models include a sedan and the Newport hardtop coupe seen here

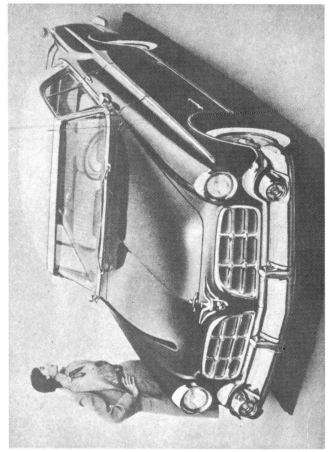

■ THE IMPERIAL

ing such a large car, even though, as a rule, I personally prefer much smaller machines. Little details distinguish this fine car. The parking lights, set low and far outboard in the distinctive bumper, are given an individualistic touch with protective chromed cross bars. The grille suggests kinship to the Chrysler line, but is deeper and is more detailed with an extra horizontal bar in each of the divided sides. The chrome line around the bottom of the body and around the fender cutouts wraps around the front, over the parking lamps, and increases the illusion of great width. But perhaps the most interesting styling note is the tail-light treatment which hails directly from the *d'Elegance* show car. Up high, and actually a thing apart from the rest of the car, these tail-lights are easily seen from the driver's seat.

The instrument panel is exactly like that of the Chrysler so the comments on the

panel need not be repeated. The steering wheel, too, is like that of the smaller car, thumbplates and all. But elsewhere inside, the Imperial is given distinctive styling with color combinations and materials not duplicated in the Chrysler line. Armrests actually form ledges built into the doors; these ledges hold ashtrays, power window controls, and are faced, on portions, with chrome which is duplicated in facing plates for the door handles.

Rich blues and greens and somber grays predominate in the interiors; seat back facings are usually heavy broadcloths which carry down toward the seat center as a background for the regal appearing crown symbol which is worked into the decor. Bolsters are pleated, as is the back of the front seat. Carpeting is very thick pile and removable footrests for rear seat passengers fit snugly against the bottom of the front seat back. Chrome is everywhere, but it has

been used tastefully to a greater degree, perhaps, than ever before in the interior of a domestic car.

The performance was not surprising, although it was extremely good for a large car. But the handling was a surprise. I had been quite pleased with the Chrysler New Yorker's handling, for ordinarily I feel inhibited by the usual roll and sway of the ultra-soft riding large cars. The Imperial, however, cornered every bit as well as the Chrysler, if not a bit better. Power steering of course—and I would prefer faster steering, but in spite of increased weight and size, the Imperial will get around with surprising agility. In traffic too, the car handled very well, and excellent visibility, probably the best in the Chrysler Corporation's expanded line, made driving a pleasure.

My objections to the Imperial reflect, largely, my personal beefs on the four other

cars in this line: the position of the Power-Flite gear ratio selector lever, the indicator, key starting, clock too far right for easy reading, etc. As in the Chrysler, the instruments are complete, well lighted, etc., but are so low on the dash as to require much eye shift from the normal driving position. I found the turn signals do not cancel when turning back from a less than 90-degree turn (not an exclusive by any means), the wipers leave large blind spots at each side of the windshield, and at night there is more windshield reflection from the instruments and dash panel chrome than there should be on such an expensive car.

The Imperial will perform like a whirlwind; it's in good taste, but does look rich; and even though it's large, the standard 130-inch wheelbase version tested is a remarkably maneuverable car, giving you the feeling of riding in luxury, yet having the capabilities of the fleetfooted smaller cars.

36

Engine: Duplicates the New Yorker Firepower V8.

Styling: No front-end facelift for the Imperial leaves it with a distinctive 2-piece grille (which it shared last year with Chrysler's semi-split metalwork) for '56. To the rear, the Imperial picks up the "dart" form with a climbing fenderline, on top of which is mounted, naturally, the unique "microphone-like" tail light. A subdued chrome rub strip leads to a wedge-shaped backup light. The rear end is finished off with the New Yorker Deluxe's bumper, rather than with the '55 Imperial's handsome interpretation of integral exhaust ports. For this year, exhaust is routed almost to the inner edge of the rear bumper, without a trace of pipe tips visible to dual-exhaust-port lovers (true of all cars in the Chrysler line).

An Imperial exclusive is the gas tank filler. Pushing the right-side reflector button above the backup light releases a catch that lets a spring-loaded door swing to the side, exposing

THE '56 IMPERIAL

the filler-neck within the fender. Not entirely new, but good.

Chassis: The single change in suspension components for the new Chrysler line is in the Imperial rear-end layout. For '56 it has a modified Hotchkiss-type drive with a pair of rear axle control struts running from the top of the axle rearward to the frame. About 2½ inches wide, the leaf-spring-like struts give, in effect, an increase in rear spring rate, and their position limits the travel of the differential case (allowing a smaller tunnel to clear the housing). This strut installation serves to take some torque off the rear springs, permitting the use of soft suspension units with more powerful engines; in addition, an advantageous by-product (and one that was noticeable in our demonstration Imperial) is resistance to rear-end sway and body roll.

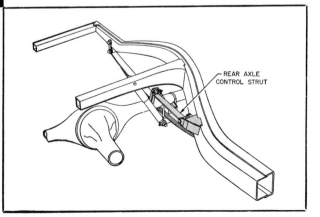

REAR AXLE
CONTROL STRUT

The IMPERIAL

"Luxury, top performance" is Tom's verdict on this 280-hp prestige car.

By Tom McCahill

"Exclusive Imperial" measures a long 229 in.

"In my personal opinion," says Tom, "this car is undoubtedly one of the handsomest ever built in America. I've never driven anything that received more voluntary compliments."

IMPERIAL, according to Webster's Dictionary, means quite a few things including "supreme, superior, of unusual size or excellence." To the Chrysler Corporation, as every TV-viewer has plainly heard, it also means "exclusive." Chrysler's "Exclusive Imperial" is their answer to GM's Cadillac Eldorado and Ford's Continental, meaning it is the top hack in the Chrysler barn. How does it compare with the others? Placing these three on a pedestal for investigation brings out many interesting facets.

The Imperial won't give way an inch in quality or comfort to the other two except that the Continental's chromework has a slight edge and both it and the Eldorado are more expensive. (Factory delivered prices, roughly: Imperial 2-door hardtop $5,400; Eldorado $6,700; Continental $9,600—*Editor*.) In performance the Imperial is quite a few blocks ahead of the others. In appearance these three top-level cars are as different as George Gobel, Clark Gable and Jimmy Durante. (It's up to you to figure out which one is Gable.) The outstanding style gimmicks, as you all know, are the Continental's tire mount, the Eldorado's Space Cadet tail fins and the Imperial's now-famous Sparrow-Strainer taillights, which means all three cars have rear-end features that make them distinctive.

My personal opinion of the Imperial's looks, which may not agree at all with yours, is that this is undoubtedly one of the handsomest cars ever built in America—depending on the paint job.

In hard turns and bends Tom found car bit in and held on "like a bat in a wind tunnel."

SPECIFICATIONS

MODEL TESTED:
1956 Chrysler Imperial hardtop convertible

ENGINE:
V8 cylinder, OHV; bore 3.94 inches, stroke 3.63 inches; maximum torque 380 foot pounds @ 2800 rpm; brake horsepower 280 @ 4600 rpm; compression ratio 9.0 to 1

DIMENSIONS:
Wheelbase 133 inches; overall length 229 inches; tread 61.3 inches front, 60.4 rear; width 78.8 inches; height 60.4 inches; weight 4,530 pounds; standard tire size 8.20x15; gas tank 20 gals

PERFORMANCE:
0 to 30 mph, 4.2 seconds
0 to 50 mph, 8.2 seconds
0 to 60 mph, 9.8 seconds
0 to 70 mph, 13.9 seconds
Top speed, 115-120 mph, depending entirely on tune-up

SPEEDOMETER ERROR:
At 60 mph on speedometer, actual speed 59.7 mph

angler's club), it created quite a sensation among the Continental and Eldorado Set.

One day in the Keys when the temperature was pushing 100, I snapped the air conditioning on to Full and felt like a roasting US#1. In a snowstorm that dumped 18 inches on my New Jersey mountain, I found this big car had a lot better traction and plow-through than many other American models I have driven in the last few years under such conditions. The power plant is Chrysler's big 354-cubic-inch mill developing 280 hp. The transmission with pushbuttons has been changed on the Imperial models of just a few months ago. On the late model '56 Imperials an extra third speed has been added (see photo) which gives it a lot more flexibility and dig than when it was first introduced. Engine-wise, this is basically the same car as the Chrysler New Yorker. The original models, due to their extra size and weight, were not up to the New Yorkers in traffic light get-away. With the addition of this third-speed button control the big Imperial will now out-nose the New Yorker by just a whisker in fast passing or in getting away from an angry mother-in-law on a motorcycle. These Imperials, when properly tuned, will get up to a full 120 mph and will cruise at 80 with no more effort than it takes to down a milkshake.

The proof of any car's real roadability comes in putting it over the road. I left Florida one night on my northern test leg with the car loaded like a paddy wagon after an Irish wedding. Hour after hour, this big Imperial ate up the road towards [Continued on page 42]

Extra third-speed button on transmission gives big car much more boff for passing.

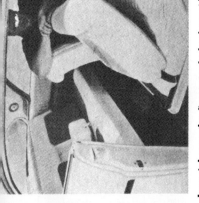

Fine upholstery made Tom wonder where harem girls were when he opened door.

Imperial uses the finest grade leather with nylon tapestry trim, reports our Uncle Tom.

I have never seen a car that can change its character quite as much as this one does through various combinations of colors. To me, some of the two-tone jobs only look like distant cousins of the same car in a solid color. Color combinations actually give the impression of changing the design of the entire automobile.

My test car was a solid white two-door hardtop and though this might be garish on some lesser automobiles, on the test car it seemed to give even more meaning to the name Imperial. The upholstery was the finest grade white leather with nylon tapestry trim. It made you wonder on opening the door, "Where are the harem girls that must go with this Sultan's barouche?" The top-priced three, slopes down so that your eyes can get a sizeable bite of the road immediately ahead. This vision is not cluttered with any gee-gaws to distract

the driver. The only forward ornament on the car is good old Herman The Coot in jump position—and he can only be seen by walking around front.

This is a big car—make no bones about that. It has a wheelbase of 133 inches, an overall length of 229 and an overall width of 78.8. It hits the scales, dry as a bar car going through South Carolina, at 4,530 pounds.

As this is an important entry in the race for America's Top Prestige Wagon, my tests were a lot longer than I usually make and covered over 5,000 miles in *extreme* conditions that varied from 18 inches of snow to tropical late-spring heat in the Florida Keys. In my many years of driving, at times in some pretty fancy cars, I've never driven anything that received more voluntary compliments than this one. At the Angler's Club in Key Largo where I went for some shooting (dig that, *shooting* at an

Gas tank filler cap is hidden behind hinged part of tail fin.

Now famous "Sparrow-Strainer" taillights are a distinctive mark of Imperial. Tom liked the air-conditioning unit, too.

39

CUSTOM STYLING FOR WELL-HEELED CUSTOMERS

Imperial has a restrained and dignified look, and new "control struts" help give riding ease to match it

IMPERIAL

■ Our test Imperial, a luxurious 4-door hardtop finished in light blue and gunmetal, was loaded with every piece of power equipment its makers offer. Lacking only air conditioning (which was certainly not missed due to the wintry blasts), this car was heavier than the 1955 model we had tested.

Imperial is in many ways a deluxe version of the Chrysler New Yorker, and is put out (as always) by the Chrysler division. But there are distinguishing differences. Most important, the Imperial is larger and heavier than the biggest Chrysler. Last year's Imperial was built on a 130-inch wheelbase chassis. For 1956 this big car has a wheelbase of 133 inches while its overall length has grown from 223 to 229-6/10 inches. Conversely the overall width (for some unexplained reason) has been slimmed ever so slightly from 79-1/10 to 78-8/10 inches. The tread of the front and rear wheels is unchanged as are principal suspension components.

Because large cars are inclined to sway, the rear end geometry has been improved, and resistance to sway built in by means of two control struts. These struts, one on each side, attach to the frame forward of the rear axle and are then anchored, flexibly, to the ends of the rear axle housing immediately inboard of the rear springs. Mounted longitudinally so as to resist sideway, these control struts improve the car's handling characteristics, their steadying action being noticed at once when you round the first corner. These struts look something like short leaf springs. The front suspension, with the shock absorbers mounted inside the coil springs, is still basically the same and leaf springs with steeply slanted shock absorbers are still used in the rear. Due to the increased weight of the larger new model, there has been considerable beefing up of the various members.

The *Crown Imperial*, the "block long" (149.5 inch wheelbase) limousine, formerly used disc type brakes; these have been discontinued in

Chrysler Corporation's finest is nearly seven inches longer overall than last year (now 19 feet plus). It boasts many custom features.

IMPERIAL "gunsight" tail lights, and changes under the hood

favor of the newly developed "floating shoe center-plane" brakes mentioned previously under De Soto and Chrysler. Requiring less maintenance, resisting fade to the great extent, bringing a larger percentage of the lining area into contact with the brake drums, these new conventional type brakes are said to be at least the equal of the disc type used until this year on the Crown Imperial. Last year the effective lining area was 201 square inches; increased to 251 square inches for 1956, the braking action like the decreased rear end sway is immediately noticeable to the driver. Power brakes of the new vacuum reserve type reviewed earlier in this Chrysler Corp. section are standard on Imperials. Repeated fast braking for a dozen hard stops left the pedal still reasonably easy to operate and stopping distances were not noticeably affected.

The aforementioned rear axle control struts have an additional benefit too: they evidently provide a little more stiffness aft and prevent the rear end from rising as much as previously on a fast stop, for nose dipping is less on the '56 model when the brakes are slammed down hard. The brake pedal is large and set low for the quick action so necessary today.

Styling is important, and the Imperial has its share with special attention having been devoted to a distinctive approach to the famed

"Forward Look." The tail lights, or illuminated gunsights if you prefer, are the Imperial's hallmark and descend from the successful K-310 show car of a few years back. For 1956 they are redesigned and look more streamlined. The rear fenders are upswept and have the same general lines as those of the Chrysler and De Soto lines, but a special streamlined piece of formed metal terminates the fenders taking the place of the conventional tail lights. The rear bumper is new, the guards being smoothly formed to mate with the slant of the fenders. The back-up lights are set into the extreme tail of the fenders above the guards, and the right fender tip hinges outboard of the car for entry to the fuel tank filler when a small button above the back-up light is pushed. A dual exhaust system is standard equipment, but unlike last year, the tail pipes are modestly kept out of sight beneath the car instead of being piped through the bumper tips, as the 1956 cliché would have them.

While the rear of the Imperial has a completely new look, the front is changed only slightly. The grille, divided into two separate and functional openings, is unchanged as is the basic fender line. The headlights, however, have been given new bezels which have less chrome and come to a more pronounced and pointed hood above the lights. The front

bumper still contains the parking and turn signal light combination in rather rugged looking bomb-like guards while the front chrome strip below the grille wraps up and over the bumper guards and over the wheel openings and along the bottom side of the body. The belt line chrome trim along the side is new, more simplified, and has a sculptured look.

Inside the driver faces an instrument panel that is almost identical to that of the Chrysler line with the front radio speaker to the extreme right and the moderately sized glovecase adjacent. The clock is a bit on the small side for easy driver reference and is above the glovecase. The entire dash top is padded, like last year. Auxiliary controls are grouped horizontally below the padded top and in the center; these range from panel and dome light switches to the single (front seat) cigar lighter and require some reach. The heater and ventilation controls are also centered but are below the radio. The test Imperial was equipped with the new transistor-type radio which requires no warm-up time; there was a rear seat compartment speaker as well, and tone quality was excellent —superior in fact to the conventional tube type radios. Of course this luxury car had the new Highway Hi-Fi record player. Mounted in the ultra-smooth-riding Imperial the player gave a much better performance than did the unit in one of our two test Plymouths, and never missed a beat in spite of bumps for the fifty-minute duration of a single record.

The interior space afforded by the Imperial is almost identical to that of the Chrysler. As

Imperial's engine is identical to that in Chrysler New Yorker. With 354 cubic inches, this is the year's fourth largest engine. Power is 280 with bigger potential for '57.

Longer front fenders permit distinctive pointed hood over headlights. The grille is unchanged.

MI Tests The Imperial

[Continued from page 39]

New York with all the comfort of riding in the lushest Pullman. In hard turns and bends I found it biting in and holding on like a bat in a wind tunnel.

Jim McMichael who was behind me in my own car finally found out the real reason for the Mars-type taillights. On this trip we ran mile after mile with almost zero visibility through smoke caused by a series of forest fires that came right up to the road's edge. Jim told me, when we stopped for coffee, that those taillights stood out like Gina Lollobrigida in a Boy Scout's suit. When these lights were first introduced on the original Imperials they resembled moose antlers on a canary. They are now a distinctive trademark of the car and a useful one, too.

Due to the full-time power steering, this is the easiest-handling-and-controlling car of mastadon proportions that I've ever driven in city traffic where you grunt and groan two feet at a time. Whether you like power steering or not, in traffic with a big car it's real great. If you're going to have power steering, then go all the way and have it full-time, like Chrysler's. Anything less is like playing catch with an ice cube to save the price of an air-conditioning unit. There was a time when guys with little wives never expected them to drive big-sized family buckets because the sheer physical strength needed just to park would have developed her into an Olympic discus-throwing champ in a matter of months. As all you old-time readers know, I've been a booster of small cars for many years and haven't wavered from this point one inch, even now. But when we do have big cars it's nice to know that from a physical output standpoint there is no difference in the handling, regardless of size.

I still get in a lot of arguments regarding power steering and especially Chrysler's full-time power. The arguments usually center around the fact that "you don't get the road feel" that you do without power steering. This is absolutely true and no argument could change it. You do get more road feel without power steering. But after several thousand miles with full-time power steering, if you're a good driver you become sensitized to this new effortless

method and suddenly you find you have as much road feel and knowledge of what's going on as you ever did, only the sensation is coming to you differently. It's like a piston pilot of many years' experience going into jets for the first time. It's a different feel but the end result is the same—and much faster. For real competition and hard road driving I would still prefer non-power steering and a correctly-balanced car. However, power steering has advanced and after more than 50,000 miles of driving cars so equipped I'm finally convinced that there is a definite place for it, especially in luxury liners where ease of operation is more important than how the car could get through White House Corner at LeMans at full throttle.

In summing up, the Imperial is a full-bore luxury car, jammed full of goodies for everyone who has the price and is not interested in winning the next steeplechase at Belmont. There isn't a car made in America today offering more interior luxury, combined with top performance, than the new Imperials. Mechanically they are sound, gutty and reliable, using the same power plant as the world record-holding Chrysler 300 tamed down for civilized use. •

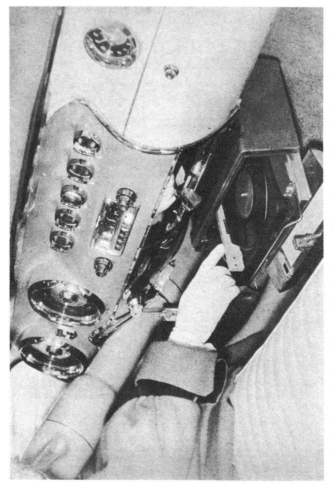

Optional record player slides out for placing a record on the turntable. One has only to push pickup arm to right where it stops automatically at start of record. Soft ride kept needle in place.

a matter of fact the depth of the trunk is only about 1½ inches greater in the Imperial. Where then is the value received for the extra cost? Beyond the distinctive styling, Imperial gives this: smaller production, hence a prestige born of owning a car that is practically custom built. The principal interior fittings used in the Imperial are identical with those used in the Chrysler, but the assembly of such a car as the Imperial is more closely inspected because it is a top prestige product that is pitted against the Lincoln, Cadillac and the big Packards in the competitive scramble for the top dollar.

The Imperial, being about 8½ inches longer than the Chrysler New Yorker, will be a bit more clumsy to park; it will require a slightly larger (but no wider) garage. The tires are larger, front and rear overhang is more, but

mechanics will find the car's innards to be duplicates of the Chrysler New Yorker's with engine and transmission the same except for a change in rear axles due to the increased weight. Strangely the Imperial shares with Cadillac the distinction of giving the best overall mileage of all V-8's (15.5 m.p.g.) during the brief mileage tests that the time allowed. The state of tune of the modern V-8 high compression engine both as to ignition and carburetor can vary quite widely. In other words such a large car, conditions being equal, will be more expensive to run and to maintain than smaller cars.

The Imperial's appeal is to the connoisseur, the person of means, who buys for the prestige inherent in owning a distinctive car. Chrysler Division has improved this car's sales chances for 1956 by giving it greater styling distinction.

THE IMPERIAL
LE BARON

*America's Most
Distinguished Car*

The Le Baron, a four-door body type, retains, of course, all of the superb, exclusive styling and the engineering excellence of the new Imperials. Its distinction and charm lie in the ultra-conservative design and decor of the interior; in the long list of standard equipment; and in several distinguishing marks of identification on the exterior of the car. It is available only in solid colors for the exterior and luxurious, conservative monotone interiors of the finest broadcloth. The Le Baron was created especially for a very distinct clientele, and will be available only in limited numbers.

THE IMPERIAL FOUR-DOOR SEDAN

THE IMPERIAL FOUR-DOOR SOUTHAMPTON

THE IMPERIAL TWO-DOOR SOUTHAMPTON

CROWN TWO-DOOR SOUTHAMPTON

THE IMPERIAL CROWN SEDAN

You will not find a car, anywhere in the world, that looks like the Imperial Crown Sedan, illustrated above. Whether or not *you* think it is the *most beautiful* car in the world is entirely a matter of your own decision. However, if you are tired of the similarity of all other cars, and want *something different*, something with *smart individuality* we suggest that you see, carefully inspect, and *drive* the Imperial.

On the right is shown a new design feature—the *curved* window frame of extruded aluminum and the *curved* window glass, which maintain the smooth flow of the body line from the roof to the bottom of the side sill, giving the car a low, sculptured look.

45

THE IMPERIAL CROWN FOUR-DOOR SOUTHAMPTON

THE IMPERIAL CROWN CONVERTIBLE COUPE

Gas filler cap can't get lost.   Direction signals are below pushbuttons.   Inside latches are like aircraft throttles.

Restraint has gone out the curved window of the

IMPERIAL

'57

SINCE IT BROKE AWAY from the Chryslers, at least name-wise, the haughty Imperial has been working toward a true character of its own. With 1957, it truly establishes a separate identity. To our surprise, it has abandoned its former stately quality to become the most distinctive, and we think the most attractive, '57 car.

This one deserves a walk around it before entering. Only subtle differences set the four-door sedan body shell apart from the line's other four cars; it has the wrap-over-as-well-as-around, and fantastically expensive, new windshield that other Chrysler products use only on convertibles. Vent and roll-down windows curve inward at the top, and you can have the false but handsome "tire cover" on the rear

deck if you like. Two- and four-door hardtops use a dual-sectioned roof (will it be transparent for '58?) that really sets them apart. And there's a convertible that could make Eldorado buyers think twice.

Through the new wheel with its padded spokes, you command an instrument panel with more than a touch of the classic. Giant twin dials are supremely readable. Black light helps at night. Torqueflite buttons, including the neutral start control, are disposed vertically—1, 2, D, R, N, reading up at the left edge, and below them is a curious new teeter-totter turn signal. You press the top for a right turn, the bottom for a left, the middle if you change your mind. We don't see the advantage in taking your hand off the wheel to signal. Heater and air conditioner controls are also vertical, opposite the Torqueflite buttons. The foot-operated emergency brake should be extended to the rest of the line.

The luxury touches haven't been spared elsewhere inside. Window ledges are still leather covered, and each rear passenger has his own ashtray and lighter on the more expensive versions. There are now an Imperial Crown and an Imperial LeBaron (no relation to the original classic), differing only in trim and equipment, as well as the "ordinary" Imperial. These have opening armrests for extra storage. Some models have center armrests in the rear only, and some provide them in the front as well.

Outside of a double-jointed driveshaft, the chassis of the Imperial is essentially that of the Chrysler New Yorker. With greater weight and the same Firepower engine (4.0 x 3.9 bore and stroke, 392 cubic inches, 9.25 compression ratio, four-barrel carburetor, 325 horsepower) its performance will lag behind the strongest Chrysler. But top performance isn't its function. Luxury is what this one has to offer, and it gives full measure.

IMPERIAL

By JAMES WHIPPLE

CHRYSLER Corporation shot the works in designing and engineering the 1957 Imperial, which represents the first major style change since the car made its debut as an independent make.

With a price range of $4,700 to $5,600 at the factory (including automatic transmission and power assists), Imperial comes squarely into competition with Cadillac and Lincoln as a full-fledged luxury car.

As soon as we compared the Imperial with the '57 Chrysler we realized that it was a completely different car rather than a longer wheelbase version of the Chrysler New Yorker with different grille and trim. Every body panel, strip of trim and piece of glass in the '57 Imperial is new; not one a duplicate of a Chrysler part.

Only the massive, 392 cubic inch FirePower V-8 and the new three-speed TorqueFlite transmission are shared with the Chrysler New Yorker. The Imperial's chassis and suspension

is basically the same as that found on all '57 Chrysler Corporation cars, with ball-joint-and-torsion-bar front suspension and asymetric, outboard-mounted rear springs. However, the Imperial frame is its own, designed for the car's 129-inch wheelbase and 224-inch overall length.

Although these dimensions are longer than the Chrysler's, they represent a reduction in both length and wheelbase over last year's Imperial, which was 229 inches overall and had a wheelbase of 133 inches. The result of the shortening job has been to eliminate the eight-passenger limousine and sedan from the line.

This does not mean that the Imperial is cramped by anyone's definition of the term. With the front seat moved as far to the rear as possible, there's still leg-stretching room for six-foot plus passengers in the rear seat. This roomy rear compartment is found on the four-door hardtops as well as the full-fledged sedan.

Chrysler executives evidently felt that the limousine market was so small that it did not warrant the extra expense of two chassis of different wheelbases with different-sized bodies. Nor did they feel that it warranted limiting all models to the longer wheelbase necessary for the eight-passenger cars which are more difficult for the owner-driver to maneuver.

The '57 Imperial looks like a much bigger car than last year's even though it is shorter. There are two reasons for this; one is the finned, "Flight-Sweep" styling with its unbroken line from headlight to tail-light which makes the car look longer, the other is the fact that the '57 is four inches lower and 2½ inches wider. The car appears to be tremendously wide, but once behind the wheel we felt no greater psychological hazard maneuvering in close quarters than in any other luxury car.

The '57 Imperial is the first of the large luxury cars to produce a really

48

Price range (Factory list price)
$4,762.50 (Imperial four-door sedan)
to $5,667.50 (LeBaron four-door sedan and
LeBaron Southampton hardtop)

IMPERIAL
is the car
for you

if... You appreciate sleek, beautiful lines and a car that's dashing and elegant without being flashy, bulky-looking or overtrimmed with chrome.

if... You want a really big, roomy car that has the most powerful performance in its field.

if... You would rather have a car that's extremely steady when rounding curves or traveling over bad roads at high speeds than a car that soaks up all road vibration yet sways and rolls on turns.

if... You want a car that's generous in every dimension yet as easy to maneuver as one of the low-priced cars.

IMPERIAL SPECIFICATIONS

ENGINE	V-8
Bore and stroke	4 in. x 3.9 in.
Displacement	392 cu. in.
Compression ratio	9.25:1
Max. brake horsepower	325 @ 4600 rpm
Max. torque	430 @ 2800 rpm
DIMENSIONS	
Wheelbase	129 in.
Overall length	224 in.
Overall width	81.2 in.
Overall height	56.7 in.
TRANSMISSION	TorqueFlite

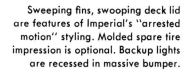

Sweeping fins, swooping deck lid are features of Imperial's "arrested motion" styling. Molded spare tire impression is optional. Backup lights are recessed in massive bumper.

low-slung sedan. (Imperial is 56.7 inches high compared to 59.1 for Cadillac and 60.2 for Lincoln.) The lowering job was done with no sacrifice of interior headroom. Door dimensions remain ample although it is necessary to stoop a bit more when climbing into the car.

Seating positions have given way somewhat in the interest of maintaining sufficient headroom in the lowered car. Rear seat passengers in the '57 Imperial will find that their knees are higher because the cushion has been placed closer to the floor than in the '56 models. With six-way power control the front seat can be adjusted to any height and position comfortable to the driver.

Some luxury car owners may find the lower seating position a bit different, but few if any will find it uncomfortable.

As far as looks are concerned, we think that the Imperial is outstanding among the cars of the upper-medium and luxury-price groups. It is the sleekest of the really large cars, with a tremendous amount of passenger space enclosed in a very smooth and graceful body shell.

Vision is excellent from the power-adjusted front seat which permits drivers of short or tall stature a comfortable, relaxed driving position. The

windshield of the Imperial tested showed some distortion at the sharply-wrapped lower corners

It's probable that this distortion problem will be eliminated later in the model run as has been the case with wraparounds in the past.

The door and rear quarter windows provide better-than-average vision for a conventional sedan. This is because the frames are extruded aluminum enabling thinner sections than conventional pressed steel frames

These side windows also represent a "first" for American production cars, as the glass is formed in a gentle curve inward to top of the frames. This permits a tapered effect from door to roofline with a correspondingly narrower roof and a wider view of the scenery for all passengers.

Once under way, the Imperial proves the superior combination of handling, stability and ride inherent in the lower center of gravity and Chrysler Corporation suspension systems.

Imperial has a flat ride with almost no tossing or pitching on very sharp bumps.

The performance of the Imperial belies its great weight and bulk. The 325 horsepower V-8 driving through three-speed TorqueFlite transmission will snap the 4,800-pound sedan from a standing start to a true 60 mph in

just ten seconds.

Action in the middle speed ranges is equally fast, especially when the acceleration is made below the maximum "kick-down" of second gear.

With TorqueFlite you can hold the Imperial in second by depressing the "2" button on the panel. The car will then operate in second regardless of the throttle opening until the automatic upshift point is reached at 70 mph. The engine and transmission are satisfactorily quiet

Operation of TorqueFlite on the Imperial is about average in the luxury field. The positioning of the transmission control buttons in a long line on the edge of the instrument cluster hood is a good deal less convenient than the compact grouping in the control head at the left corner of the windshield found on all other automatic transmission-equipped Chrysler products.

Power steering was very satisfactory on the Imperial, principally because there is more resistance to turning than on other Chrysler cars; it's not as easy to swerve the wheel more than you intend to. Also, the front wheels have greater caster action and tend to return to straight-ahead position as you complete a turn.

The push-button directional signal switch on the Imperial was a source

Imperial's grille and hood emphasize width and lowness. Effect is also stressed by optional dual headlights. Conventional headlights are housed in chrome cylinders, balancing grille.

of considerable annoyance because it cannot be switched off except by turning the steering wheel for a considerable distance in the reverse direction. This means that when moving out to pass another car at cruising speeds you can't stop the blinking lights unless you swerve the car sharply. The only other alternative is not to use the signals. This is the sort of engineering "goof" that is all the more surprising when it appears on a top-of-the-line luxury car.

There were a few loose ends in the finishing of the car that spoiled the otherwise high standards of workmanship. Door latch and window lifts rattled considerably in both front doors when we travelled over bumpy roads or rough surfaces. There was some leakage into the trunk after driving through a steady rain, and the springs in the back seat cushion popped whenever a passenger shifted his weight.

SUMMING UP: Imperial is the most rakishly-styled luxury car in America —a car with excellent interior room, vision for driver and passengers and the steadiest ride in its class. Performance is second to none, although not quite the smoothest. Quality of workmanship falls a bit short of the standards of perfection expected in an automobile of this price. ●

IMPERIAL CHECK LIST ☑☑☑☑☑ — 5 CHECKS MEANS TOP RATING IN ITS PRICE CLASS

	Imperial checks out as the most powerful performer in the luxury field. Acceleration time from 0 to 60 is just 10 seconds. TorqueFlite transmission is very responsive in the passing range.	☑☑☑ ☑☑
STYLING	The new Imperial stands out as the sleekest, most gracefully-styled of the large luxury cars. The design makes the car look lower and longer than it really is yet provides superior vision, good headroom and luggage space.	☑☑☑ ☑☑
RIDING COMFORT	Lower center of gravity and new Chrysler Corporation suspension system gives the Imperial the steadiest ride at high speed of any of the luxury cars. However, the car does not absorb vibration from rough road surface quite as well as the other big luxury cars.	☑☑☐ ☑☑
INTERIOR DESIGN	Shoulder, hip and legroom in the new Imperial is more than ample. Headroom is satisfactory even in this extremely low car. Seating positions are lower than other luxury cars but very comfortable. Vision is the best in the luxury group while luggage space is above average.	☑☑☐ ☑☑
ROADABILITY	In its class, Imperial has the edge, giving a very stable, flat-cornering ride at high speeds on rough roads as well as taut control of rebound on sharp dips and bumps.	☑☑☑ ☑☑
EASE OF CONTROL	An excellent power steering system, responsive engine and transmission combination, plus easy-acting power brakes make the Imperial a very happy car to operate in parking lots or on superhighways.	☑☑☐ ☑☑
ECONOMY	With its large (392 cu. in.) engine and heavy weight, Imperial cannot be expected to be an economical car as far as gasoline mileage is concerned. Like all other 1957 luxury cars it uses premium grade gasoline. TorqueFlite transmission doesn't have as favorable a high gear ratio as one of the other luxury cars.	☑☑☐ ☑☐
SERVICEABILITY	Normal service operations are no more difficult on the Imperial than any of the large luxury cars. Imperial spark plugs are buried in valve covers but are easier to reach than some others.	☑☑☐ ☑☑
WORKMANSHIP	Quality of workmanship on the Imperial has improved since the first cars appeared (they had "orange peel" paint and misfit window frames) but it still falls below that found on another of the three luxury cars.	☑☑☐ ☑☐
VALUE PER DOLLAR	Imperial is a soundly engineered well-built car with styling that will stay "up to date" for several years. In the past, Imperials have depreciated faster than some other luxury cars.	☑☑☐ ☑☑

IMPERIAL OVERALL RATING...4.1 CHECKS

CHRYSLER IMPERIAL IS UNQUESTIONABLY ONE OF THE SMARTEST, AND LARGEST PACKAGES TO COME FROM DETROIT IN A LONG TIME.

IMPERIAL ROAD TEST

MOST Beautiful Car of the Year was the title many people felt the new Imperial deserved after seeing all the 1957 models last fall and winter.

That opinions like this were not just passing ones is evidenced by the tremendous sales reception Imperial has received since then. In fact, it is the most improved car of the year in that respect!

At the end of the first five months of this year, well over 14,000 Imperials had been registered by proud buyers—as compared to something over 4,000 for the same period in 1956. That was good enough to vault from 18th to 15th position in the sales race.

A sales gain of that nature is a pretty

good indication that the car in question is a desirable one!

A major factor in Imperial's 1957 success story, of course, is the undeniably good looks of the car. Its sweeping, long and low lines give it a graceful appearance not always achieved in an automobile of this size. It's a big car—and looks it—but its designers managed to avoid the excessively bulky, almost clumsy appearance that is all too often a characteristic of king-sized luxury jobs.

Nor is this impression of gracefulness lost when you ride or drive in an Imperial.

The big 392-inch V-8 puts out such ample quantities of power and torque that the Imperial is clearly the best performer in its class. Yet the car's nearly two and one-half tons are propelled along so smoothly and effortlessly that it's hard to realize it goes as well as it does.

There is little clumsiness about its handling qualities, either. Despite the fact that Imperial has one of the longest wheelbases of any standard 1957 model, it is surprisingly easy to drive. Obviously it is not as nimble as low-priced cars with wheelbases of from 18 inches to two feet less.

Cornering characteristics are excellent and it is surprisingly maneuverable in view of its bulk. It is at least as good as any current U.S. car of nearly similar size and is far superior to some of its competition. In fact, it makes some cars

in the medium price class look silly in this respect.

It's often been said that no car is perfect, however, and that is true of the Imperial. It has flaws—most are merely minor annoyances, but others are rather serious.

Into the latter category fall complaints about quality. The expensive radio didn't play properly. Weatherstripping came loose, the trunk was poorly sealed, one door handle was defective.

It must be granted that this particular car came out of the factory and was promptly put into service as a company courtesy car, so it didn't get the normal dealer pre-delivery check.

Other complaints noted during the test were not so important and conceivably would be eliminated by greater familiarity with the car (although the test period covered more than a week and 1000 miles).

The pushbutton turn signal control was not nearly as convenient as a normal column-mounted lever. It was located at the lower left side of the dash, requiring the driver to move one hand from the steering wheel to signal a turn. In addition, the control is a single button pivoted in the center and it was sometimes hard to hit it correctly, without a downward glance, to signal the direction in which the turn was to be made.

Transmission pushbutton controls, grouped in a line at the far left side of the instrument cluster, seemed to be less

IMPERIAL TEST DATA

Test Car: Imperial two-door hardtop
Basic Price: $4735.50
Engine: 392-cubic-inch ohv V-8
Carburetion: Single four-barrel
Compression Ratio: 9.25-to-1
Horsepower: 325 @ 4600 rpm
Torque: 430 @ 2800
Dimensions: Length 224 inches, width 81.2, height 56.7, tread 62 front and 60 rear, wheelbase 129
Shipping Weight: 4650 lbs.
Transmission: TorqueFlite (torque converter)
Acceleration: 0-30 mph in 4.1 seconds, 0-45 in 7.1, 0-60 in 10.4
Gas Mileage: 13.8 mpg tank average
Speedometer Corrections: Indicated 30, 45 and 60 mph are actual 29, 43 and 56, respectively

BEAUTIFUL UPHOLSTERY and folding armrest in Imperial rear seat present a plush appearance, coupled with solid comfort, to those who ride in Chrysler Corporation's new prestige car.

HI-WAY HI-FI is listed among extras for Chrysler Corp. cars. Turntable revolves at 16⅔ rpm, or half speed of conventional LP units, to minimize possibility of needle jumping from grooves.

IMPERIAL GRILLE is relatively simple and uncluttered. Concensus of opinion is that car looks better with the optional dual headlight treatment. The bumper design is extremely well done.

CURVED SIDE GLASS retracts fully into door and body panels, like other hardtop designs, eliminating center post. Pull type door handles offer no chance to snag clothing. Note the roof styling.

convenient to the driver than other push-button setups.

Getting back to the plus side, it would be unfair to leave out mention of the absolutely tremendous vision driver and passengers have in an Imperial. The windshield, curved back at top as well as around the sides, makes it easy to spot overhead traffic lights and signs set high above the road. Passengers liked the way they could get a virtually unobstructed look at the scenery in almost any direction.

The Imperial did not prove to be overly thirsty. In fact, gas mileage was good for a car of this size. It averaged about 15 mpg on the highway at cruising speeds of 55 to 60 mph—and with much stop and go driving through small towns on the route. Overall city and highway average was just under 14 mpg.

The test car was equipped with three-speed TorqueFlite automatic transmission, full-time power steering and power brakes—all three are standard items and are included in the base price quoted in the data panel. It also had power seats, power windows and similar options which have come to be the same as standard on cars of this class, except that they add to the price!

The TorqueFlite unit was as smooth as most of its type—torque converter with auxiliary gearsets—in going through its shift points. It is a much more satisfactory unit than the two-speed transmissions Chrysler formerly used. Being able to select second gear manually (below approximately 70 mph) is an aid in decelerating for corners and downhill grades.

Full-time power steering is a necessity on a car of this size at almost any speed if any sort of medium-fast steering response is desired. The Imperial steering seemed to have more self-centering action after turns than some Chrysler products tested in the past.

All in all, it's not difficult to see why Imperial is attracting a record number of buyers this year after driving one. The attractive appearance catches your admiration at first and the car's other sterling qualities hold it as you become acquainted.

The most irritating thing about the car was the assembly defects. It certainly would not have taken much to correct them, however, so they detracted nothing from the intrinsic character of the Imperial.

Even if this automobile is not changed greatly in the next year or so, it seems likely that it has a winning combination —one that will keep winning it new friends and customers. ●

IMPERIAL

By JIM WHIPPLE

CHRYSLER Corporation's big Imperial is basically a refined version of the car that caused such a sensation in the luxury car field during the 1957 model run. Sales of the '57 Imperial zoomed to more than three times the '56 total.

Last year, the Imperial offered really exciting new styling of a kind which brought to mind the classic Marmons, Packards and Duesenbergs of 25 years ago.

Then, too, there was roadability and handling ease superior to anything that had come before. And to top it off, Imperial offered higher torque (430) and horsepower (325) than any of the competition.

Having taken these engineering and styling giant steps with the '57 Imperial, Chrysler Corporation has taken 1958 to consolidate its gains and make sure that its production people are able to assemble brilliantly engineered components into a solid, flawless and enduring automobile.

After spending a weekend with a '58 Imperial, we are happy to be able to report that great gains have been made in quality control since the early months of 1957 model production.

All the annoying imperfections that showed up in some of the '57 Imperials have been eliminated (We draw our conclusions on the basis of examinations of a half dozen or so '58 Imperials spot checked in dealers' showrooms).

No longer do door handles rattle, windows stick and window frames not meet perfectly at their joints. Paint, finish and trim are now up to standards expected in a car costing upwards of $5000.

After testing the "Big Three" last year, we came to the clear-cut decision that Imperial offered a superior combination of riding quality, roadability and ease of control. It was simply able to take you over more difficult roads faster, with greater comfort and less driver effort, than either Cadillac or Lincoln.

On the basis of such superiority, Chrysler Corporation evidently felt that all it needed to keep abreast of its 1958 competition was a number of detailed refinements and improved quality control.

After testing the new Imperial, we've come to the conclusion that Chrysler was pretty near right.

However, both Lincoln and Cadillac have come a long way toward closing the gap left by the dramatic advances made by Imperial in '57. In a few respects the competition has passed Imperial.

The most significant improvement is Lincoln's unit body and frame structure in which every part except the doors, hood, trunk lid, engine and running gear are welded into one rattle-free unit. This construction eliminates body shake caused by the "whip" of the car's frame resulting from road shocks transmitted by the suspension.

(Continued on page 56)

As the silhouette indicates, Imperial underwent less of an exterior change than any other '58. The car's excellent '57 sales were result of a wide public acceptance.

IMPERIAL
is the car
for you

if... Your eye is pleased by sleek, sweeping body lines that make the Imperial different from others in its field.

if... You are willing to accept lower seating positions as the price of outstanding vision and a sway-free ride.

if... You appreciate the outstanding maneuverability that stems from Imperial's "quicker" power steering and push-button transmission.

IMPERIAL SPECIFICATIONS

ENGINE	V-8
Bore and stroke	4.0 in. x 3.9 in.
Displacement	392 cu. in.
Compression ratio	10.0:1
Max. brake horsepower	345 @ 4600 rpm
Max. torque	450 @ 2800 rpm
DIMENSIONS	
Wheelbase	129 in.
Overall length	225.8 in.
Overall width	81.2 in.
Overall height	57 in.
TRANSMISSION	Torqueflite

When Imperial does not have optional "Continental" cover, trunk lid has chrome strip splitting it down the middle. Carpeted tire cover is available to cover spare and keep luggage unbruised.

Imperial engine has a four-barrel carburetor puts out 345 bhp at 4600 rpm.

Imperial's suspension is good enough to absorb a great percentage of road shock before it reaches the frame and the frame in turn is rigid enough to prevent the body parts from shaking against each other.

Considering pure riding comfort without taking into consideration roadability or handling ease, Imperial's torsion bar and leaf spring suspension matches the comfort of its steel spring competition.

However, both Cadillac and Lincoln offer optional air suspension systems. Coil springs are replaced with air-filled bags whose pressure can be regulated to provide just enough resistance to keep the frame a certain distance from the road, regardless of the passenger and luggage weight that may be added or subtracted. The result is that there need be no "compromise" between desirable softness (low spring rate) and the stiffness (high spring rate) necessary to properly support the maximum load.

With compromise springing, even when it is as good as Imperial's, you get maximum comfort only when you are under average load conditions (e.g. about four or five passengers).

Imperial's springing is not quite as soft as the '58 Cadillac's (with steel springs) on rough pavement such as broken concrete or cobblestones, but the freedom from jounce in the Imperial gives a total picture of slightly superior comfort. However, Imperial's tendency toward a greater amount of body shake slightly clouds the picture.

Compared with the steel sprung Lincoln, Imperial has a slightly flatter ride in travelling over high-crowned, sharply-curving roads. But this is equaled by Lincoln's ability to absorb road shocks coupled with its freedom from body shake.

One of the major reasons for buying a "Big Three" luxury car, other than intangibles such as prestige, pride of ownership, etc., is for greater room and comfort.

In respect to interior roominess, Imperial (and Cadillac) must take second place to the '58 Lincoln, a cavernous automobile. (Unfortunately, Lincoln's extra large interior requires proportionate increase in exterior dimensions). Standard Cadillac (6 passenger) sedans are about as roomy as similar Imperial models.

However, the Imperial's silhouette is lower and in order to provide equal headroom, Imperial seats are nearer to the floor.

For the middle-of-the-seat passenger in both front and rear of the Imperial, the transmission hump and tunnel offers more of a problem than in the competition cars. It's chiefly a problem of legroom for these center passengers although the cushion is stiffer due to lack of spring depth in the center.

Overall passenger vision is better in Imperial than in either of the other cars, although there is still a good deal of distortion in the corners of the wraparound windshield.

From the driver's standpoint, the '58 Imperial offers little ground for complaint. Of all the "Big Three," Imperial is our choice as the easiest and most enjoyable to drive.

The principal reasons for our choice are the Imperial's new power steering mechanism and the top notch road-holding and stability of the suspension system.

Imperial's power steering has a lower ratio requiring fewer turns of the wheel in swinging from full left to full right than any of the other large

One of few exterior changes on Imperial occurred on grille with introduction of "floating" rectangles as part of design. Dual headlamps are standard.

cars. It is hard to imagine what a difference this "quicker" steering makes in man handling a 129-inch wheelbase automobile in heavy traffic.

Out on the open road, Imperial's power steering has now a much more comfortable action, with much greater "feel" of the road, resistance to cornering so that the driver can proportion his effort.

Summing Up: The '58 Imperial is a sleek, smooth-riding and powerful car with exceptional roadability and handling ease. Its performance is quiet but extremely powerful and equal to anything in its class. Its quality of manufacture now equals the overall excellence of its engineering. It adds up to a well-balanced package of luxury transportation with unbeatable pleasure for the driver. ●

IMPERIAL CHECK LIST

5 CHECKS MEAN TOP RATING IN ITS PRICE CLASS

		Checks
PERFORMANCE	Imperial, with an engine of 345 horsepower, is the second most powerful performer in the luxury field. Its 0 to 60 mph time is 9.9 seconds. Under full throttle Imperial's engine is satisfactorily quiet but not as quiet as its competition.	✔✔ / ✔✔
STYLING	With improvements and major changes in the styling of its competition, Imperial is no longer as outstanding as in '57, but it still has the most graceful styling of any car in its field.	✔✔✔ / ✔✔
RIDING COMFORT	Here again, Imperial's competition has been catching up. Although it still has the flattest cornering and most completely sway-free ride. Lincoln is free from body shake and Cadillac's suspension absorbs surface roughness more completely.	✔✔ / ✔✔
INTERIOR DESIGN	Imperial has as good shoulder, head, and hip room as any car in its field. Legroom is also good except for the center positions of front and rear seats where the tunnel intrudes. Vision is tops, but seats are lower than some people find comfortable. Rear door openings could be wider for easy entry and exit.	✔✔ / ✔
ROADABILITY	Here, Imperial still has the edge with its stable, flat-cornering, sway-free handling characteristics at high speed. Lincoln "tracks" a bit better but Imperial has a slightly surer-footed feel under most conditions.	✔✔✔ / ✔✔
EASE OF CONTROL	An improved power-steering system which gives the driver greater "road sense," yet retains the lower numerical ratio and "quicker" action, makes Imperial the easiest to handle of the big luxury cars.	✔✔✔ / ✔✔
ECONOMY	Penny-pinchers don't wind up in the luxury field and if they do they won't find Imperial the most economical. It will give just about as good (or bad depending on your viewpoint) as Lincoln which has a larger engine but more favorable axle ratio.	✔✔ / ✔✔
SERVICEABILITY	Imperial's big engine with its buried spark plugs isn't as easy to service as some other Chrysler Corporation cars but is no more difficult than other cars with accessory-loaded engine compartments.	✔✔ / ✔
WORKMANSHIP	Although Imperial has made tremendous gains in the quality of finish and precision of assembly since the hastily produced Imperials of the early '57 model run, it still lags behind the near perfection of Cadillac and Lincoln.	✔✔ / ✔✔
VALUE PER DOLLAR	The tremendous gains in public acceptance of the Imperial will do a great deal toward evening out the car's steeper rate of depreciation. From the standpoint of engineering and overall performance, Imperial stands right up with the leaders.	✔✔ / ✔✔

IMPERIAL OVERALL RATING...4.1 CHECKS

Imperial, a real big seller in 1957, has lost a considerable share of the pie in 1958. Down by more than 50 per cent, this luxury liner offers a brand new engine—manufactured at a new automated plant in Trenton, Michigan—some revamped styling, and swivel front seats. These and many more "extras" are part of the plot to get some of that lost pie back!

THE 1959 IMPERIAL

STYLING

FRONT end appearance has been transformed by a new grille, headlamp and bumper treatment. The grille consists of a large horizontal chrome bar with five heavy vertical cross pieces—unlike any past Imperial grille. Headlights are placed lower in the front end and the front bumper is large and styled low to give the car a low, wide and thrusting appearance.

The rear bumper is larger than in the past and has a clean, semi-oval appearance that blends in with the Imperial's fin treatment. Rear end appearance is enhanced by a large chrome deck lid medallion with an Imperial eagle design. The medallion is the largest ever used by this company on any of its cars.

Side appearance of the Imperial has been improved by a new side sweep molding of gleaming chrome. The molding appears to be an extension of the wrap-around rear bumper as it begins at the base of the rear fender and extends forward to the front wheel opening.

Imperial introduces three new optional hardtop roof treatments for 1959. The Silvercrest Landau roof consists of a stainless steel front and a simulated leather canopy; the Silvercrest roof consists of the stainless steel front roof area; and the Landau roof consists of the simulated leather rear canopy.

The new Imperial instrument panel features the use of textured aluminum and a new horizontal speed indicator. A transparent cover is fitted over the instrument cluster with words and letters for each instrument etched upon it.

A roll of protective padding has been added to the top of the front seat back as a standard feature of the Imperial Crown and Imperial LeBaron for rear seat passenger safety.

New seat and door panel designs have been created for Imperial interiors and a wide choice of new fabrics, vinyls and leather are available.

The Imperial is available as a two-door

IMPERIAL GRILLE is highlighted by a large horizontal chrome bar with five heavy vertical cross pieces. Headlights are at a lower position in the grille arrangement than in past years. Note parking lights in lower section of bumper and medallions set on fenders.

CHRYSLER'S entrant in the prestige field is offered in a two-door hardtop, four-door hardtop and four-door sedan. The new Imperial assembly plant has gone into operation stressing quality control, an element which has been somewhat of a sore point in past.

hardtop, four-door hardtop and four-door sedan. Imperial Crown is made as a two-door hardtop, four-door hardtop, four-door sedan and convertible. The Imperial LeBaron, most luxurious of all Chrysler's cars, comes as a four-door hardtop and four-door sedan.

Big optional offer for 1959 are the swivel seats. Company engineers and stylists are betting that this development will be as popular with the public as the power seat adjustment. Individual seats are provided for the driver and front seat passenger. Each seat swivels outward in a 40-degree arc to facilitate ease of entrance and exit. The center portion of the front seat is stationary. Without a doubt, most Imperial buyers will call for them.

ENGINEERING

Imperial's power for 1959 is a completely new V-8 manufactured at the company's automated engine plant in Trenton, Michigan. Design features of the all-new engine include a deep-skirted block, wedge-shaped combustion chamber —as opposed to the hemispherical—one-piece rocker arms, and in-line overhead valves with hydraulic lifters.

Outstanding achievements with this new design are reduced engine weight (it is more than 100 lbs. lighter), improved economy (the previous Firepower V-8 was one of the most costly engines to manufacture), improved performance and simplified servicing.

The Imperial, Crown Imperial and Imperial LeBaron for 1959 are powered by a 413-cubic-inch engine with compression ratio of 10.0-to-1, bore of 4.16 and stroke of 3.75 inches. A four-barrel carburetor and dual exhaust are standard.

This new V-8 which is so much lighter than the 392-cubic-inch V-8 it replaces, will help improve gasoline economy, performance and weight distribution.

An outstanding feature of the 1959 Imperial engine is a new cooling system design. The amount of coolant required is reduced to 16 quarts, as compared with the 25 quarts required in the past.

This sizeable reduction in the amount of coolant pays off in speeded engine warmup time, which reduces engine wear, and gives noticeable improvement in fuel economy on short trips. An additional cold weather benefit is faster heater warmup.

The short stroke and big bore of the engine is designed to accommodate an unusually heavy and rigid crankshaft. The additional rigidity is obtained from almost an inch of journal overlap in the forged-steel crankshaft. This should about eliminate engine noise originating from crankshaft vibration.

Company engineers report that the rigid, deep-skirted design of the cylinder block in these new engines makes them sturdier than engines of the past. The structural rigidity of the design achieves durability capable of withstanding the most severe engine use along with a new level of smoothness.

Servicing has also been simplified. The most frequently serviced engine components—the distributor, spark plugs and other electrical parts—are easily accessible. In addition, the oil pump is externally mounted and an oil filter of the throw-away type is located on the front of the oil pump and can be replaced by hand.

Air suspension is also introduced for the first time in 1959 as an optional feature. It is a modified system used in conjunction with the Torsion-Aire unit. The system is used only on the rear of the car, with an improved Torsion-Aire system at the front.

The ingenious new suspension system utilizes air springs in the rear of the car as well as leaf springs. In the event of air spring failure, the leaf springs still provide adequate support for driving the car and for towing it.

Low-rate leaf springs support most of the weight of the rear axle, and the air springs support the remainder of the load. The air springs provide automatic car leveling, regardless of load, and a smoother ride.

Principal components of the air suspension system are a high pressure air compressor which is located in the engine compartment, a storage tank at the front of the frame, a low pressure air reservoir above the rear axle, rugged rubber and nylon air springs and a height control valve.

Air springs are used only in the rear because that is where principal advantage is obtained and, say Chrysler's engineers, because the rear installation is possible without detracting from the basic design advantage of Torsion-Aire. ●

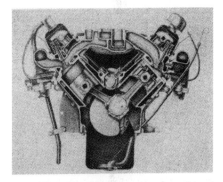

ALL NEW V8 engine boasts a deep-skirted block, wedge-shaped combustion chamber, in-line overhead valves, one-piece rocker arms.

OPTIONAL HARDTOP ROOF treatments are new for 1959. The Silvercrest Landau roof consists of a stainless steel front and simulated leather canopy; the Silvercrest roof consists of the stainless steel front roof area; the Landau roof is offered in the simulated leather roof canopy. The new side sweep molding has improved the side appearance of the luxury conscious Chrysler Imperial.

Road Impressions . . .

OPULENT

The Chrysler looks every bit of the ornate luxury wagon it is.

. . . an ALAN GIBBONS feature

WHETHER you prefer English or Continental vehicles, after one look at the latest American Chrysler Imperial, you've got to agree it is one of the most eye-catching and impressive looking cars on the road today.

It is a car which offers every possible comfort; and after driving it, one's dominant impression is that it is so modern it tends to take most of the fun out of motoring.

Here is a vehicle in which you could drive non-stop from Brisbane to Melbourne and arrive as fresh as a daisy. If you didn't drift off to sleep with sheer boredom, that is.

Should you wish to change gear, you simply press a button.

If there is too much draught through the rear windows you again just press a button; while if the seat is a fraction high, again a magic button will adjust it to the correct height and angle.

Perhaps radio reception isn't the best. Simply press another button and the antenna extends skywards. And for those long trips where the driver needs the additional comfort of a central arm-rest, that too is provided in this luxurious model.

Externally, the custom built body by "Le Baron" features glorious lines which flow back towards the high, elongated tail fins.

These, however, are not as exaggerated as on some American cars.

The squarish bonnet is enhanced with a generous amount of chrome, while the bubble-type wraparound windshield not only wraps around the sides but up and back at the top as well. The large rectangular door handles will appear unusual to Australians. Each is large enough for all four fingers to hold, and the door is

opened by lifting the handle. At last, motor car manufacturers seem to be getting away from the conventional type of handle, which has often been a source of danger in cases of accidents to pedestrians.

Luxury . . .

Inside the Chrysler, the roominess and luxury are striking.

The bench type seats appear to be divided, but this is only an impression brought about by the lower height of the flush-fitting arm rests in both front and rear seats. These are deliberately made low so as not to impede rear view mirror vision. The seating accommodation is wide enough to carry four persons in each compartment at a pinch, while for normal travelling a six-passenger load is comfortable. The interior trim is pastel green — the seats being covered with a "felt" type of material, while the crash padding around dash, door sills and head trim is in a matching leatherette. (Clear plastic seat covers were being tailored for the car when "Wheels" inspected it.)

The front seat may be adjusted electrically to any position. The height, as well as the angle of tilt and the distance from the controls, may be altered by a touch on a switch.

Electric Windows . . .

The doors, which have their sill portions padded with plastic covered foam rubber, also house electric operative mechanisms for all windows. These may be raised or lowered by touching a button. The rear doors also house large ash trays, fitted with cigarette lighters.

Both front doors have armrests, the tops of which can be raised to permit access to convenient map compart-

ments. All doors have chrome kick-plates along their lower edges — no more foot marks on the trim for this car!

The dash is one of the most elaborate we've seen. It is a maze of chrome knobs and dials, yet strangely enough it is easy to read.

Gadgets . . .

Let's examine this control centre and learn the purpose of all these gadgets and switches.

Facia has distinct aircraft influence; all dials are large and clear and hooded against reflections. Wheel is foam-rubber padded. Buttons at left are for gears.

IMPERIAL BY *Chrysler*

Only one of its kind in this country is this 1958 Chrysler Imperial

—high priced prestige-wagon owned by an overseas Consulate.

As our Imperial is a left-hand-drive vehicle, we'll start from the steering wheel side and work our way across the facia to the right.

The extreme left has a group of five press buttons, set vertically, which are the gearshift controls. The Torque-Flite automatic transmission with which the car is fitted is similar to that of the Plymouth Belvedere described in last month's issue.

About two inches below the gear selector panel there is a chromed two-way switch, which operates the winking directional indicators.

A recessed hooded panel houses the main instruments.

There are two large dials set immediately below the driver's line of vision. These denote: (1) speedometer complete with total and trip meters, and (2) fuel, oil pressure, and temperature gauges and ammeter.

Immediately above the steering column there are three gauges. The left one is the high beam indicator; then comes a small but easily read clock, and finally a telltale light which informs the driver if the hand-brake has not been fully released.

A line of six chromed switches extends along the lower section of this hooded area. Reading from the left, these are: head and panel light switch: hand brake release; power antenna control, heater, defroster, and air-conditioning control, wind-screen wiper control, and finally the key-type ignition switch.

On the extreme right of this panel, in a corresponding position to that of the press-button gear selector panel there is another vertical-slide type of control. This is the heater and air conditioning regulator.

In the centre of the sloping dash panel and close to the windscreen is a large chromed vent. This is for the supply of warm air to demist the windscreen.

The remainder of the dash is divided into two sections.

The centre partition houses a press button radio; while that in front of the passenger contains a deep, lockable glove box.

The steering wheel is set low and has a single, deeply dished, thickly padded spoke. A half-circle horn ring is conveniently positioned on the lower half close to the rim.

Although not on the facia, there are four more buttons within easy reach of the driver. These are on the driver's door, just below the sill, and are the electric window controls. These operate not only the driver's window but all other windows in the car as well. In addition, each window can be operated independently by the passenger if required.

Neatly shaped tail makes car look much smaller than it really is. This is the view most drivers would get of the Imperial on the road—it can cruise easily at 90-100.

Comfortable motoring the American way! Note deeply dished wheel; curved glass (electrically operated) in all doors.

OPULENT IMPERIAL BY CHRYSLER

Foot Controls . . .

The Imperial is of course, a two pedal car, and, being left hand drive, has its accelerator on the right, towards the centre of the car. The huge brake pedal (it's at least six inches by two inches) is a dominant floor feature. At left a white-tipped pendant type pedal operates the electric windscreen washers (standard fitting on this model). Two small foot switches on the extreme left operate the dipper switch and direction indicator cancelling.

To start the car it is necessary to have the transmission in neutral (press "N", the top button of the gear selector bracket) before turning the key-start switch to the right. The fuel mixture is automatically adjusted to provide correct engine starting, warming up, operating mixtures, and consequently there is no choke fitted.

Overdrive . . .

The overdrive with which the Imperial is fitted is controlled from the instrument panel. With the control in its full-forward position the automatic overdrive comes into operation.

The overdrive engages automatically on releasing the accelerator momentarily when travelling at above cut-in-speed, approximately 25 m.p.h. It can be kicked out at any time by depressing the accelerator quickly to its limit; then readjusting the engine speed as required. When decelerating, the overdrive will automatically cut out (downshift) at approximately 22 m.p.h. If the car is in deep sand, or

descending a steep grade, say, and it is necessary to cut out the overdrive completely, this can be done by use of the manual control.

The Imperial features Torque-Flite transmission as in the Plymouth Belvedere, and little more need be said about it beyond remarking on the different press-button layout—vertical instead of grouped.

The same ranges do exactly the same things, and as in the case of the Plymouth, there is a safety provision with reverse. If the car is moving forward above a predetermined speed, any attempt to reverse direction by pushing the reverse or forward button will cause the transmission to automatically select neutral. This prevents damage to the gearbox, and, following its having happened, it is necessary to re-select the range required by again pressing the button, to place the car under propulsion.

Torque-Flite transmission cars are certainly a joy to drive, once the operator has become accustomed to all this button-pushing business, but if the car has to be towed any distance it is a different story. The makers recommend that the propeller shaft should be removed for any long tow. Conversely, the spark plugs can be withdrawn and the car towed in gear.

Engine . . .

So much for the exterior, interior and transmission of this luxurious limousine. Let's lift the bonnet and peer dazedly into the maze of mechanisms beneath.

The V-eight cylinder motor which is rated at 51.2 horsepower develops 345 b.h.p. It is almost square, the bore being 101.6 mm. and the stroke 99.06 mm. Displacement is 392 cubic inches, and compression ratio is

10 to 1.

The manufacturers claim that the 126 inch wheelbase automobile will return 15-18 m.p.g., and will attain a top speed of 110 m.p.h. This we do not doubt. Brief pressings of the pedal indicated the following (speedometer) accelerations:

0-30 m.p.h.	3.8 sec.
0-40 m.p.h.	6.5 sec.
0-60 m.p.h.	9.6 sec.

It was in city traffic that we felt best the full surge of power, as well as the smoothness of the Torque-Flite transmission. There was no jerk whatever as the car slid silently into a higher or lower range. Even in a full power take-off and savage power braking there was complete absence of curtsey from either end of the car.

Another feature of this American aristocrat is its quietness of operation. Even at highish speeds there was no indication that the huge motor was exerting itself.

Four Barrel Carb. . . .

The four barrel carburettor was first introduced by Chrysler on this model—as was the automatic choke, now called the "Economy Choke." This choke has a three stage vacuum piston, designed to match the choke position more accurately to engine needs during warm-up. This prevents over-rich mixtures during part-throttle operation. It is said to improve fuel economy, and to cut down engine wear by reducing entry of raw fuel into the engine bores.

We found that on tram lines, over loose bumpy roads, and on slippery surfaces there was virtually no tendency for the Imperial to roll, to pitch, or to wiggle its tail. This results no doubt from the excellent torsion-aire suspension, and from the giant six-ply tyres which are fitted to the car. These 14 in. "rubber cushions" measured eleven inches across at the tread! With so much rubber on the road, it is little wonder that the Chrysler clings tightly to the tarmac—but ooh, what a lot of rubber to wear!

Prestige Car . . .

Inside and out, it is a quality car. The paintwork, for example, looks better than on any of the other big U.S. cars we've seen, and has a rich, Rolls-like depth about it. The points where body panels join together—always a dead give away of sloppy workmanship—are completely free of bare spots, gaps, and blobs of weld.

However, for an Australian (or even for an Australian-resident Consul) there are several disadvantages to owning such a vehicle.

Foremost, there occurs the position of spare parts. In Australia these would be non-existent. Not even a tyre can be bought for this car here! Then there are parking problems—imagine trying to park this gigantic automobile in a busy city street during peak periods, or even to fit it into a normal parking-metered space! Why—you'd even have to build yourself a special-width garage in which to stable it!

But if you **are** prepared to put up with such problems, and if you're able to wangle yourself an import licence, the Chrysler Imperial would indeed be a magnificent motor to have in your garage. ●

Luggage boot is lined with high-grade carpet; has automatic interior lighting. Spare can be fitted in alternative position on underside of boot lid, which is heavily spring-loaded.

LUXURY AUTOMOBILES ON TRIAL

WHICH LUXURY AUTOMOBILE produced in America today is really the finest and best of all the prestige cars? To find out, MOTOR TREND has made a complete comparative road test of the three top family cars, all four-door hardtops. More expensive models are produced by the manufacturers of the Lincoln, Imperial, and Cadillac, but they are in the limousine or special class, hence do not generally come into consideration for ordinary family use.

Each of the three cars tested is competitive in price, with each manufacturer considering his particular model the most logical choice for the man on the way up. Which fine car should you buy? The choice must inevitably remain with the buyer, but here are a few conclusions drawn after living with each of these cars for more than a week and driving them at a time of year when the worst points of a car manifest themselves more quickly than do the good features.

If you want the widest car, you'll be surprised to learn your choice will be the Imperial. To own the longest, you'll have to make your deal on the Lincoln; it is also the lowest. The quickest away from the light, according to our test, is the Lincoln. The big Cadillac gets the blue ribbon for the best fuel consumption. For the softest ride, Cadillac takes the honors, but for handling and roadability, the Imperial can't be beat.

The brakes on these cars are not too good. The total contact brakes of the Imperial allowed but five slowdowns from 60 to 20 mph before fading (four each for Lincoln and Cadillac) and seven stops before braking effectiveness was totally gone (seven for Lincoln and six for Cadillac).

Steep driveways can cause trouble on all three cars with the long overhang on each the culprit; this can also cause parking problems, of course. The Imperial, especially, suffers from a combination of long front overhang and the lowest *front* angle of approach if dips or some railroad crossings are taken at critical speeds. As the photographs to the left prove, all dip with their nose to the ground over rough crossings.

For the most silent riding car, Cadillac is our choice, but as to wind noise on the open road, there's little choice. Most impressive car of the group is strictly up to you and the car's general reputation in the fine-car field.

What is wrong with these prestige cars? There are faults, many of them inexcusable in such costly machinery. For instance, the Lincoln did not make use of the principal virtue of unitized construction; the entire body possessed many rattles. Driving over rough road surfaces produced pronounced shaking of body panels. Fortunately, these vibrations were not communicated to the passengers, but the noise was objectionable. Doors fitted too tightly; the left rear door closed so tightly that the weatherstripping was mutilated and torn away. Windshield wipers had the poorest sweep and worked with difficulty. The Imperial indicated poor inspection, for the right rear door was incapable of being opened from the outside. The Cadillac had a creaking dashboard which made noises on every bump, and the right front door could not be locked electrically or manually.

Yet, even for these correctible criticisms, all three cars are worthy of being called America's finest automobiles. The one which satisfies the individual whims of the buyer is *his* best buy. They do differ, however, and you'll be better equipped to judge by reading the detailed test report of each car on the following pages.

LINCOLN PREMIERE

ACCELERATION

From Standing Start
0-45 mph 6.2 0-60 mph 10.8

Passing Speeds
30-50 mph 4.3 45-60 mph 4.9
50-80 mph 11.4

FUEL CONSUMPTION

Stop-and-Go Driving
8.8 mpg for 162 miles

Highway Average
12.0 mpg for 186 miles

Overall Average
10.7 mpg for 348 miles

Fuel used: Mobilgas Special

BRAKING

Withstood 4 slowdowns from 60 mph to 20 mph before fading appeared

COMPLETELY NEW, the Lincoln is built in an equally new factory designed especially for the construction of unitized bodies. Thousands of separate welding operations fabricate a combined body and under-frame of great strength and rigidity. The entire unitized body, before final fitting and painting, is dipped in a tank where rust resisting primer flows over and into every nook and cranny.

We tested the Premiere Landau, Lincoln's finest four-door hardtop. It was fitted with a 375-hp engine, Turbo-Drive torque-converter automatic transmission, power steering, and vacuum-assisted power brakes — all of which are standard equipment and are included in the base price. The test car also had a heater and defroster, a radio with an optional station changing floor-mounted step-switch, power windows, six-way power seat — all extra-cost accessories.

In the Lincoln, you step down when entering, unlike the other two luxury automobiles tested, making the low roof less of a hazard. Elderly persons especially will find the Lincoln rear seat the easiest entered of the three cars, largely due to the lowered floor. Instruments and controls are the best located of the three cars. The driver need never stretch as all controls for heater, fresh-air ventilation, radio, lights,

IMPERIAL CROWN

ACCELERATION

From Standing Start
0-45 mph 6.6 0-60 mph 11.9

Passing Speeds
30-50 mph 4.8 45-60 mph 5.5
50-80 mph 11.8

FUEL CONSUMPTION

Stop-and-Go Driving
8.6 mpg for 144 miles

Highway Average
12.7 mpg for 173 miles

Overall Average
10.9 mpg for 317 miles

Fuel used: Mobilgas Special

BRAKING

Withstood 5 slowdowns from 60 mph to 20 mph before fading appeared

MT'S TEST IMPERIAL was the luxurious Crown Southampton four-door hardtop. Standard equipment included the TorqueFlite automatic three-speed transmission, power steering, and power brakes; the extra-cost accessories installed on the test car included the radio with floor station-switch, heater, air-conditioning system, six-way power seat, and power windows.

Since the floor was level, not recessed as in the Lincoln, we found ourselves ducking our heads slightly to avoid knocking against the top sill when entering the car. Rear seat entrance is made less difficult because of the unusually wide door opening.

Instruments and controls run a close second to the Lincoln with one exception — there's little logic in the clumsy placement of the turn signal switch at the bottom end of the vertically-arranged transmission pushbuttons. This requires one to remove the left hand from the steering wheel, glance quickly, and reach about nine inches down and to the left. Window controls are in the door panels, and the electric door-lock switch (optional) is positioned for easy left-hand operation. Instrument lighting is the best of the three cars — the black lighting does not glare, makes reading the large dials

CADILLAC 60 FLEETWOOD

ACCELERATION

From Standing Start
0-45 mph 6.9 0-60 mph 12.6

Passing Speeds
30-50 mph 4.9 45-60 mph 5.6
50-80 mph 12.2

FUEL CONSUMPTION

Stop-and-Go Driving
9.8 mpg for 109 miles

Highway Average
13.6 mpg for 204 miles

Overall Average
11.6 mpg for 313 miles

Fuel used: Mobilgas Special

BRAKING

Withstood 4 slowdowns from 60 mph to 20 mph before fading appeared

THE BIG, FLEETWOOD 60 SPECIAL was MT's test Cadillac. Available only as a four-door hardtop, this car has 3.5 inches more wheelbase and a scant two inches more overall length than the variety of models available in the more popular 62 series. The 60 has greater rear legroom than the smaller cars, but the same space in front. The test car was equipped with radio and heater, air-conditioning, a six-way power seat, power windows (including the vents), electric door locks, and air suspension. Its engine was the 310-hp unit equipped with the standard single four-barrel carburetor. An optional "Q" engine uses an improved intake manifold mounting three two-barrels, raising the hp to 335, with the same rpm torque.

Entry and exit are on a par with the other large cars tested, but the front seat cushions are on the short side, giving less leg and thigh support than on the other cars. Power seat controls are in the driver's armrest, making adjustment easiest of the three cars. Floors are level with the door sill, making entry into the rear more difficult due to the downward sweep of the roofline at this point.

The electric door locking controls are impossibly positioned far back on the door sills, requiring difficult hand etc. are neatly gathered into the bottom half of the instrument group which occupies a separate panel directly in front of the steering wheel. The instruments, while excellently placed, reflect badly in the upper left half of the windshield at night; however, only half this glare is the fault of the panel lighting — the real culprit is the prism-like transmission quadrant.

Driving position is excellent and the seats are deep enough to give genuinely comfortable support. In traffic, the steering is quickly responsive, although we found the test car cruised with better than one-half turn of free play in the steering wheel over the specified 3.3 turns lock-to-lock. One is amazed at the maneuverability of this huge car. We found that setting the transmission lever to "L" (low) would drop the speed gently to second gear without jerking; when the speed is dropped to about 20 mph, first gear comes in with greater engine braking, but very smoothly. The more you drive this big, heavy car you become aware that it does not ride as easily as you had expected. Although bumps are felt only slightly, you feel them more than in the other two cars tested. Roadability is almost superb — directional stability is the best I have ever experienced in any car, small or large.

Corners at speed are easy, the car's trailing arm rear suspension giving just the right amount of understeer. Although there is considerable lean on sharp or fast corners, this is not too apparent to drivers or passengers. Such heeling-over is less than that of the Cadillac, more than the Imperial.

Luggage space on the Lincoln is cavernous, the most usable capacity of any of the three cars tested. Once warmed up, the heating and defrosting system will run you out of the place. Especially good is Lincoln's method of piping heat to the rear passengers. The defrosters were the best of the three and covered the greatest expanse of windshield.

The Lincoln has a feel of luxury; its leather upholstery is carefully fitted over seats that were the softest of the three cars tested, and folding armrests in the centers of both front and rear seats add greatly to highway comfort. The rear center armrest, however, should have a pull tab of some sort to facilitate unfolding it from its very tight fit in the backrest. The rolls and pleats of the upholstery have a custom look and feel, and the carpeting is thick and soft. Separate lamps at each extreme end of the dash light, with the dome light, when either door is opened, giving this car the best interior lighting of the three. /MT

---

easy, and there is almost no annoying reflection at night in the windshield.

The steering wheel, in our opinion, is the best of the three; the straight-across spoking allows a relaxing change of hand positions on a long trip. The power-seat controls are positioned handily at the bottom left of the seat; with the seat in the far aft position, there's a disturbing space of uncovered steel floor plainly visible beneath the front edge of the seat. Newly positioned left of center, the rear-view mirror does give improved view aft, if there is no-one sitting in the middle of the rear seat. This mirror, along with several others checked, failed to stay put after adjustment.

Driving position ranks, in my opinion, the best of the three cars tested. The depth of the seats from front edge to the backrest gives fine leg and thigh support. Armrests are comfortable; the front rests feature a hinged top surface which discloses a roomy space for maps and other small items like flashlights, fuel coupons, etc.

In driving, we often had the feeling, when catching sight of either fin in the corner of our eye, that another driver was too close. Fast 3.5-turn steering makes traffic maneuverability good; the lack of any free play in the steering made

this car the quickest to respond of the three. The Imperial, with its torsion-aire suspension system, handles like a well-trained quarter horse on all road surfaces. On the test car were the optional 11.00 x 14 tires which give a softer ride. Unfortunately, however, these fatter tires, though they increase traction, do not help roadability. On the contrary, they sometimes cause a slight rear-end sway on quick turns. Power steering is quick and responsive; there is slight understeer, just enough to facilitate high-speed travel in greater safety. Cornering lean is slight, less than the other two cars. We noticed a hint of road wander, brought on most likely by the large tires.

Heating and ventilation are good, but defrosting is the least effective of the three cars tested. Heat, however, comes within three minutes after a cold start.

The feel of luxury in the Imperial is emphasized by the metallic-threaded nylon upholstery; it looks and feels rich. Warmer than the leather in the Lincoln in cold weather, this upholstery is matched by the finest looking door panelling, the best formed and most comfortably located center armrests. Chromeplating on the instrument panel has a better look of quality than on the other two cars. /MT

---

maneuvering. The outside rear-view mirror is controlled by a handle from the inside. The parking brake gave trouble on freezing mornings; the release trip is on the left of the pedal and sometimes release is not positive. Instruments are surrounded by too much chrome; at night, unless the panel light is dimmed well, reflections in the windshield are bothersome. Foot pedals for throttle and power brakes are close enough for simple foot pivoting.

Since the Cadillac had air suspension, we used the height control lever to raise the car to climb a curb when it was pinned into a parking slot by a double-parked car. It takes two or three minutes to raise the car; the tail end rises first, followed more slowly by the front end. Road clearance can be increased by more than four inches for emergencies.

The steering wheel has two spokes with nearly the shape of a knife edge, not making them a safe resting place for the driver's chest in case of an accident. As in the Lincoln, we favored the automatic transmission control lever over the dash-mounted pushbuttons that are on the Imperial; you do not have to remove either hand from the wheel to operate this or the turn signal switch.

Driving position is good, although the driver is the least

comfortable of the three because of the short seat design. Front armrests on the doors are not positioned for best comfort; a recess for pulling the doors closed is located exactly where the elbow rests. The transmission selector indicator is centered immediately below the horizontal speedometer face, best for viewing of the three. In traffic, only disturbing factor is the slow steering which requires considerable winding, nor does the steering wheel effectively center itself after a sharp turn as on the other two cars tested. Downshifts for safer braking are smooth. Visibility to the rear is best from behind the wheel of the Cadillac.

On trips, the air suspension gives a beautiful ride, but road bumps, dips and paving strips are still felt. The Cad has greater lean on corners than the other two; nose diving on an emergency stop is greater, also. Road feel through the steering wheel is less, however.

Heat circulation is good; there were no leaks around doors or windows, and defrosting of the windshield was excellent.

As to the feel of luxury, the test car had beautiful nylon upholstery in a dull gray tone to lend subtle charm to the interior. Rear passengers now have manually-operated vent panes in the windows. /MT

1959
ROAD TEST

W HERE there once was a wide range of choice in upper bracket American-made luxury cars, the field in recent years has been reduced to just three names: Cadillac, Lincoln and Imperial. This trio is likely to remain unchallenged by any domestic newcomer, at least in significant volume, and each make seems to have a promising future.

The chief objective in this limited class, aside from the prestige of driving a more costly vehicle, is massive luxury, supported by a higher degree of quality. On the massive luxury point there is some threat from the middle priced cars which have constantly been raising their stand-

1959 it has undergone major changes that accompany a new design. Only unaltered components are the engine, which has been carefully refined over a 10-year period, and the pioneer Hydramatic transmission.

The rest of the chassis was new in 1958 and its principal distinguishing feature is the cruciform or "hourglass"-type frame. Although air springing is available, the test car had the traditional coil and A-arm in front, matched by coils with trailing links at the rear.

In a straight line at moderate speeds, or in city cruising, the Cadillac is masterfully smooth. Flaws are noted only at high speeds, when some swaying motion sets in, and in fast corners when the tires protest loudly as the heavyweight goes through a bend. Under certain conditions on rough roads it appeared that the frame was actually flexing, as the car developed an overall quiver. During hard acceleration runs there was no wheel spin.

Fuel consumption was creditable for a

car of this size. While the average for all driving was 11.7 mpg, with cautious operation during one phase of the testing a top of 22 mpg was registered for 150 miles from the center of a metropolitan area.

Cadillac's strongest claim to superiority is its unmatched feeling of luxury and quality. When riding in this car, the almost soundless operation coupled with rich materials and fine assembly produce the desired effect: you know that this is an expensive and luxurious automobile. One is never in doubt.

The interior is Cadillac's best to date. The instruments are the most legible of any GM car, deeply recessed in padded cavities. Electric latches, not an exclusive feature, permit locking of all doors with one switch, which is surprisingly handy and convenient.

Imperial in its 1959 model has some advantages. The major one is better handling qualities, although not as good as some of the lighter Chrysler Corporation

CADILLAC AND IMPERIAL

ards. As yet, however, the prestige trio is more secure in its position than any other category of U.S. cars.

The real differences between these cars are often subtile and slight. Performance is relatively adequate by today's averages, with no apparent effort at outstanding accelerating ability in keeping with the conservative requirements of dignity. Distinctive features are largely on the surface, a matter of styling and appointments rather than extreme basic design.

Two of these luxury cars, a Cadillac four-door hardtop of the most popular series, and the rarer Imperial convertible, were recently tested. While two such body types were certain to produce different results, they do make an interesting study.

Cadillac is the more noteworthy this year, not only because it still is the undisputed leader in this class, but because in

CADILLAC FRONT AND REAR is massive as ever, but sleeker. The flamboyant fins are as controversial as they were 10 years ago.

IMPERIAL LOOKS GOOD but needs greater distinction from the Chrysler line in order to match its rivals in the luxury class.

One is nearly all-new—and one is not. But the differences that count are not revolutionary features. Solid luxury is the word

a heavy steel plate X-member assembly for the convertible body type. It is this and similar strengthening elsewhere that adds to the car's weight.

The Imperial's handicap in its field is not that it is a lesser car, which it positively is not, but that it is a comparatively new name alongside Cadillac and Lincoln. Some years will be required to develop its personality. Another limiting factor is Imperial's close relationship with Chrysler —much closer than, say, Cadillac is to Buick or Lincoln is to Mercury. A greater separation is necessary for prestige and distinction.

Cadillac, in 1959, unquestionably remains the leader in this exclusive class and it has earned the right again through production quality and engineering of details. Imperial may be more roadable and may even possess some advantages in style, and in performance potential, but these are almost secondary factors. Magnificent massive luxury is the mark. ●

vehicles. Nonetheless it corners well, travels at high speeds with a surer degree of control.

The acceleration figures for the test convertible do not reflect the normal ability of the Imperial, which in lighter body types would be a second or two quicker.

The Imperial, of course, is much the same car it was in 1958. The minor facelift included lowering of the headlights and locating them in the dual chromed pods which project forward of the front fender. The grille has been dressed up so that it no longer consists of the simple patterns of straight bars. In general, the alterations have not improved the appearance of the car, and it might have been better left as it was in the preceding year.

The instrument panel is definitely less desirable than 1958, when it was a more logical arrangement. Night reading of dials is easier than by daylight.

Frame of the Imperial is conventional boxed outside frame rails, universal in Chrysler products, with the addition of

Test Data

Test Car: 1959 Imperial
Body Type: Convertible
Basic Price: $5773
Engine: V-8
Carburetion: Single four-barrel
Displacement: 413 cubic inches
Bore & Stroke: 4.18 x 3.75
Compression Ratio: 10.1-to-1
Horsepower: 350
Horsepower per cubic inch: .84
Torque: 470 lb.-ft @ 2800 rpm
Engine speed: 2000 rpm @ 60 mph
Test Weight: 4910 lbs. without driver
Weight Distribution: 55 per cent on front wheels
Power-Weight Ratio: 14.02 lbs. per horsepower
Transmission: Torqueflite
Rear Axle Ratio: 2.93
Steering: 3½ turns lock-to-lock
Dimensions: overall length 226 inches, width 81, height 57, wheelbase 129
Springs: Torsion-bar front, leaf rear
Gas Mileage: 11.5
Speedometer Error: Indicated 30, 45 and 60 mph are actual 32, 46½ and 61 mph, respectively
Acceleration: 0-30 mph in 4.0 seconds, 0-45 in 7.2 and 0-60 in 12.2

Test Data

Test Car: 1959 Cadillac
Body Type: Four-door sedan
Basic Price: $5498
Engine: V-8
Carburetion: Single four-barrel
Displacement: 390 cubic inches
Bore & Stroke: 4 x 3.875
Compression Ratio: 10.5-to-1
Horsepower: 325 @ 4800 rpm
Horsepower per cubic inch: .83
Torque: 430 lb.-ft @ 3100 rpm
Engine speed: 2200 rpm @ 60 mph
Test Weight: 5160 lbs. without driver
Weight Distribution: 52 per cent on front wheels
Power-Weight Ratio: 15.8 lbs. per horsepower
Transmission: Dual Range Hydramatic
Rear Axle Ratio: 2.94
Steering: 4 turns lock-to-lock
Dimensions: overall length 225 inches, width 81, height 56, wheelbase 130
Springs: Coil
Gas Mileage: 11.7
Speedometer Error: Indicated 30, 45 and 60 mph are actual 26½, 39 and 52 mph, respectively
Acceleration: 0-30 mph in 3.8 seconds, 0-45 in 6.4 and 0-60 in 10.3

IMPERIAL

By JIM WHIPPLE

ONCE AGAIN when we picked up our 1959 Imperial test car we realized how really good its basic design is. When Chrysler's chief stylist Virgil Exner laid out the basic design for the '57 model, he created an automobile shape that is dignified and yet exciting. He proved once and for all that sweeping lines with considerable aerodynamic basis can be successfully combined with the large, formal sedan body without sacrificing anything but the ease of entrance associated with high-ceilinged cars.

Imperial's lines are maintained in good order on the 1959 model with very little damage from that Detroit malady, creeping chromism. That's the disease which overtakes the most beautifully styled cars whenever the manufacturers attempt to conceal the fact that no major changes have been made in the body sheet metal.

Imperials have picked up a swatch

of chrome below the belt line on their rear fenders, and the new grille is a massive chromed divider borrowed from the world's largest ice cube tray.

Most of the changes made in the '59 Imperial lie beneath the sleek and glassy-smooth enamelled surface. First of all, there's a brand new engine, lighter in weight and, it seemed to me, quieter in action. This engine is the largest version of Chrysler Corporation's new "B" type introduced last year on De Soto.

It's a short-stroke design of 413-cu. in. displacement, developing 350 horsepower. With a rear axle ratio of 2.93 to 1, this powerhouse rarely needs to be opened up. As a result, cruising on superhighways is a very quiet and restful process.

Helping to eliminate weariness on long trips is Chrysler's Auto Pilot, a remarkably efficient speed governor that takes over operation of the accelerator and maintains an even speed

set by the driver on an instrument panel dial. A touch on the accelerator pedal will over-ride Auto Pilot and permit you to speed up for passing. A touch on the brake pedal unlocks the governor and closes the throttle instantly.

Torqueflite automatic transmission is standard equipment on all models. It's a good smooth transmission with three pushbuttons governing operation in forward speeds.

The "D" button, used in all normal driving, permits the transmission to shift into high gear whenever car speed and throttle position permit—at 20 mph with slightly open throttle and at 65-70 under full-throttle acceleration all the way.

Pushing down the "2" button keeps the transmission locked in Intermediate speed no matter what the throttle position, until an automatic upshift is forced at 65-70 mph.

The "1" button is primarily for use

IMPERIAL
is the car
for you

if... Its smooth and distinctive styling pleases you.

if... The excellent maneuverability that results from the quickest steering in its field stands high on your list.

if... You appreciate the levelest, most sway-free ride rather than a suspension which absorbs more surface vibration.

if... You find it difficult to get in and out of today's low-slung automobiles and appreciate the convenience of Imperial's swivel seats.

IMPERIAL
SPECIFICATIONS

ENGINE	CROWN IMPERIAL	IMPERIAL CUSTOM
Bore and stroke	4.00 in. x 3.90 in.	4.18 in. x 3.75 in.
Displacement	392 cu. in.	413 cu. in.
Compression ratio	10.0 to 1	10.1 to 1
Max. brake horsepower	325 @ 4600 rpm	350 @ 4600 rpm
Max. torque	460 @ 2800 rpm	470 @ 2800 rpm
DIMENSIONS		
Wheelbase	129.0 in.	
Overall length	226.3 in.	
Overall width	81.0 in.	
Overall height	56.9 in.	
TRANSMISSIONS		
TorqueFlite		

Wide, wide styling of '59 Imperial Southampton is apparent; stainless steel roof is available as option.

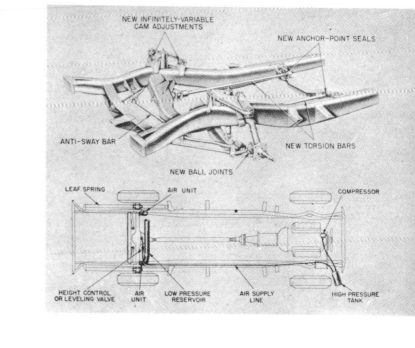

Electronic rear view "Mirror-Matic" provides the ultimate in driving comfort. Schematic shows how photo-electric cell reacts to light, changing mirror angle. Compact unit is entirely self-contained.

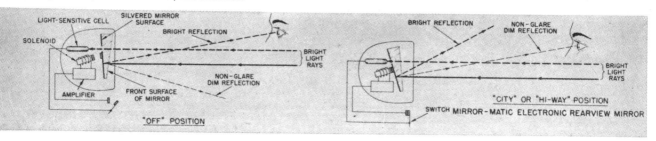

in slowing the car on steep downgrades—it locks the transmission in low gear until full-throttle limit in that speed.

CHASSIS IMPROVEMENTS

A number of improvements have been made in and around the chassis of the '59 Imperial. For one thing, the ball joints of the Torsion Air front suspension have been improved and infinitely variable cam-type adjusters have been incorporated into the upper control arms. Torsion bar anchors have been improved to make them absolutely squeak-free.

Back at the rear axle are Imperial's long, smooth-acting, outboard-mounted leaf springs and axle locating struts. But, for $156 extra, you can add Chrysler Corporation's True Level supplemental air suspension system. This setup consists of an air-compressor, piping, a levelling valve and a hollow air chamber, plus two heavy rubber air suspension bags mounted between the rear springs and the frame.

When the car is empty, or very lightly laden, the conventional leaf springs alone are just right to support the car and its one or two passengers

in optimum comfort. As more passengers and luggage are added, air under pressure is admitted to the rubber suspension chambers and additional support is given to the body so that it is held on an even keel and full rear-axle bump travel is available. This means that the ride is equally comfortable, whether the car is near-empty or fully laden, and maximum roadability is maintained at all times.

As a road car the Imperial is as good as ever—maybe even a bit better—with the aid of the supplemental air suspension

Insulation of body mounts, large section tires and rubber insulated suspension have shut out the vibration that sometimes shows up on lesser Chrysler Corporation cars when they're driven on rough surfaced pavement like broken concrete.

RIDE

The Imperial rides very steadily. There is no car giving less vertical motion over large bumps. In freedom from sway in cornering, Imperial stands absolutely alone. You can pour it on around sharp curve after sharp curve while the tires scream, but you'll get very little lean or bobble.

However, Imperial comes in as a tie for second in the ride-and-comfort sweepstakes simply because there is a bit more body shake and shudder on rough going—torsion bars notwithstanding—than you'll find in its chief competitor. Although the body doesn't jounce or sway as much as most other cars, certain rough surfaces induce more of a rubbery juddering into the body and frame.

On narrow, winding, high-crowned country roads the Imperial is truly king of the road. Its quick steering, which requires only 3.5 turns lock to lock, plus its glue-like roadability, enables the alert driver to set remarkably high averages of speed—55 instead of 40 for example—without nerve strain, danger or discomfort. The chassis engineering on the Imperial—and other Chrysler products—stands second to none. The only flaw seems to be in lack of sufficient body rigidity.

INTERIORS

Imperial's interior is as lush as ever for '59, but the most important development for my money is the swivel seat, which makes entry and exit twice as easy for driver and front-seat passenger.

Imperial has a brand-new instrument panel this year which, in my opinion, is disorganized and gadget laden. Various instruments peep through a pale grey enamelled panel which in turn is housed behind a broad expanse of glass and lighted in its entirety. It is flanked by vertical rows of pushbuttons—transmission control to the left and heating controls to the right. There are six minor league controls governing operations like the raising of the radio antenna, which are nearly hidden below the panel's edge. Of great advantage to the curious however, are Imperial's full four gauges telling not only how much fuel is in the tank but how the electrical system is doing, how high the oil pressure is and how hot the fluid in the cooling system has become.

SUMMING UP

Imperial is a sleek and beautifully styled car, albeit a bit chromy up front, and one that provides an extremely stable and comfortable ride and a truly luxurious, if somewhat showy, interior. Its only flaws are a moderate amount of body shake on rough road surfaces and less than perfect workmanship in respect to trim and finish. Its performance is outstanding. ●

IMPERIAL CHECK LIST

5 CHECKS MEAN TOP RATING IN ITS PRICE CLASS

PERFORMANCE	Imperial's smooth and efficient new engine, coupled with powerful Torqueflite transmission, gives it very lively performance for a heavy car. It will accelerate to 60 mph from a standing start in 10.1 seconds.	✓✓ / ✓✓
STYLING	Imperial's sleek lines, virtually unchanged since the car's introduction, have made it one of the really outstanding cars in the U.S. and the leader of its class.	✓✓✓ / ✓✓
RIDING COMFORT	Imperial is still the smoothest cornering car in its class and has a really fine, level, jounce-free ride, but its competitors have done a lot of catching up and in one case have overtaken it by a narrow margin.	✓✓ / ✓✓
INTERIOR DESIGN	The wide Imperial has excellent shoulder and hiproom with good headroom and legroom. High tunnel for transmission and driveshaft makes center of seats somewhat uncomfortable. Swing-out front seats are a great and exclusive convenience feature.	✓✓ / ✓✓
ROADABILITY	Imperial's low, low center of gravity and sway-free cornering make it the match of its competition in this important category.	✓✓✓ / ✓✓
EASE OF CONTROL	Imperial's quick power steering, smooth, powerful brakes and convenient pushbutton transmission control make it very easy to handle.	✓✓ / ✓✓
ECONOMY	Imperial will hold its own with its competition. It will, under comparable conditions, use less gasoline than Lincoln, more than Cadillac.	✓✓ / ✓✓
SERVICEABILITY	Imperial's new engine with spark plugs and other components mounted on top and at the front has made routine service operations much easier.	✓✓ / ✓
WORKMANSHIP	The quality of trim finish and assembly in the Imperial has improved steadily to a point where it trails only one of its competitors.	✓✓ / ✓✓
VALUE PER DOLLAR	In excellence of engineering and overall performance, Imperial stands with the leaders of the industry. However, it s less favorable (i.e. faster) rate of depreciation puts it below its competition as an investment.	✓✓ / ✓✓

IMPERIAL OVERALL RATING... 4.1 CHECKS

THE **IMPERIAL** FAMILY

Chrysler's prestige car sticks to tradition in both styling and body-and-frame construction

TRADITION, a strong factor in luxury car design, has played a great part in shaping the 1960 Imperial. Unlike the radically changed Chrysler, De Soto, Dodge and Plymouth, it continues as the same basic car that has been gaining a larger market since 1957.

Though it contains many innovations and improvements, the new Imperial is essentially a face lift of the previous model and does not share the unit body-and-frame construction of its 1960 corporate brothers.

Styling changes are still impressive; interiors favor lush comfort with an attention to detail seldom found in any automobile. Seats have as much as six inches of foam rubber, with a separate seat back for the driver which supports shoulders and spine like few production cars ever have. There's a non-glare instrument

panel with electroluminescent light (metal dials coated with glowing phosphor), an improved Auto Pilot and swivel seats that chase doors open and closed. Series designations are the same as 1959 (Custom, Crown and LeBaron) as are engine capacity and major exterior dimensions.

Best of the new features are a double-padded instrument panel, improved seat belt design and a wonderful emergency warning flasher system. No matter whether the ignition is on or off, the owner of an Imperial can flip a special switch and start all four turn signals flashing on and off as a warning to oncoming traffic. Borrowed from the truck lines, this is a feature that could well be on all passenger cars.

Some styling changes are obvious, others not. There are satin-finish stainless steel inserts on the roof of LeBaron models, which also have a sharp appearing small rear window for greater rear seat privacy in both sedans and hardtops. Inside, there are power-operated vent windows and a new elliptical steering wheel. The unique shape of the wheel and spoke placement permits a full view of the instrument panel, while flattened upper and lower arcs provide greater leg clearance and improved forward visibility for short people. For old-fashioned

DISTINCTION between expensive Le Baron and other Imperial models is sharpened for 1960 by using smaller rear window, as shown at far left. Greater interior privacy is also claimed.

RESTYLED GRILLE, left, has lighter look, resembles that of previous Chryslers more than Imperials. Front bumper is also new but continues to include parking lights and turn signals.

OVERALL DESIGN, lower left, continues traditional Imperial features with detail refinements. Regular body and frame are used, rather than unit structure like other new Chrysler cars.

folks, a conventional full circle wheel is available.

The automatic speed control (Auto-Pilot), introduced by Imperial in 1958, has been updated but good. Early models held the speed well, but if the unit was cut off by touching the brake, the driver had to engage the control again manually. On 1960 Imperials the control is cut off only temporarily when the brake is applied. When the dialed speed is reached again, the control engages itself automatically. There are few changes under the hood, except for detail improvements made to ease servicing and production problems.

As usual, interior trim materials seem almost too nice to sit on. Full leather, custom designed nylon-viscose body cloths and a new doeskin vinyl are all available. The last material has all the feel and appearance of high quality chamois, except that the nap doesn't fuzz when you rub it. It is lovely and will certainly set a new trend when custom car fans get their hands on the bolt material. The Imperial Custom series uses the nylon-viscose, Crowns offer many combinations of cloth and leather (or full leather) while the LeBaron features soft, tailored woolen broadcloth combinations. Deeply set buttons increase the impression of rich depth while LeBaron coat-of-arms decorates head bolsters of the back and driver seats.

Driving the Imperial proved only that, like all previous large Chrysler products, it handled and rode better than anything else of its size on the road. For all its mass, it feels like a light car, with TorqueFlite transmission, power steering and power brakes doing everything they can to eliminate labor from driving. Compared to last year's Imperial, the 1960 is quieter, more comfortable, and even easier on the eye. But compared to a 1960 Chrysler (with unit body) the 1960 Imperial will likely suffer. Its frame and separate body construction will probably pass more road noise and shock to the driver. Sound control does not seem as good as on the Chrysler, with the result that more engine and transmission noise are to be expected. At a high speed, from 75 to 100 mph, wind noise rises to the point where conversation becomes difficult. This may have been better than average for 1959 cars, but for 1960, Imperial suffers by comparison with its running mates.

Still, it is an Imperial. The car is big, with all the lush comfort of our best transportation from the Chrysler Corporation. It handles like a dream for such a large car, with huge tires and measured suspension soaking up chuckholes like a thirsty sponge.

Maintaining its successful engineering and widely accepted styling, the 1960 Imperial comes into the showroom as one of the most thoroughly proven cars in its class. ●

FLATTENED WHEEL allows better visibility above and greater leg clearance below; regular type is also available. Electroluminescent lighting makes instruments more legible at night.

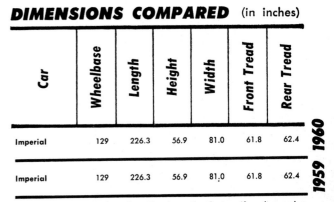

1960 ANALYSIS
IMPERIAL

DIMENSIONS COMPARED (in inches)

Car	Wheelbase	Length	Height	Width	Front Tread	Rear Tread	
Imperial	129	226.3	56.9	81.0	61.8	62.4	**1960**
Imperial	129	226.3	56.9	81.0	61.8	62.4	**1959**

NOTES—Series and body styles offered are the Custom (four-door sedan, four-door hardtop, two-door hardtop), the Crown (four-door sedan, four-door hardtop, two-door hardtop and convertible), the LeBaron (four-door sedan and four-door hardtop). Body dimensions are all identical.

ENGINES

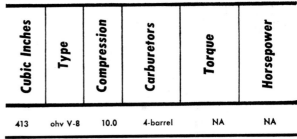

Cubic Inches	Type	Compression	Carburetors	Torque	Horsepower
413	ohv V-8	10.0	4-barrel	NA	NA

NOTES—Engine has identical bore and stroke as 1959 models and should produce similar torque and horsepower ratings. 1959 horsepower: 350; torque: 470 lb. @ 2800 rpm.

LINCOLN CONTINENTAL

TESTING THE

F OR SHEER luxury, Detroit provides three magnificent choices, Cadillac, Imperial and Lincoln. No other car in this country and a few from overseas can equal the refinement of these.

Perhaps the best way to characterize the three is in contrast to another car in the same price class, the Chrysler 300-F. It, too, is refined but in an entirely different way. It has been engineered to put the driver in intimate touch with the machine and the machine with the road. By luxury car standards, it has rough, noisy operation.

Cadillac, Imperial and Lincoln are just the reverse. Everything about them isolates their occupants from the road; the whole emphasis is on smoothness and silence. This, as the tests reveal, has its effects on their merits as automobiles.

Each of the three is a different solution to the problem of including a luxury car within a broad corporate line. Cadillac shares its body shell with other General Motors makes but has its own engine and chassis. Imperial and Lincoln follow an opposite policy, using the same mechanical components as their medium-priced running mates with their own distinctive structures. And distinctive they are. Imperial is Chrysler's sole product with a separate body and frame while Lincoln is Ford's only full-sized car with unit construction.

In their regular lines, each offers three series. Cadillac has the 62, Fleetwood 60 Special and Eldorado, Imperial the Custom, Crown and Le Baron and Lincoln the plain Lincoln, Premiere and Continental Mark V. Prices range from $4892 to $7401 for Cadillac, $4922 to $6318 for Imperial and $5252 to $7056 for Lincoln.

All of the closed Cadillacs are hardtops while Imperial and Lincoln each use the same bodies and charge the same prices for four-door sedans and hardtops.

They all build formal cars as well, Cadillac the 75 eight-passenger sedan and limousine costing up to $9748, Imperial the eight-passenger Crown limousine at $15,600 and Lincoln the six-

passenger Continental town car and limousine reaching $10,230.

Finally, Cadillac has the Eldorado Brougham at $13,075. Both the Brougham and Imperial limousine have bodies built in Italy so the Lincoln Continental limousine is left with the title of the most expensive car made in this country.

Turning from high finance, the cars actually tested for this report were a Cadillac 62, Imperial Le Baron and Lincoln Continental. Strictly speaking, Cadillac's equivalent to the Le Baron and Continental is the Fleetwood 60 Special but, because the 60 and 62 are the same mechanically, the test results are still comparable.

In every other respect, the three cars were similar. All were four-door hardtops with complete power equipment and air conditioning to equalize any weight advantages. It would have been difficult to have them unlike because so many accessories, power steering, power brakes and automatic transmissions as well as minor niceties like electric clocks, windshield washers, remote control outside mirrors and back-up lights, are all standard. Lincoln goes all the way and even includes radios and heaters at no extra cost.

This may well be a last look at the high-priced field as it has long existed. Just as the Rambler has revolutionized popular car concepts, the Thunderbird has pointed the way to new ideas in luxury. Specifically, it has dispelled the notion that a relatively expensive car must be big.

CADILLAC

For 1960, Cadillac continues the basic design introduced last year with important changes in its suspension and braking systems.

It proved the best performer of the trio, even though it had the smallest engine. From 0-to-60, the 62 test car averaged 10.7 seconds, beating the Imperial and Lincoln by 1.6 and 3.5 seconds, respectively.

The 390-cubic-inch engine is essentially an enlarged version of the first ohv V-8 offered by Cadillac 11 years ago. It develops 325 hp with 10.5-to-1 compression and single four-barrel carbure-

74

Checking the big ones - from their polite performance to their gorgeous gadgets

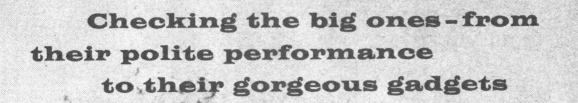

Luxury CARS

IMPERIAL

CADILLAC

CADILLAC interior is least ornate of the tested trio, but basic quality and solidity make it most outstanding within this area.

LINCOLN dash is impressive but confusing home of buttons and dials. Driver has trouble just scanning full range of panel.

IMPERIAL instruments are carried out in same massive proportions as rest of car. Some are more for style than function.

TESTING THE LUXURY CARS

tion. For those who want a bit more spirit, there is a 345-hp modification with triple two-barrel carburetion, standard in the Eldorado and optional in other series.

Behind this particular Cadillac's superior acceleration was lower gearing. With air conditioning, the factory installs a 3.21 rear axle ratio instead of the normal 2.94. This, of course, increases fuel consumption; the 62's 10-to-13 mpg range was poorest of the luxury cars.

At first, the 62 does not feel as lively as it really is because engine noise and vibration levels are so low. An important factor here, and a good example of Cadillac's attention to detail, is the radiator fan fitted to air-conditioned cars. It has a temperature-controlled clutch to reduce fan noise at high speeds.

The coil springs, front and rear, have 10 per cent softer rates this year. As a result, riding qualities are smoother but less stable. The car behaves beautifully on even surfaces at moderate speeds. Across dips and around corners, however, it floats and sways badly.

When travelling fast on a narrow country road, proper control is quite difficult. The car seems to feel, literally, all over the road.

Another annoyance, even on well-paved surfaces, is a vibration that occurs between 60 and 70 mph. Apparently it is caused by a point of resonance in the "X" frame because it disappears beyond 70 mph.

The brakes, too, have been altered. They now adjust themselves, taking up any slack when the car is driven in reverse. At the rear, extended and finned drums improve cooling and allow slightly bigger cylinders. Most interesting of all is a new vacuum release for the parking brake. It operates automatically when the engine is running and the car is placed in gear.

This has several advantages. It makes it impossible for the car to be driven with the brake on, it prevents accidental release when the ignition is off and it provides a true emergency brake. Since the parking brake will not lock with the car in gear, it can be used as a supplementary source of stopping power when the car is in motion.

The 62 four-door hardtop, called a Sedan de Ville in its more lavishly trimmed version, comes in two shapes at the same price. One has a flat roof and four side windows, the other a sloping roof and six side windows. The test car was an example of the latter, which seems more practical because it has more interior height, providing space for a higher seat cushion and greater head room in front.

Generally, the Cadillac does not give the impression of being

an unusually roomy car, though its interior dimensions compare favorably with those of the Imperial and Lincoln. One difficulty is its awkward entry and exit, hindered in front by the windshield dog leg and in back by a narrow door opening and deep floor wells.

Interior details are very well planned. The instrument panel is recessed to eliminate reflections and includes the shift quadrant. Minor controls and switches all seem out of the way, yet easy to reach. An interesting touch is the removal of the turn indicator lights from the instrument cluster. There is now an amber light in the chrome strip above each front fender that lets the driver know he is signalling for a turn.

But perhaps Cadillac's most impressive feature is its quality. Not just the excellence of finish or the fact things work but the way they work. Take the power windows, for instance. In most cars, they raise and lower with a whirr, then a clunk. In the Cadillac, they operate with only the slightest hum.

The tremendous popularity of the make (Cadillac sells three times as many cars as Imperial and Lincoln combined) causes

CLEVER DESIGN of the Continental's front doors allows air conditioning tunnel to extend to the rear passenger area. It is the best solution thus far offered to this annoying problem.

a low rate of depreciation. This same popularity, however, virtually eliminates the possibility of a discount on the original price, so a Cadillac would not necessarily be the least expensive buy in its class.

A final note: Cadillac is the only one of the three luxury cars available with any mechanical options and even it has very few, the engines and axle ratios mentioned earlier plus air suspension. Other equipment parallels that offered by Imperial and Lincoln and includes an automatic speed device called Cruise Control.

IMPERIAL

Imperial's latest model features extensive restyling of its four-year-old structure but no major changes in its fundamental engineering.

The Imperial engine, most powerful in the luxury class, is the same 350-hp, 413-cubic-inch V-8 used in the Chrysler New Yorker and serves as a basis of the 375-hp unit in the Chrysler 300-F. It has a 10.1-to-1 compression ratio and a single four-barrel carburetor.

The Le Baron recorded a good balance of acceleration and economy for a car of its weight. It averaged 0-to-60 mph runs at 12.3 seconds and fuel consumption between 11 and 14 mpg.

For roadability, the Imperial is at the head of its class. Its suspension system, torsion bars at the front and semi-elliptics at the rear, proves a comfortable ride can be achieved with a definite feel of control. It is smooth on the boulevard yet steady on the highway.

All Chrysler products are noted for their roadability. Throughout the line, their high-speed handling surpasses that of their competitors by a significant margin. However, except for the stiffly sprung 300-F, it is a virtue that lessens as size increases. In other words, an Imperial is not going to keep up with a Plymouth or Dart over a road racing circuit.

But it will stay well ahead of a Cadillac and safely in front of a Lincoln. It has the most stable suspension of any such big, heavy car built today. Float at cruising speeds and sway in corners are both within limits that enable the driver to keep track of the car's placement on the road. If traction weakens in a turn, the classic technique of increased accelerator pressure puts the Imperial right back on course. It responds to correction far more precisely than its two rivals.

This exaggerates a common characteristic of the luxury cars, the ease with which they can be driven faster than intended. Because they operate so quietly, a driver is often startled by the reading on the speedometer. And in the steadier handling Imperial, such a thing is especially true.

All of which makes the Auto Pilot, Imperial's automatic speed device, a most useful accessory. It was the first unit of its kind and, in an improved form for 1960, has become the best.

Basically, it is a governor that can be locked at a pre-selected speed. The original Auto Pilot, together with the present Cadillac Cruise Control and Lincoln Speed Control, had to be re-set manually every time the brakes were applied. The latest version eliminates this slight inconvenience and will re-engage automatically as soon as the car is returned to the desired cruising speed.

Another interesting new feature is an emergency warning light system. With the flip of a switch, all four turn indicators start flashing. The purpose is to make the car visible when it is stopped on dark roads.

Increased emphasis on quality shows up strongly in the 1960 model. For nearly two years, the make has been built in a separate plant where it can be given more careful attention and the policy is beginning to pay off. The new Imperial has the highest quality of any to bear the name in years. It is not yet the equal of Cadillac but, on the basis of the particular cars tested, it seems to have gained an edge over Lincoln.

The four-door hardtop, listed as a Southampton in the Imperial catalog, now shares its shell with the sedan. Aside from the latter's fixed window frames on the doors, there is no real

MOTOR LIFE TEST DATA

1960 CADILLAC

Test Car

Test Car: Cadillac 62
Body Type: Four-door hardtop
Base Price: $5498

Maneuverability Factors

Overall Length: 225 inches
Overall Width: 79.9 inches
Overall Height: 56.2 inches
Wheelbase: 130 inches
Tread, Front/Rear: 61 and 61 inches
Test Weight: 5130 lbs.
Weight Distribution: 54 per cent on front wheels
Steering: 4 turns lock-to-lock
Turning Circle: 47.8 feet curb-to-curb
Ground Clearance: 5.9 inches

Interior Room

Seating Capacity: Six
Front Seat
  Headroom: 34.2 inches
  Width: 61.7 inches
  Legroom: 45.9 inches
Trunk Capacity: 16.4 cubic feet

Engine & Drive Train

Type: ohv V-8
Displacement: 390 cubic inches
Bore & Stroke: 4.0 x 3.875
Compression Ratio: 10.5-to-1
Carburetion: Single four-barrel
Horsepower: 325 @ 4800 rpm
Torque: 430 lbs-ft @ 3100 rpm
Transmission: Four-speed automatic
Rear Axle Ratio: 3.21

Performance

Gas Mileage: 10 to 13 miles per gallon
Acceleration: 0-30 mph in 4.0 seconds, 0-45 mph in 6.6 seconds and 0-60 mph in 10.7 seconds
Speedometer Error: Indicated 30, 45 and 60 mph are actual 28, 42 and 57 mph respectively
Power-Weight Ratio: 15.8 lbs. per horsepower
Horsepower Per Cubic Inch: .83

1960 IMPERIAL

Test Car

Test Car: Imperial Le Baron
Body Type: Four-door hardtop
Base Price: $6318

Maneuverability Factors

Overall Length: 226.3 inches
Overall Width: 80.5 inches
Overall Height: 56.7 inches
Wheelbase: 129 inches
Tread, Front/Rear: 61.8 and 62.2 inches
Test Weight: 5260 lbs.
Weight Distribution: 54 per cent on front wheels
Steering: 3.5 turns lock-to-lock
Turning Circle: 48.2 feet curb-to-curb
Ground Clearance: 5.6 inches

Interior Room

Seating Capacity: Six
Front Seat
   Headroom: 34.4 inches
   Width: 61.0 inches
   Legroom: 46.9 inches
Trunk Capacity: 17.8 cubic feet

Engine & Drive Train

Type: ohv V-8
Displacement: 413 cubic inches
Bore & Stroke: 4.18 x 3.75
Compression Ratio: 10.1-to-1
Carburetion: Single four-barrel
Horsepower: 350 @ 4600 rpm
Torque: 470 lbs-ft @ 2800 rpm
Transmission: Three-speed automatic
Rear Axle Ratio: 2.93

Performance

Gas Mileage: 11 to 14 miles per gallon
Acceleration: 0-30 mph in 4.3 seconds, 0-45 mph in 7.3 seconds and 0-60 mph in 12.3 seconds
Speedometer Error: Indicated 30, 45 and 60 mph are actual 30, 44 and 57 mph respectively
Power-Weight Ratio: 15.2 lbs. per horsepower
Horsepower Per Cubic Inch: .85

difference between the two. Previously, a different four-door, six-window sedan had been available.

A unique feature of all Imperial body styles is curved glass for the side windows. The Le Baron has the further distinction of an unusually small window, creating an effect of privacy for rear seat passengers but restricting visibility for the driver. He has to be extra cautious about things behind him. Fortunately, the fins and taillights are within his view and serve as some guide when reversing the car.

Two circular dash housings contain a complete set of instruments, including generator, temperature and oil pressure gauges. Thanks to non-glare electroluminescent lighting, they are even easier to read at night than during the day.

Placement of some controls seems to have been dictated by styling rather than function. A particularly irritating case in point is the turn indicator switch. It is on the dash, just to the left of the instrument cluster, where it neatly balances the appearance of the heater lever at the right. However, it is quite awkward to reach. A subtle touch of symmetry hardly seems worth making a frequently-used control less accessible.

Other features for 1960 include the square steering wheel also used by Plymouth and the high-backed driver's seat now offered on all full-sized Chrysler products, both items which have been discussed in earlier tests. And Imperial has finally caught up with Cadillac and Lincoln in another detail; power vent windows have been made available as an option.

LINCOLN

Lincoln has carried its current design into a third year with reduced power and new rear springing.

Its engine has the biggest displacement, 430 cubic inches, and now the lowest output, 315 hp, of the luxury cars. A change from four-barrel to two-barrel carburetion accounts for the drop from last year's 350 hp. The compression ratio remains the same at 10-to-1. Variations of the Lincoln engine power the 310-hp Mercury and the 350-hp Thunderbird.

With a 2.89 rear axle ratio, the Continental Mark V test car was good for no better an average 0-to-60 time than 14.2 seconds. This is the slowest figure recorded this year by any V-8, regardless of price or power. Economy was on a par with Imperial's at 11 to 14 mpg, leading one to wonder why Lincoln did not

VENTILATION of the Lincoln is greatly improved by the roll-down rear window. Driver controls the power operation from his seat. The glass slides into the area behind the rear seat.

challenge the big Chrysler product in the Mobil Economy Run. It was the only make not entered in the 1960 event yet seems capable of a very good showing.

The rear suspension of the 1960 Lincoln is completely new. Previously, coil springs were used but these have been replaced by conventional semi-elliptics. The coil system had been designed so that air suspension could be installed with a minimum of difficulty. However, the option is no longer available.

With the same spring rates, the ride is just as smooth and much steadier. The car does not squat as badly as it did under hard acceleration nor does it dive as sharply when the brakes are applied. There is still some float at high speed but considerably less than there used to be.

In corners, the new Lincoln handles better, though it is still no match for the Imperial. Tires squealing and body leaning, it tends to plow through turns because of its nose heaviness. Approximately 57 per cent of the weight is on the front end.

A redeeming factor, though, is the steering. It is one of the best power-assisted units available. It has enough road feel to please the skilled driver and is remarkably quick. In normal driving, it is even faster than its 3.2 turns lock-to-lock might indicate because the car has a smaller turning circle than either Cadillac or Imperial.

Under traffic conditions, the Linclon is surprisingly easy to maneuver for a car of its size. Crisp fender lines make it less difficult to place in crowded situations than its competitors.

All this is despite its immense bulk. It is the longest, heaviest (and costliest) six-passenger sedan built in this country. It is within an inch of being 19 feet long and has a shipping weight over 5,000 lbs. As tested, it was the heavyweight champion of the year at 5300 lbs.

Interior dimensions are consistent with its overall size. Lincoln has higher seat cushions and more head room, front and rear, than either Cadillac or Imperial. Much of this can be attributed to its unit construction, which allows a greater distance between ceiling and floor because no thick frame members take up space under the passenger's feet.

When the body and frame are combined, a car can become more subject to noise and vibration from road shock. Lincoln has avoided this problem with thorough insulation. Even on the roughest surfaces, it is a quiet car. The Continental tested did have some wind noise at high speeds but this was due simply to an ineffective window seal.

Lincoln calls its four-door hardtop a Landau and, like Imperial, uses the same shell for its sedan.

The Continental series has an exclusive roll-down rear window controlled from a console in the driver's arm rest. The glass slides immediately behind the rear seat so there is no room for a rear radio speaker but it provides wonderful ventilation. On all but the hottest days, it is more pleasant to leave the air conditioning off and lower all the windows to enjoy the forced breeze that comes through the car.

Turning to the dash, instruments and controls are gathered together on a single, flat panel in front of the driver. Heating, ventilating, defrosting and air conditioning are all combined in one of the simplest, easiest arrangements possible. A single knob controls fan level and a dial setting for the kind and temperature of air wanted.

The parking brake has a vacuum release, similar to Cadillac's, that will not function unless the engine is running. However, it is operated by a pushbutton rather than by placing the shift lever in gear.

Two small features will appeal to the family man. The electric door switch is on the dash, right below a red light that goes on if any door is unlocked. Thus, if a child unlocks a rear door, which he must do before he can open it, the driver is immediately warned and can relock it with the dash switch. And the master control for the power windows has a control that cancels operation of all but the windows in the driver's door, preventing small hands from playing with them. ●

MOTOR LIFE TEST DATA

1960 LINCOLN

Test Car

Test Car: Lincoln Continental
Body Type: Four-door hardtop
Base Price: $6845

Maneuverability Factors

Overall Length: 227.2 inches
Overall Width: 80.3 inches
Overall Height: 56.7 inches
Wheelbase: 131 inches
Tread, Front/Rear: 61 and 61 inches
Test Weight: 5300 lbs.
Weight Distribution: 57 per cent on front wheels
Steering: 3.2 turns lock-to-lock
Turning Circle: 45 feet curb-to-curb
Ground Clearance: 6 inches

Interior Room

Seating Capacity: Six
Front Seat
  Headroom: 34.9 inches
  Width: 60.4 inches
  Legroom: 44.0 inches
Trunk Capacity: 17.2 cubic feet

Engine & Drive Train

Type: ohv V-8
Displacement: 430 cubic inches
Bore & Stroke: 4.3 x 3.7
Compression Ratio: 10-to-1
Carburetion: Single two-barrel
Horsepower: 315 @ 4100 rpm
Torque: 465 lbs-ft @ 2200 rpm
Transmission: Three-speed automatic
Rear Axle Ratio: 2.89

Performance

Gas Mileage: 11 to 14 miles per gallon
Acceleration: 0-30 mph in 4.9 seconds, 0-45 mph in 8.3 seconds and 0-60 mph in 14.2 seconds
Speedometer Error: Indicated 30, 45 and 60 mph are actual 28, 42.5 and 54.5 mph respectively
Power-Weight Ratio: 16.8 lbs. per horsepower
Horsepower Per Cubic Inch: .68

Close-up shows new grille of the Imperial and the free-standing headlamps.

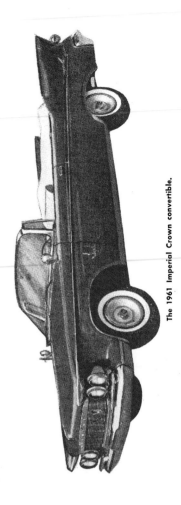

The 1961 Imperial Crown convertible.

· IMPERIAL

Imperial continues traditional styling and construction but has a few new wrinkles

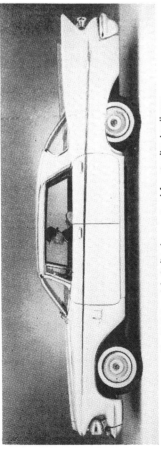

The 1961 Imperial. Stylists have restored free-standing headlamps.

IMPERIAL for 1961 has not been radically changed—either in styling or mechanical components—in line with its policy of maintaining continuity of design. However, there is a new grille, and there are unique free-standing front headlamps.

These headlamps are inset in niches provided at each side of the grille, which consist of thin horizontal bars.

Fender ends are flatter and squarer with parking lights in their overhang. Hood line is flatter and on the same plane as the fender tops, giving the front end a much more integrated appearance. The new bumper runs straight across in one piece and wraps around

the lower end of the fender.

Rear deck lines are smoother and the traditional Imperial tail lamp is mounted in the notch formed where the fin sweeps up from the fender line.

Imperial continues separate body and frame construction despite the switch to unitized bodies in other Chrysler lines. It also continues the Chrysler torsion bar suspension in front, with leaf springs in the rear.

Engine in the Imperial is the 413-cu. in. V8 which has a 10:1 compression ratio and develops 350 hp. Chrysler's AC alternator, which replaces the DC generator for better current output at low engine speed, is stand-

ard equipment this year.

Imperial uses the new Chrysler-built distributor. Carburetors are fitted with rubber tipped needle valves in the float bowl to reduce likelihood of flooding from dirt particles on the needle valve or seat. The rubber tip squeezes around the particles, forming a more nearly perfect seal.

A new parking brake release lever must be pulled out and pushed down to release the brake, thus reducing possibility of inadvertently releasing it.

Imperials are undercoated at the factory and a thick fiberglass pad under the hood screens out engine noises from the passenger compartment. Anti-corrosion treatment of

bodies has been extended, with all body sills coated with wax in a new 3-step process.

The Custom series includes 2- and 4-door hardtops, while the Crown series has 2- and 4-door hardtops and a convertible. Leather trim, standard equipment in the convertible, is optional in the two hardtops. The new Le-Baron hardtop has a limousine style rear window and a canopied effect in the roof.

A new electrically-operated windshield washer sends four jets of water against the windshield under high pressure for better spray pattern and more efficient washing.

A much wider choice of upholstery colors and materials is available, and a total of 13 exterior colors are offered.

Rear end of the Imperial.

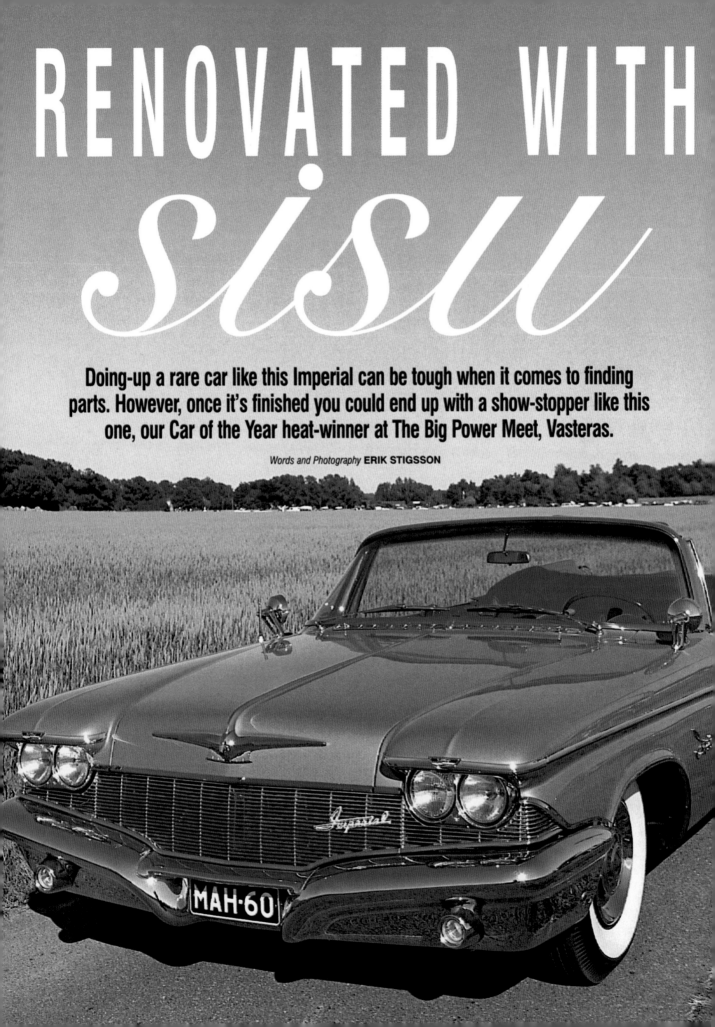

RENOVATED WITH
Sisu

Doing-up a rare car like this Imperial can be tough when it comes to finding parts. However, once it's finished you could end up with a show-stopper like this one, our Car of the Year heat-winner at The Big Power Meet, Vasteras.

Words and Photography **ERIK STIGSSON**

THE Finnish word 'sisu' can be translated as 'extreme perseverance', which is exactly what Jouko Haapala from Voikka, Finland needed during his rebuild of this 1960 Chrysler Imperial. Jouko bought this car in January 1993, little guessing that the work needed to bring the car back from the brink would take six years. He'd spent many years working on American cars, so he was no rookie, but the rebuild turned out to be much more difficult than even he could have imagined.

The main obstacle he faced during the restoration was the scarcity of good-quality parts. He now reckons that this is probably the reason why the gentleman who imported the Imperial back in 1987 wanted to sell the car. He had only managed to fix some interior details before giving up on the whole project and selling it to Jouko.

Luckily, the rust in the bodywork was not the biggest problem; there was plenty of it, but he'd seen much worse. The main problem was the number of bits missing from the car when he bought it, coupled with the fact that most of the reproduction parts Jouko found were of very poor quality. In fact some of the repro parts were so bad that they were unusable, whilst others needed a great deal of reworking before they could be fitted.

The situation was not much better when Jouko ordered used parts from the States. Some arrived in such poor condition that they were beyond salvage, whilst others turned out to be from a different make or model entirely! For instance, the upper windscreen frame moulding alone took three years to find. When Jouko finally found one, the seller wanted $900 for it! He refused

RENOVATED WITH *Sis*

to drop the price at all, but promised that it was in excellent condition.

The guy must have been blind, as when the frame arrived in Finland it was in terrible shape and took a lot of work to make it usable, which sorely tried Jouko's patience. Many restorers would have given up by now, but not him, he just pressed on regardless and that's what the Finns mean by 'sisu'; relentless perseverance.

Quite often during the restoration, parts were unavailable, so it was necessary to fabricate them at home. Friends of Jouko's helped out by making emblems and other cast parts, whilst new glass has not been a problem at all; Kattilan Autolasi in Finland can make windows, even front and rear screens, from scratch. In fact it's not unknown for Americans to order their glass from Finland for hard-to-get models or customs (see John D'Agostino's Cool Cadinental in last month's magazine).

It came as no surprise to anyone to find that the 413cu.in. V8 needed a complete rebuild. It was seized when he bought the car, but with help from his friend Petri, he has completely restored it to its former 350bhp glory. The automatic transmission was 'a complete mess', as Jouko put it, but another friend, Esa, managed to salvage it after many hours of work.

After the chassis was restored, the car at last began to look like an Imperial again. Auto Tanskanen in Helsinki resprayed the body in its original Powdered Bronze colour, whilst another

'MANY RESTORERS WOULD HAVE GIVEN UP BY NOW, BUT NOT HIM, HE JUST PRESSED ON REGARDLESS AND THAT'S WHAT THE FINNS MEAN BY 'SISU'; RELENTLESS PERSEVERANCE'

ABOVE: SIX-WAY POWER SEATS EVEN SWING OUT OF THE CAR FOR EASY ENTRY AND EGRESS.
LEFT: RED INTERIOR COMPLETELY RETRIMMED

company reupholstered the red leather interior, using the old material as patterns. Jouko went around several different electroplaters until he found one whose results he was happy with, and almost all the chrome parts have now been replated. Yet another friend, known as 'Detail' Timis, lent a hand to finish the car off, and his extremely particular nature has resulted in the perfectly detailed car you see here.

Imperials were a luxury marque, but the Crown was the most luxurious in the line, with such fittings as six-way power seats as standard. Jouko's car has plenty of options too, such as air conditioning, swivel seats, automatic beam-dipper and central locking. The fake spare wheel moulding on the boot lid was not standard even on the Crown, and neither was the passenger side mirror. In fact Jouko's Imperial did not come from the factory with all these options, which means that some of them must have been retro-fitted at a later date.

The Imperial was ready just in time to debut at the Hot Rod Show in Helsinki in March '99, where it won first prize in its class, along with the People's Choice trophy. The car ended up winning 10 trophies at the first three Finnish shows it participated in. Jouko even bought the car to the Power Big Meet in Sweden, and he did not go home empty-handed then, either; the Imperial took the *Classic American* / AMPAR Car of the Year heat-winner trophy home to Voikka. Proof, were it needed, that 'sisu' does pay off in the end! ⭐

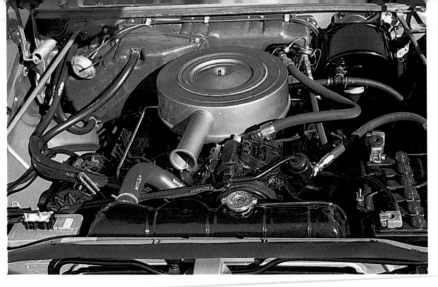

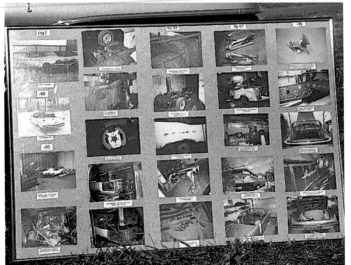

ABOVE: 413CU.IN. V8 GIVES 350BHP
LEFT: A PHOTO ALBUM THAT WON'T EMBARASS YOUR CHILDREN
BELOW: AN APPROPRIATE REGISTRATION PLATE FOR SUCH A RARE CAR...

RENOVATED WITH *sisu*

CAR LIFE ROAD TEST

CHRYSLER IMPERIAL

Intangibles are America's best car-selling lures, with those contributing to status the most successful of all. In this maze of mechanized symbolism, where does the $7000 Imperial fit in?

There are those who (unlike the writer) do not go right up the wall when someone says the price of a car is $7000. These people are the ones who buy Cadillacs, Lincoln Continentals, and—Imperials. The three makes mentioned are the prime American cars for the select market of people who either have it made, or at least hope the car will make everyone think they do. It was thus with no little trepidation that we approached the Imperial, for although we had road tested status symbols before (Cadillac, Continental), the car under scrutiny this time was one with which we were far less familiar.

We needn't have been concerned, it developed, for driving the Imperial seemed like renewing an acquaintance of long standing, since our experience with products of the Chrysler Corporation is rather extensive. From behind its odd-shaped wheel (which we didn't like, and don't think you will either) the Imperial drives like its lower-priced brethren, albeit more smoothly due to an increase in weight not accompanied by an increase in spring stiffness. Obtaining a boulevard ride in this manner is cheap, reliable, and for the most part, satisfactory, except that roadability is, of course, inferior to that of a car having either slightly harsher riding characteristics, or an equally good ride obtained through more exotic (and expensive) suspension systems.

85

The penalty one must pay for an ultra-soft ride while retaining conventional suspension made itself evident during our road test very seldom, but when it did, it was noticeable. One occasion was during the speedometer calibration tests. To ascertain speedometer error, it is necessary to run the car through a quarter-mile timing trap, maintaining a steady speed according to the speedometer, meanwhile actually clocking the car's true speed. Comparison of the two readings (clocked time and speedometer time) will show up the amount of speedometer error. We usually do this in 10-mile-per-hour increments, and the last few runs in the upper speed ranges are usually quite revealing of the car's inherent high-speed stability—or lack of same. We found the Imperial's soft springing to be doubly deceptive. During the 100-mph run, my co-driver remarked that it didn't seem as though we were traveling anywhere near that speed, although so far the speedometer had proved no more a liar than those of most contemporary cars. My retort was that although *his* side of the car might not have felt as if it were traveling 100 mph, *mine* certainly did. The soft suspension, slow steering (more than five turns, lock-to-lock) and tremendous power boost to the steering all combined to totally eliminate road feel altogether, thus giving us the impression that a portion of our sensory apparatus had gone dead. Spooky, indeed.

It may be argued that Imperials aren't designed for high-speed cross-country travel, and shouldn't be expected to handle well at such speeds. This may or may not be true, but the fact remains that the Imperial, in order to sell in the U.S., must stand comparison with the Lincoln Continental and the Cadillac, both excellent open road cars. As it now stands, the Imperial is running third in a three-car race as far as its road manners are concerned, and whether or not the purchaser will either notice or care is not our concern, since our task is merely to observe and report.

In other aspects of our road testing procedures the Imperial made a better showing, keeping in mind the inevitable comparison with those "other two" prestige cars. On acceleration, it proved to have surprising initial lunge, equaling the Cadillac and exceeding the Lincoln up to 80 mph. Beyond this point, the Cadillac takes over with the Imperial and Lincoln falling behind. This is principally due to Cadillac's trend toward a more compact configuration in recent years, thus resulting in less mass to accelerate, rather than any deficiency in either the Lincoln or Imperial powerplants.

Readers who read the Cadillac and Lincoln Con-

tinental road tests in *Car Life* will recall that on both of these cars, best acceleration figures were attained by letting the automatic transmissions shift for themselves at their pre-set points, with no intervention from the driver. The Imperial, by contrast, improved mightily when shifted manually, compared with the times obtained when letting the transmission select its own shift points.

Unfortunately, the manual shifting is limited to controlling the shift point between first and second ratios only. Even if the 2 button is left depressed indefinitely, a shift to 3 will be made automatically at the pre-set speed, as a prevention against accidental overspeeding. Naturally, speed-equipment firms are producing modified valve bodies for the TorqueFlite transmission which will allow the driver to leave it in either of the two lower ratios as long as desired, but we seriously doubt that this

is of any import whatsoever to potential Imperial owners. It is, however, of some technical interest, for the improvement brought about in acceleration times by manually controlling the first shift makes one wonder how much better the pick-up would be if both changes-up

could be selected at will. The following illustrates the difference:

	Automatic shift	Manual shift
0-30	4.0	. . .
0-40	5.6	5.3
0-50	7.5	7.0
0-60	10.0	9.4
0-70	12.5	12.0
0-80	16.6	15.7
0-90	22.7	21.5
0-100	35.0	. . .
¼ mi. e.t.	17.0	16.6
trap speed	81.0	82.0

As is usual in our test regimen, we evaluate the car's ability to stop by the way its brakes react to the repeated abuse they are subjected to in bringing the car to a halt after each acceleration or speedometer run. We don't

lock them up at 100 mph and slide to a halt, because, in spite of being spectacular, this proves little if anything, except perhaps how big a flat spot you can grind on the bottom of the front tires. No, we merely snub them down quickly and firmly, and continue doing so until we have to suspend our acceleration runs to let the brakes cool enough so that we know we will be able to stop quickly after we resume.

With the Imperial, no refreshing pause was necessary. Although this car's weight is considerable in proportion to its lining area, the effectiveness of the Chrysler Corporation's "Center-Plane" brake design is undeniable. But efficient brakes aren't enough in themselves, for brakes are merely a device for turning forward motion into heat. Unless this heat may be dissipated so that repeated use may be made of the braking system's effectiveness, it is akin to a sports car having a powerful engine but no cooling system. Happily enough, Chrysler, unlike so many of the other manufacturers who have adopted a "head in the sand" attitude toward brake fade, has taken steps to see that the effectiveness of the Imperial's brakes will withstand repeated usage. Not the end of the line by any means, it is still a laudable effort in a field conspicuous by the absence of any concern at all in this direction. Simple to a fault, it consists of the use of 15 in. wheels and properly designed hubcaps, that's all!

The photograph on page 58 shows better than any amount of words how the Imperial hubcaps are designed to circulate air about the wheel itself, thus helping dissipate the heat built up within that area by the effectiveness of the brake. Ordinarily, the full-wheel-cover type of hubcap does nothing more than act as a heat trap, reducing the effectiveness of the brakes, rather than aiding it, but by a simple and inconspicuous design change, Imperial has turned a deficit into an asset—and that's the kind of engineering for which American automobile makes used to be famous, all over the world.

We found that the Imperial's performance in the Mobilgas Runs wasn't at all freakish, since we were able to record 15 miles per gallon in normal driving, which included some city, some turnpike, and quite a bit of air conditioner use. The cooling system for the car's interior naturally doesn't run on personal magnetism, so the power required to run it must eventually be noticed in

additional fuel consumed. We consider 15 mpg under these conditions from a car of this weight a real achievement—but to what end, we don't know, since anyone who can afford to buy an Imperial should be no more concerned over the price of gasoline than the Aga Khan.

The source of this ability to obtain excellent mileage from a big car is the TorqueFlite transmission, but the manner in which it performs this feat is objectionable to us. This 3-speed planetary transmission, plus torque converter, makes you feel as though the old "free wheeling" feature is back when you lift your foot from the throttle. Although coasting is *verboten* in the Mobilgas Run, this transmission does the next thing to it, thus

explaining the run of "luck" enjoyed by Chrysler products in this particular type of competition. You may think this is fine down in the flat lands, but even with the Imperial's better-ventilated-than-most brakes, I'd hate to make a habit of driving a car of this girth in the mountains with no help from the engine in retarding it on downgrades. Since the Imperial's avowed purpose is conveying socialites to the opera, this is probably a lint-picking comment but, again, our chore is to report; the readers, to evaluate—so we'll leave it up to you.

The interior of the Imperial is fitted out in fabrics obviously costing many $$$ per yard, along with quantities of leather and/or leatherette, with a smattering of chrome

to set it off. This, along with the external styling differences, is what sets the "Big I" apart from the rest of the Chrysler line. The slogan "America's Most Carefully Built Car" was neither proved nor disproved during the 1500 miles we had the Imperial in our possession, so we're in no position to cast any light on its validity. Our final impression of this car, after some pleasant surprises in the areas of acceleration, braking, and economy, was that the Imperial is for the man who believes that he should be driving a car that costs *twice* as much as a Chrysler, but likes the Chrysler-type of car. Personally, we'd just as soon have *two* Chrysler Newports—you know, one for summer and one for winter. ∎

CAR LIFE ROAD TEST

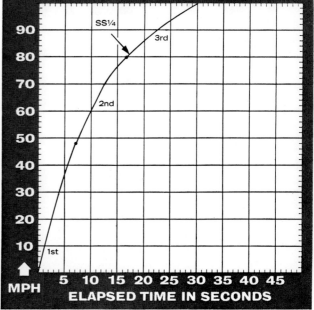

IMPERIAL

SPECIFICATIONS

List price	$5647
Price, as tested	6503
Curb weight, lb	5110
Test weight	5400
distribution, %	54.5/45.5
Tire size	8.20-15
Tire capacity, lb	4900
Brake lining area	251
Engine type	V-8, ohv
Bore & stroke	4.19 x 3.75
Displacement, cc	6771
cu in	413.0
Compression ratio	10.1
Bhp @ rpm	350 @ 4600
equivalent mph	122
Torque, lb-ft	470 @ 2800
equivalent mph	74.3

GEAR RATIOS

3rd (1.00), overall	3.23
2nd (1.45)	4.68
1st (2.45)	7.91
1st (2.45 x 2.2)	17.4

DIMENSIONS

Wheelbase, in	129.0
Tread, f and r	61.8/62.2
Over-all length, in	227.3
width	81.7
height	56.7
equivalent vol, cu ft	610
Frontal area, sq ft	25.7
Ground clearance, in	5.6
Steering ratio, o/a	15.7
turns, lock to lock	3.5
turning circle, ft	48.2
Hip room, front	61.0
Hip room, rear	60.2
Pedal to seat back, max	46.0
Floor to ground	12.5
Luggage vol, cu ft	34.1

PERFORMANCE

Top speed (est), mph	120
best timed run	n.a.
3rd ( )	
2nd (4360)	80
1st (4430)	48

FUEL CONSUMPTION

Normal range, mpg	13/15

ACCELERATION

0-30 mph, sec	4.0
0-40	5.6
0-50	7.5
0-60	10.0
0-70	12.5
0-80	16.6
0-100	35.0
Standing ¼ mile	17.0
speed at end	81

PULLING POWER

3rd, lb/ton @ mph	300 @ 45
2nd	445 @ 30
1st	off scale
Total drag at 60 mph, lb	175

SPEEDOMETER ERROR

30 mph, actual	31.4
60 mph	58.7
90 mph	86.2

CALCULATED DATA

Lb/hp (test wt)	15.4
Cu ft/ton mile	.100
Mph/1000 rpm	26.5
Engine revs/mile	2260
Piston travel, ft/mile	1415
Car Life wear index	31.9

ACCELERATION & COASTING

(Graph: MPH vs. ELAPSED TIME IN SECONDS, showing 1st, 2nd, 3rd gear acceleration curve with SS¼ marked)

THREE

for the MONEY

AMERICA'S LEADING LUXURY CARS — CADILLAC, IMPERIAL AND THE LINCOLN CONTINENTAL — REFLECT SUMPTUOUS STYLE AND TASTE.

Luxury personified: Cadillac, Imperial, Lincoln...
"A look, a feel, a state of mind"

by Bob Russo

THE LEADING LUXURY CARS in America today — Cadillac, Imperial and Lincoln — share one significant point. Each has dignity, that unmistakable characteristic which sets a thoroughbred apart from the cow pony. This quality may be expressed and reflected differently by each manufacturer but it has a common appeal in "look, feel and state of mind" for those who drive these cars — or those who wish they could drive them.

In this test of the Cadillac de Ville, Imperial LeBaron and Lincoln Continental, our purpose is not to evaluate them by comparison but to pick out the major points of each model on which the greatest emphasis has been placed.

The 1961 Cadillac de Ville, in keeping with the entire Cadillac line, emphasizes *greater* comfort. This has been achieved through a change in chassis and frame construction which permits more head- and legroom, and an improved ride through a new front suspension system. Body style has taken on only a slight change, noticeable mostly in the rear where tail/back-up light pods are now in a horizontal position rather than vertical. Power steering and brakes and Hydra-Matic transmissions are, of course, standard on all 1961 Cadillacs.

steel appliques at the roof insert area and a "town car" rear window which offers greater privacy to passengers.

The instrument panel is one of the most functional in any car, regardless of price. The entire interior, in fact, shows good taste and careful planning. There is no cramping for leg space, even for rear seat passengers, when the front seat is in its rearmost position.

Considerable styling changes this year give the LeBaron a classic look. Tail fins have been subdued, but the trunk lid with the familiar wheel cover is still available as an option. Emphasis has shifted more to the front of the car, where crisp lines are met by a distinguished grille and free-standing headlights.

Driving the LeBaron provides every bit of the big car feel one would expect from a luxury vehicle such as this. But despite this big car feel, the Imperial handles exceptionally well. Our one objection was vision, side and rear. Not being able to see the right front fender takes a bit of getting used to, while the vision restriction created by the town-car rear window requires extreme caution when leaving a parking place or moving into a busy street from a side road.

The Continental, available as a sedan or convertible and

If a comparison were to be made, the de Ville has a more racy appearance with its sweeping fins, large windows and peppy performance — in contrast with a slight trace of European styling found in the Imperial and Lincoln.

The luxury of a smooth, quiet ride for which Cadillac has always been famous, has been further improved with a redesigned frame and chassis, permitting use of a new suspension system, front and rear. Road bumps are better absorbed through the new single lower control arm in front, while noise is dampened with generous use of rubber mountings throughout the frame and chassis.

The same 390-cubic-inch V-8 engine with its 325-hp rating has been retained for '61. It packs a surprising amount of wallop despite the weight of the car, and will make the 0-60 run in 11 seconds.

Vision, from all angles, is excellent from the driver's seat, and the de Ville is a true comfort to drive. Despite its size, it moves through traffic easily, has plenty of reserve power if needed for passing, and will brake to a halt from 60 mph in 175 feet.

The Imperial LeBaron, most elegant of the four Imperial models available this year, contains just about every luxury ever invented for an automobile, and most of these are standard equipment, including power seats, windows, brakes and steering, automatic transmission, and windshield washers. One of its most striking points, perhaps, is the smooth body finish. Almost flawless, it complements the fine styling of the LeBaron which is emphasized by sculptured stainless

the only Lincoln model now made, has been designed to fit its name. Inside and out, it has the continental touch. Massive bumpers, slender roof and unbroken body lines give it a distinctive look that is all Lincoln. Seating, especially from a driver's standpoint, is more comfortable than the most expensive easy chair, with a small, thin-rimmed steering wheel well positioned for maximum comfort.

Although not lacking in power, the 430-cubic-inch V-8 engine could use a bit more top-end punch, especially for passing. Its 0-60-mph rating is 13.5 seconds, as compared to 11.0 and 11.1 seconds respectively for Cadillac and Imperial.

Pointing out the Continental's reliability, Henry Ford II revealed at announcement time that the warranty on all 1961 models has been increased to two full years or 24,000 miles — double that offered by other U.S. manufacturers, and an expression of confidence that this is the finest, most reliable luxury car ever produced by the Ford Motor Co.

As mentioned at the beginning, this test of the three leading luxury cars is not meant to compare one against the other. However, one factor that should be pointed out is fuel economy. As expected, none of these cars is easy on gas. The Cadillac averaged nine to 10 mpg, as compared to eight to 10 by the Lincoln and 10 to 12 mpg by the Imperial.

However, fuel economy is not the main reason owners purchase a Cadillac, Lincoln or Imperial. There is a *luxury feeling* that comes with riding in a luxury car that cannot be defined — but it can be bought.

Imperial Le Baron

New in overall appearance, Imperial styling has now taken on the look and feel of a true classic car.

PHOTOS BY BOB D'OLIVO, PAT BROLLIER

Overhead view of the Imperial reveals its new styling. Featured are stainless steel appliques on both sides of the roof insert area as part of new look. These are standard on the LeBaron.

A limousine-style roof and rear window seclude rear passengers but restrict side and rear view for driver. Top-quality safety glass is used in all windows. Heat-absorbing glass is optional.

IMPERIAL LE BARON

4-door, 6-passenger hardtop

OPTIONS ON CAR TESTED: Air conditioning, power seats and windows, remote control side-view mirror, power antenna.

ODOMETER READING AT START OF TEST: 428 miles

PERFORMANCE

ACCELERATION (2 aboard)

0-30 mph	4.1 secs.
0-45 mph	6.9
0-60 mph	11.1

Standing start ¼-mile 18.6 secs. and 79.5 mph

Speeds in gears @ 4200 rpm
1st .... 38 mph
2nd .... 79 mph

Speedometer Error on Test Car

Car's speedometer reading	31	47	54	65	75	85
Weston electric speedometer	30	45	50	60	70	80

Miles per hour per 1000 rpm in top gear (actual meter reading) ....24.5 mph

Stopping Distances — from 30 mph, 37 ft.; from 60 mph, 158 ft.

SPECIFICATIONS FROM MANUFACTURER

Engine
Ohv V-8
Bore: 4.18 ins.   Stroke: 3.75 ins.
Displacement: 413 cubic inches
Compression ratio: 10.1:1
Horsepower: 350 @ 4600 rpm
Ignition: 12-volt battery/coil

Gearbox
TorqueFlite automatic with pushbutton control

Driveshaft
Open

Differential
Hotchkiss drive with hypoid axle
Standard ratio 2.93:1

Suspension
Front: Independent with torsion bar springs, Oriflow shocks

Rear: Tapered-leaf outboard springs with interliners and rear axle strut, Oriflow shocks

Wheels and Tires
Steel safety-rim wheels with 8.20 x 15 tubeless tires; white sidewalls standard

Brakes
Total-contact, power operated
Front and rear: 12-in. drums

Body and Frame
Wheelbase 129 ins.
Track, front 61.8 ins., rear 62.2 ins.
Overall length 227.3 ins.

Perfectly grouped instruments include rare oil and battery gauges in place of warning lights. Air conditioning system can be directed various ways: toward rear seat, cowl or floor.

Quality handling and smooth ride were evident in bump test. Despite high speed and a severe dip, Imperial remained level and true. Shocks have been improved for quieter, easy operation.

(Above) Generous trunk will hold more than an average need. Covered spare mounts flat (left).

Compressor, alternator and power steering unit plus Imperial's 413-cubic-inch V-8 leave very little extra room under the hood. Waterproof ignition and dual exhausts are standard items.

IMPERIAL

IN SELECTING Chrysler's Imperial LeBaron four-door Southampton hardtop, we picked the biggest of the big in the luxury field. And with LeBaron we had the top of the Imperial line — the plushest, fanciest automobile that Chrysler manufactures. We didn't have to take the measurements to realize that it is longer, wider and taller than anything else currently in the passenger car field. Massively proportioned, it looks big and impressive.

Yet, after checking exact dimensions, we found that it is only five inches longer overall than the Cadillac (actually a half-inch shorter in wheelbase), and less than two inches wider than the Cad. Its size, therefore, is partly an illusion. But only partly, as we learned while threading through narrow traffic lanes with what seemed zero clearance on the sides. So right off we were able to determine what seems to be about the only disadvantage of this car, the very thing that makes it desirable to most purchasers — its bigness. After a while, of course, the size became less noticeable and drivers compensated by driving a little less aggressively.

The modest rear window, providing considerable privacy for rear seat passengers, creates a town-car roof and a completely distinctive appearance that attracted a great deal more attention than we anticipated. Ordinarily, our domestic test cars never get a second glance, but there is something distinguished about the LeBaron that made people stare (we got the same treatment in the Rolls-Royce) — not so much at the car but at its passengers, as if onlookers were expecting to see a real live celebrity.

Actually, there have been no significant mechanical changes in the car for '62. The engine remains Chrysler's extremely potent 340-hp, 413-inch powerplant, so beloved by Chrysler owners and hot rodders alike. That much punch is not wasted; it is essential in a car that can easily scale over 6000 pounds, loaded with six passengers and luggage. At that, acceleration should please the most critical. The feeling was strong, smooth power all the way up the speed range.

The three-speed automatic transmission operates and acts just like the old TorqueFlite it replaces but it has been redesigned internally, is more compact, giving more cockpit space, and is 60 pounds lighter, due in part to an aluminum case. Shifts were perceptible but seemed exceptionally smooth, in keeping with the way we believe a luxury car should perform. One other change this year is the use of a single exhaust system instead of the duals formerly used. A single system operates hotter and should lengthen muffler and tailpipe life.

The biggest changes (for the better, we felt) have been in styling. The fins have been chopped and the rear fender line flows easily, topped by the famous gun-sight taillights. The only other appearance change worth noting is the divided grille. On the inside, everything remains as it was in '61. The instrument panel is recessed between a series of transmission and heat/cooling control pushbuttons on either side, and surmounted by a nearly square steering wheel. Its acceptance in use became a matter of personal taste. Some of the test crew liked it, others tolerated it, no one felt violently opposed to the unusual shape.

The chassis is not Chrysler's highly-touted Unibody construction. They utilize the more conventional method of heavy, box-section frame rails with body welded in place. This year they have followed the industry trend to sealed lube points so that 32,000-mile intervals between lubrications are standard.

The Imperial is brimming over with interior space, particularly in the rear seat. The distance between the rear seat backrest and the back side of the front seat can vary from 32 to 37 inches. With just over five feet of hiproom, there is plenty of area for three big adults to stretch out and be comfortable. Headroom, front and rear, 38.9/38.3 inches, is perfectly ample

THE LE BARON IS A BIG, BIG CAR AND ITS STYLISTS HAVE NOT ATTEMPTED TO HIDE THE FACT. IT HAS A REAL TOWN CAR APPEARANCE.

for tall men to sit upright. There are about 32 cubic feet in the handsomely detailed trunk. The spare, which has its own upholstered cover, mounts flat and would necessarily be buried under a full load of luggage. This is hardly a new problem and will be with us as long as spare tires are stored in trunks.

Chryslers have a reputation for good handling, and the LeBaron upheld it. Steering is quick, 3½ turns lock-to-lock, although the turning circle is an enormous 48.8 feet. While this type of car is not intended for successful hard cornering, it remained reasonably flat and controllable in turns, indicating its adaptability to mountainous terrain. Brakes, with 251 square inches of lining, stopped us moderately well from 60 mph. With more than enough power assist, required pedal pressure is very low but they showed considerable tendency to lock up, a not uncommon trait on heavy, power-braked cars.

The true feeling of luxury really came on at fast highway speeds. Cradled deeply into the soft cushions, windows closed, heating or cooling on as the climate dictated, we found the Imperial to be a magnificent road machine. There was just a slight wind rustle as it curled around the windshield chrome, but never enough to infringe upon normal conversation. Engine and road noises were effectively isolated from passengers. The ride was soft, verging on but not quite marshmallow, so that we found very little in driving or riding to contribute to fatigue.

Our test car was equipped with the optional ($57.45) limited-slip differential. We couldn't note any real advantage in normal operation although it's a handy device in snow, mud or sand. We found that the rear wheels would not break loose during our acceleration runs, which could be attributed either to the differential or the car's extreme weight.

Another option of interest is the Auto Pilot ($96.80). When locked on, it holds a steady pre-set speed over all terrain except steep downhills. Touching the brake releases it. It can be demonstrated that its use will actually increase fuel economy slightly but we found its biggest advantage on long trips, where we were able to shift position without having to worry about the position of our throttle foot.

Fuel economy is pretty much a matter of academic interest in the luxury field. The cars are big, heavy and powered with huge V-8's. What else can one expect except the eight to 12 mpg we experienced? The 2.93-to-1 axle ratio is about as far as one can practically go into an economy gear. The only answer is to keep the 23-gallon fuel tank filled.

Although it is the most expensive single option, the dual air conditioner and heater ($777.75) does an outstanding job. Temperature, heating or cooling, may be adjusted and held to precise limits and while using it we were quite unconcerned about outside weather conditions. With this type of system we found very little necessity to ever open the windows.

The extra-cost options bumped the LeBaron's price from a base of $6422 to a total of $7735.90. Destination charge added $205, making the car's delivery price $7940.90, plus tax and license. For this kind of money one expects something awfully close to the best. We can only add that anyone seeking dignified, quiet luxury really need look no further than the Imperial LeBaron.   /MT

The mammoth control console relies on the Chrysler pushbutton theme. Note the squared steering wheel.

Tall men will breathe a sigh of relief when they board the Imperial. There's even hat room on the inside.

CHRYSLER IMPERIAL LE BARON
4-door, 6-passenger hardtop

OPTIONS ON CAR TESTED: Dual air conditioner and heater, Auto Pilot, Sure-Grip differential, power door locks, automatic beam changer, radio and power antenna, seat belts, tinted glass, 8.20 x 15 rayon whitewall tires, door edge protectors, remote control mirror

BASIC PRICE: $6422

PRICE AS TESTED: $7940.90 (plus tax and license)

ODOMETER READING AT START OF TEST: 4051 miles

PERFORMANCE

ACCELERATION (2 aboard)
```
0-30 mph............................... 4.2 secs.
0-45 mph............................... 7.1
0-60 mph...............................11.0
```
Standing start ¼-mile 19.1 secs. and 79 mph

Speeds in gears @ shift points
    1st ......33 mph @ 3600 rpm   2nd .....75 mph @ 4000 rpm

Speedometer Error on Test Car

Car's speedometer reading	31	49	55	65	75	85
Weston electric speedometer	30	45	50	60	70	80

Observed miles per hour per 1000 rpm in top gear ....24 mph

Stopping Distances — from 30 mph, 41 ft.; from 60 mph, 185 ft.

SPECIFICATIONS FROM MANUFACTURER

Engine
    Ohv V-8
    Bore: 4.19 ins.
    Stroke: 3.75 ins.
    Displacement: 413 cubic inches
    Compression ratio: 10.1:1
    Horsepower: 340 @ 4600 rpm
    Ignition: 12-volt coil

Gearbox
    3-speed automatic; dash-mounted pushbutton controls

Driveshaft
    2-piece open, pre-pack anti-friction U-joint bearings

Differential
    Standard: Hypoid, semi-floating
    Optional (test car): Sure-Grip limited-slip
    Standard ratio 2.93:1

Wheels and Tires
    Steel disc, 15 x 6 L
    8.20 x 15 rayon whitewall tires

Suspension
    Front: Independent, non-parallel control arms with torsion bars, stabilizer bar, tubular shocks
    Rear: Non-independent, semi-elliptic leaf springs, tubular shocks

Brakes
    Hydraulic, power assist; total-contact brake shoes
    Front and rear: 12 in. x 2.5 in. wide
    Effective lining area: 251 sq. ins.

Body and Frame
    Welded double-channel box-section side rails, lateral cross-members, plus X-type cross-member
    Wheelbase 129.0 ins.
    Track, front 61.7 ins., rear 62.2 ins.
    Overall length 227.1 ins.
    Shipping weight 4805 lbs.

BIGGEST MECHANICAL change on the '62 Imperial is a new automatic transmission that is 60 lbs. lighter.

Imperial

Restyling of roof and rear-quarter panels has produced a cleaner look

PLENTY OF LEGROOM here, a full 14 inches from cushion to front seat.

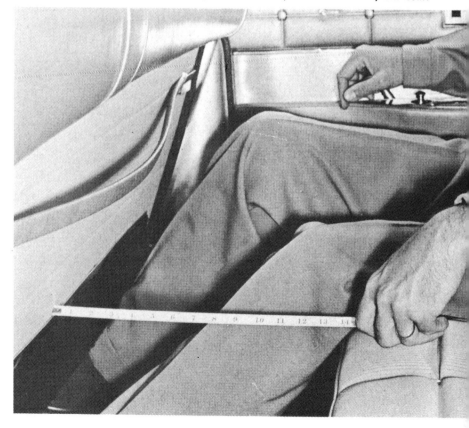

STYLING CHANGES for 1962, although not involving major body changes, have given the Imperials a new look. They still carry many of the outstanding characteristics, however, that set them apart and make them easily recognizable as Imperials.

New rear quarter panels have de-emphasized the fin effect, new moldings and a cleaner rear deck area make the car look lower and wider. Roof areas also appear "cleaned up," as the moldings that outlined the sweep areas, once two-toned, have been removed.

The Imperial lineup of models is unchanged from 1961. There are three series: the Custom with two and four-door hardtops, the Crown with two and four-door hardtops, plus convertible and the LeBaron four-door hardtop. All models are on the 129-inch wheelbase, separate-frame chassis with an overall body length of 227 inches.

As added protection against corrosion, Imperial's separate bodies receive the full seven-stage dip and spray treatment given to the other Chrysler unit-body cars.

Adoption of a new and more compact automatic transmission has made it possible for engineers to reduce the height and width of the center hump in the front compartment. This new transmission replaces the Torque-Flite automatic previously used. It has the same ratios (2.45 low, 1.45 intermediate and 1.00 direct), but internal construction is new and the case is a one-piece aluminum die casting. Not only is this transmission smaller, but it also effects a weight savings of 60 pounds. Despite this lighter weight, it has 10 percent greater torque capacity than previous transmission. Control, as before, is by push button.

Imperial's single engine is the 413-cubic-inch "senior" Chrysler Corporation V8. Installed in the Imperial with a 10.0 to 1 compression ratio and single four-barrel carburetor, this engine develops 340 horsepower at 4600 r.p.m.

A single exhaust system replaces the dual exhausts previously used on the Imperial. Because it runs hotter, the single system remains dry and resists corrosion. Cost of replacement will be halved.

Chassis-lubrication intervals have been extended from 2000 to 32,000 miles on all suspension and steering linkage items. Tie rod ends are sealed for life. Other points are refilled via plugs.

A new smaller and lighter starter has also been installed on the 1962 Imperial.

ELECTRICAL LEADS are neatly capped, plug into main terminal. Mechanism at lower right is automatic pilot control.

Custom four-door hardtop 1963 Imperial features rich styling continuity.

New 1963 Imperial Retains Styling Continuity; Adds Many Improvements

THE 1963 Imperial which went on display in dealer showrooms Wednesday, September 26, carries forward a styling continuity with design modifications which further enhance its appeal to luxury car buyers. It has a new roof structure, new styling treatment in the rear, more interior room for passengers, more luxurious interiors and additional convenience features as standard equipment.

"Imperial continues to be America's biggest car," says C. E. Briggs, vice president Chrysler Corporation and general manager of the Chrysler-Plymouth Division. "We are continuing to make Imperial the most carefully built car in the industry.

"To that end we are giving it exclusive manufacturing attention. It has its own separate shop for special coach work, and other facilities set aside for the sole purpose of making it the best car possible."

The 1963 Imperials will carry a new warranty for five years or 50,000 miles, whichever comes first, on all major power train components. This includes all cars sold in the United States and Canada. Imperial is the first of the luxury car class to offer such extended owner protection.

The 1963 model is the seventh in the modern series of Imperial cars which became a separate line in 1957. Like its predecessors, the 1963 version of Chrysler Corporation's top luxury car has its own exclusive construction which it shares with no other car.

Imperial retains many of the distinctive styling features of previous Imperials including the free standing head lamps of 1961 and 1962. There is a new grille and a more elegant rear design treatment.

Significant body changes in the 1963 Imperial include a new roof and rear window for the Custom and Crown hardtops, a restyled LeBaron roof, and new rear bumpers on all lines.

The appearance, quality and durability of interiors have been greatly improved on the 1963 Imperial.

Grain walnut door panel inserts have been added to LeBaron to impart a new note of elegance.

Fine pleating has been added to the seats of the Custom, and the Crown offers two different types of body cloth; one modern and fashionable, the other conservative and traditional.

Seats provide additional comfort and durability in the new models through use of heavier spring construction over the transmission tunnel.

The new roof silhouette allows higher rear seats and greater head room. In two-door models the rear passenger compartment has 4.5 inches additional leg room. The floor pan hump in front is lower, providing improved three-passenger comfort.

The 413 cubic inch, 340 horsepower Imperial engine is basically unchanged. However, closed crankcase ventilation will be standard on all 1963 Imperials. This reduces the amount of unburned hydro-carbons released into the atmosphere and ensures a cleaner engine.

Power operated windows, remote control left side rear view mirrors and integral arm rests with useful storage compartments hidden in front door arm rests have become standard equipment in 1963 Imperials.

Among the new features and improvements are new back windows to reduce exposure of rear passengers to sun rays, a new transmission parking lock, new automatic parking brake release, new oversize brakes with flared brake drums, and finer interiors with substantial gains in passenger comfort.

Higher braking performance is a significant new characteristic of the Imperial. Servo-contact, self-energizing brakes with 11 x 3 inch linings are introduced for 1963.

In addition, to the inherent advantages of low pedal effort, good pedal reserve, stability and quietness in operation, the new Imperial brakes offer improved cooling, higher fade resistance, and more effective sealing against ingress of water and dirt. Bonded linings are used for maximum lining life and effectiveness.

New Imperial parking brakes are on the rear wheels. The previous transmission output shaft brake is replaced by a parking system which operates the rear wheel service brakes through a cable and linkage mechanism. In addition to a sizeable reduction in the height of the transmission tunnel, adoption of the rear wheel parking brake provides higher braking capacity and smoother application.

A new, vacuum actuated parking brake release unit is featured on the Imperial. This device is operated by engine vacuum, and automatically releases the parking brake when the engine is started and the transmission placed in gear. A manual emergency override is also provided.

Higher grade stainless steels are used on exterior trim parts on the 1963 Imperial to improve life and appearance. More extensive use is made of plastic clips and fasteners for moldings and ornaments to prevent possible rusting under these parts.

New, reinforced weather-strips improve the sealing and appearance of Imperial windows and doors. Door trim panels and door openings have been realigned to reduce door closing effort and increase the effectiveness of the seals.

Additional underhood corrosion protection measures for 1963 will increase the life of components. These measures—started in 1962—include painting engine mountings, exhaust pipes, front suspension parts, and other visible items under the hood. Certain exposed components are plated for additional protection. A total of approximately 30 underhood items receive extra protection as a result of this program.

Imperial exhaust system corrosion protection is increased by using aluminized steel for all muffler parts that previously were not protected in this manner. The dual exhaust systems on the Imperial convertible model feature stainless steel for critical muffler and resonator parts in both sides of the system. Exhaust system life expectancy is considerably increased by these changes.

A parking sprag control is introduced for the Imperial's automatic transmission. The sprag mechanism is incorporated in the transmission extension and is used to lock the output shaft to the extension housing. It provides a positive and convenient method of holding the car immovable when parked. The sprag is actuated by a cable connected to a slide lever mounted on the instrument panel.

The number of Imperial model offerings remains the same. Two-door and four-door hardtops are available in the Custom and Crown series, and an improved Imperial Crown convertible is again available. The LeBaron, top of the Imperial line, is a hardtop with a distinctive town car appearance and extra luxury features. ★

The 1963 Dodge Motor Home, a versatile 26-foot vehicle designed especially for travel and recreation, is at home off the highway as well as in city traffic. A 200 hp V-8 engine, push-button automatic transmission and power brakes are standard equipment on the vehicle.

IMPERIAL

M T Road Test

by Bob McVay, *Assistant Technical Editor*

Imperial runs whisper-quiet at all speeds. Standard power accessories make driving almost too easy. The basic styling will be radically changed next year, but the size and luxury will remain.

WHEN SIX PEOPLE can climb out of an automobile after an all-day drive through stop-and-go traffic and crowded freeways without one complaint, it speaks well for the comfort of that automobile. Designed as luxurious, comfortable transportation for six, the Imperial for 1963 does its job very well indeed. Our passengers ranged from a petite five-foot-three to well over six feet, yet all had plenty of head and leg room and got out of the car as fresh and relaxed as they got in. Although it was a hot, muggy day in Southern California, our Imperial's adequate air-conditioning system kept everyone cool and comfortable throughout the day.

Comfort and luxury are the Imperial's biggest selling points. It isn't the fastest or the most economical automobile on the road, and it hasn't undergone any drastic styling changes over the past few years. But there are many changes for 1963 that make the Imperial better than last year's offering.

Our test car was the top number in the Imperial line-up — an Imperial LeBaron Southampton four-door hardtop. It's a big name that fits an equally big car, since the LeBaron is the largest car made in this country (short of a seven-passenger limousine). Only the four-door hardtop is offered in the LeBaron series, but the Crown Imperial series, next down the line, has a two- and four-door hardtop and a convertible. Rounding out the six-car line-up is the Custom Imperial series, offering a two- and a four-door hardtop. Twenty-one interior combinations of cloth and vinyl, cloth and leather, or all leather can be ordered (our test car had black vinyl and leather). Imperials come in 16 solid colors. Ten are metallic, and three are exclusive to the Imperial line.

Some of the new features on this year's Imperial include a new roof line for Custom and Crown hardtops and a re-styled roof for the LeBaron. These new roof lines allow higher rear seats, while 4.5 inches of additional leg room are available to rear-seat passengers. Here's one car a man can really stretch out in.

Two narrow vertical tail lights replace the well known gun-sight units familiar on past Imperials. Grilles and rear bumpers have been redesigned for 1963. There's a new automatic parking brake release and new rear-wheel parking brakes that no longer operate off the transmission. Aluminized steel is used extensively in the exhaust system to increase muffler and pipe life. Under-hood corrosion protection has been given a lot of attention through painting and zinc or cadmium plating. Imperials also share the five-year/50,000-mile warranty with other Chrysler products.

Base price of our car was $6434, but by the time all the options were added onto the delivered price in Los Angeles, it came to $7905.10 (including a destination charge of $205). In addition to the optional equipment listed in our

Flared brake drums increase drum mass by 37 per cent. They provide more cooling surface and help reduce drum expansion due to overheating. Brakes are self-adjusting duo-servo type.

A single-diaphragm, vacuum-suspended power brake unit is used on new Imperials. It's easier to take apart or service and is built stronger than the dual-diaphragm unit used last year. Normal stops required only light pedal pressures, but we did notice considerable fade during stops from our high-speed and acceleration runs. Panic stops from 60 mph required longer-than-average distances for a car of this size and weight.

spec chart, the Imperial came standard with such items as Torqueflite automatic transmission, power steering-brakes-windows, padded dash, remote-control left mirror (outside), arm rest storage compartments, door-mounted courtesy lamps, and front and rear arm rests (Crown and LeBaron only).

For nearly $8000, an owner expects something special — and he really gets it when he buys an Imperial, especially if it's a LeBaron. There's a 413-cubic-inch V-8 with a five-main-bearing crankshaft under that hood, putting out a whopping 470 pounds-feet of torque at 2800 rpm and 340 horses at 4600 rpm. With a 4.19-inch bore and a stroke of 3.75 inches, the engine's loafing at almost any speed. It does require premium gas, since it has a 10.1-to-1 compression ratio.

This big cast-iron engine has 5250 pounds of automobile to propel, but it manages with a smoothness and quietness that belie its potential performance. Our electric speedometer showed an actual 102 mph at 3800 rpm on Riverside Raceway's back straight, and with a longer run this car should easily top the 110 mark. From a standing start, the LeBaron clicked off speeds of 30, 45, and 60 mph in 4.1, 7.4, and 12.0 seconds respectively — quite a feat for a car weighing over 5600 pounds with two men and our test equipment on board.

Driving the big car through a 2.93 rear axle, Imperial's three-speed Torqueflite transmission proved very smooth and quiet during our test. It's a little faster off the line when the shifts are controlled by the transmission pushbuttons. Under full throttle in DRIVE, the unit shifted up at 40 mph and 3800 rpm and again at 79 mph and 4100 rpm. First range proved handy for holding the car at a crawl when descending downgrades, while 2 would hold it in the 30-40-mph area. Second also proved a good hill-climbing range. It would keep engine revs at a useful level, and power was on tap for instant passing without waiting for the usual kickdown from DRIVE to second. A parking pawl is new for 1963 on the Imperial. Mounted just to the left of the pushbuttons, the lever locks the transmission and automatically places it in neutral when the lever's pulled all the way down.

One nice thing about combining a big, powerful engine and a relatively high rear axle is that the Imperial gave us above-average fuel economy for a car of its large dimensions and ponderous weight. Our best figure was 14.5 mpg during a steady drive at 65-70 mph on the freeway. Driving the Imperial to and from work dropped the mileage to 11.2 mpg, while hard driving over winding roads with lots of stopping and starting took it down to 10. Our overall average for more than 1500 miles of driving figured out at 12.5 mpg, which isn't bad for this kind of automobile.

Our test car was fitted with a device called the Auto-Pilot. A reversible electric motor controlled by a sensor unit connected to the speedometer drives the throttle rod back and forth in response to a centrifugal governor. A dash-mounted knob controls the governor's weights and can be set at any desired cruising speed from 40 to 85 mph. What happens is this: We set the knob at the speed limit (65 mph in California), and when the speedometer needle hit 65, we felt a stiffening of the accelerator pedal as if someone had put a block under it. With the unit engaged and the knob pulled out, the car would continue at the set speed, uphill or down, and always stay within two-three mph of the set speed. To deactivate the Auto-Pilot, we had only to touch the brake pedal or push the knob in.

The stiffening of the accelerator served as a good warning that we'd reached the speed limit. Our LeBaron was so quiet

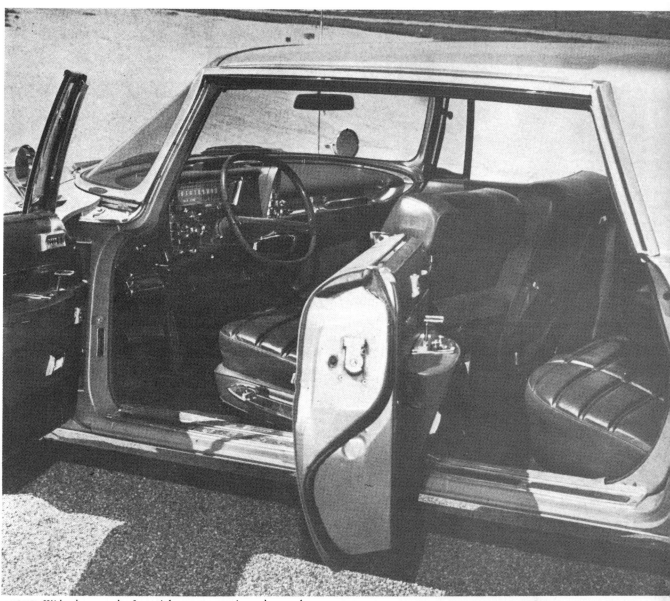

(ABOVE) *Wide doors make Imperial easy to get in and out of. Handy document cases are attached to backs of comfortable, contoured front seats. Our car had more than enough leg room.*

(RIGHT) *Dash uses easy-to-read instruments instead of warning lights. All controls are well positioned, but the squared wheel and roller speedometer are a little hard to get accustomed to.*

PHOTOS BY BOB D'OLIVO

and smooth it took a conscious effort to keep it within legal speed limits. However, the Auto-Pilot should be used only on long cruising trips or to rest one's accelerator foot. For these purposes we liked it, but, in the Imperial, the driver has so little to do anyway (and the car is so comfortable) that we preferred to use our good right foot and have control of the situation. Slightly better gas mileage is possible with the Auto-Pilot, since it's generally smoother than most drivers. It's a nice option if used as intended. The price is $96.80.

Our LeBaron proved a real road burner. The combination of a soft, comfortable ride, effortless engine, and a very quiet chassis enabled us to cover long distances without fatigue. Our golden hardtop was especially at home on the open highway but proved no problem in traffic once we became used to allowing more room when parking and making turns. A car of this size doesn't lend itself to vigorous driving, but it handled well enough on winding roads — except when hard cornering flooded the carburetor, limiting the speed at which we could take the corners.

Under a maze of hoses, wires, and accessory components is Imperial's smooth-running 413-inch V-8. It delivers 340 hp and *loafs during normal driving. A closed crankcase ventilation system is standard. Bigger air cleaner has 17-inch diameter.*

IMPERIAL ROAD TEST

We felt lots of understeer on turns when the tires were at the recommended 26 psi. With 40 pounds front and 37 rear, the car handled a lot better without any noticeable loss of riding comfort. We couldn't find a dip sharp enough to bottom the front independent torsion bar suspension, but the car did exhibit some nose dive on hard stops. At all legal cruising speeds, when the curves were wide and sweeping, the Imperial proved a responsive, easy-to-drive car, thanks to the full-time power steering and only 3.5 turns of the wheel lock to lock. All Imperials have a reduced turning circle, since the suspension strut wheel stops are now contoured to permit a three-degree increase in angular travel of the front wheels. Turning diameter is now 47.5 feet.

One of our main gripes about this car was the squared steering wheel. It measures 17.7 inches at its widest and only 14.7 inches at the narrowest. This creates a problem, since the turning force depends on where the driver rests his hands on the wheel. We got used to it, but it was disconcerting at first to be making a sharp turn and to find our hands first 17.7 inches apart and then 14.7 inches and back again. We'd like to see a smaller round wheel replace the present one.

Another important improvement announced on this year's Imperial is an increase in effective brake lining area — from 251 to 287 square inches. Our LeBaron's big 11-inch brakes featured the new flared drums that add 37 per cent more area for better cooling and quicker recovery from fade. The brakes proved adequate for normal driving, but the left rear wheel locked up on hard stopping from high speeds. Even with the improvements, there's a lot of car to stop, and our braking tests found the Imperial taking 37 feet for the 30-mph stop and 192 feet from 60 mph. All Imperials use self-adjusting brakes that set themselves when the car is backed up and stopped. We noticed considerable fade after our high-speed stops and when driving fairly rapidly over winding mountain roads. The engine died on hard stops, but it always started on the first spin and ran smoothly throughout our test period.

Inside and out, the LeBaron looked as if it was together very well, but the fit and finish weren't quite up to what we've found in other cars in this price range. Our LeBaron certainly was an attention-getter wherever we parked or drove it. People would come up and ask questions, look inside, and some would just stare. We weren't sure whether they were impressed with the sheer size of the vehicle, the luxurious appointments, or if they expected to see some celebrity driving the car. /MT

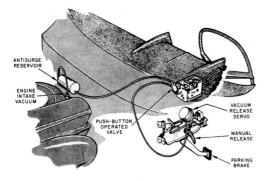

(ABOVE) New automatic parking brake release disengages parking pedal when forward or reverse gears are selected. A valve triggered by transmission pushbuttons supplies engine vacuum to a servo unit that disengages the step-on emergency brake.

(RIGHT) Imperial's trunk (carpeted) has more than enough room for several people's luggage. The larger-than-usual spare takes up some usable space, but this is a problem in all cars. A remote-control deck lid lock carries an optional price of $53.

(RIGHT, CENTER) All Imperials have curved window glass, armrest compartments for small odds and ends, and heavy carpeting.

(RIGHT, BOTTOM) New transmission parking sprag locks the rear wheels, placing transmission in NEUTRAL position. We liked the six-way power seat that added greatly to overall driving comfort by enabling us to change the seating position on long trips.

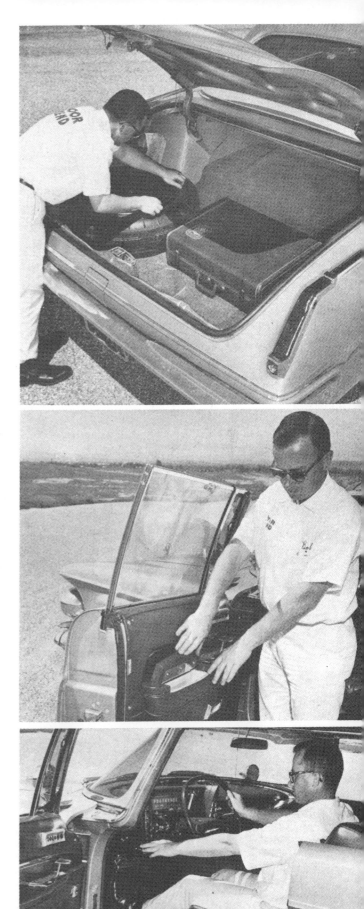

IMPERIAL LE BARON

4-door, 6-passenger hardtop

OPTIONS ON CAR TESTED: Air conditioning, radio with rear speaker, leather trim, power door locks, Auto-Pilot, remote-control deck lid lock, seat belts, whitewalls

BASIC PRICE: $6434
PRICE AS TESTED: $7905.10 (plus tax and license)
ODOMETER READING AT START OF TEST: 3676 miles
RECOMMENDED ENGINE RED LINE: 5200 rpm

PERFORMANCE

ACCELERATION (2 aboard)
```
0-30 mph.............................4.1 secs.
0-45 mph.............................7.4
0-60 mph.............................12.0
```
Standing start ¼-mile 18.8 secs. and 75 mph

Speeds in gears @ shift points
1st	....40 mph @ 3800 rpm	3rd	...............102 mph
2nd	....79 mph @ 4100 rpm		@ 3800 rpm

Speedometer Error on Test Car
Car's speedometer reading	31	45	50	64	78	90
Weston electric speedometer ..	30	45	50	60	70	80

Observed miles per hour per 1000 rpm in top gear ....26 mph
Stopping Distances — from 30 mph, 37 ft.; from 60 mph, 192 ft.

SPECIFICATIONS FROM MANUFACTURER

Engine
Ohv V-8
Bore: 4.19 ins.
Stroke: 3.75 ins.
Displacement: 413.0 cu. ins.
Compression ratio: 10.1:1
Horsepower: 340 @ 4600 rpm
Torque: 470 lbs.-ft. @ 2800 rpm
Horsepower per cubic inch: 0.82
Ignition: 12-volt coil

Gearbox
3-speed Torqueflite automatic; dash-mounted pushbutton controls

Driveshaft
2-piece — open tube

Differential
Hypoid — semi-floating
Standard ratio: 2.93:1

Suspension
Front: Independent, non-parallel control arms with torsion bars, stabilizer bar, and tubular shocks
Rear: 6-leaf, parallel, semi-elliptic springs, with tubular shocks

Steering
Rack and sector; integral full-time power
Turning diameter: 47.5 ft.
Turns: 3.5 lock to lock

Wheels and Tires
5-bolt, steel disc wheels
8.20 x 15 4-ply rayon tires

Brakes
Hydraulic, duo-servo, with vacuum power assist; self-adjusting
Front and rear: 11-in. dia. x 3 in. wide
Effective lining area: 287.2 sq. ins

Body and Frame
Welded, double-channel box-section side rails, lateral X-type crossmembers
Wheelbase: 129.0 ins.
Track: front, 61.7 ins.; rear, 62.2 ins.
Overall length: 227.8 ins.
Curb weight: 5250 lbs.

by Bob McVay

Assistant Technical Editor

IMPERIAL, that flagship of Chrysler Corporation's line-up, has a new look for 1964. One of the few all-new design offerings this year, the Imperial has taken a turn from last year's rounded styling to the sharp-edged school of design. About the only thing former Imperial owners will recognize is the familiar hood ornament. Even the dash panel has been completely redesigned.

Our test car was an Imperial Crown coupe, a hardtop with the extra vinyl roof covering. The new car's styling met with approval from most men on our staff and disapproval from others, but every woman who commented on the car's looks liked it. The engine is the reliable 413-inch, 340-hp V-8 that's proven itself well in past Imperials.

The real test of any automobile is living with it for a period of time and putting lots of miles on it. With the Imperial this was a rare pleasure. It's a luxury automobile in every sense of the word, and ours had many, many creature comforts that other cars don't offer.

With holidays ahead, we planned a visit to San Francisco. What better way to road test a luxury car designed to carry passengers from point to point in extreme comfort, no matter how far apart those points are?

Heading north on the inland route, we drove out on the freeway, accelerated to the legal limit of 65 mph, and engaged the Imperial's Auto-Pilot control. This device would hold the car at a pre-selected speed, within 2-4 mph, uphill or down. From then on, all we had to do was steer (a tap of the brake pedal or a push of the dash-mounted Auto-Pilot button disengaged the unit for normal driving).

We saw the bumps and irregularities on the road, but somehow the combination of the Imperial's fine suspension system and comfortable seats never let them through to driver or passengers. In more than 2000 miles of driving — city traffic or open highway at cruising speeds — not one bump or sharp dip caused the Imperial's suspension to bottom. Rebound after a sharp dip was mild. The car seemed to soak up every

(OPPOSITE) Imperial's familiar emblem was only thing left over from 1963 styling.
(RIGHT) Not a race car, the Imperial still handles well for its size and weight. It would understeer when pushed extra hard.

104

road irregularity, allowing us to cruise for hours in perfect comfort. For once those signs that read "Destination 412 miles" didn't bring on a discouraging feeling of the long grind ahead. We knew we only had to relax and steer — the car would take care of the rest.

Many things contribute to the total comfort offered by this year's Imperial. Normal equipment for our Crown coupe test car included TorqueFlite automatic transmission, power steering and brakes, and power windows. Also included were a padded instrument panel, center arm rests front and rear, illuminated ash tray in front, back-up lights, map, glovebox, and trunk lights, a passenger vanity mirror, remote-control outside mirror, automatic parking-brake release, variable-speed wipers, and a windshield washer. That's not all of the standard equipment either. An electric clock (an accurate one, at that), trunk carpeting, and undercoating also came with the car at its base price of $5718.

One of the car's best features was its seats, especially the front ones. Imperial's brochure calls them "executive aircraft-type seats." Well anyway, our test car's seats were top-grain black leather and used air-foam padding. They were individually power-operated and gave driver and passenger a high, commanding view of the road ahead — or let them sit lower if they wanted. Both seats had individual head rests, which could be adjusted for height or removed and stored in their own compartments in the seat backs. But again that wasn't all. A new feature of the Imperial Crown coupe is a reclining front passenger seat. It came in handy on long drives. When the front-seat passenger got tired, he had only to pull the lever and there he was, in an almost fully reclining position. Sleeping was easy, thanks again to the car's utterly smooth, utterly quiet performance.

Happy days are here again: Imperial has a round steering wheel instead of last year's square one. Needless to say, we welcome this change. The wheel's relation to the driver is quite comfortable, and a number of positions are possible, thanks to the power seat's adjustability. We enjoyed the big Imperial's full-time power steering. Its 3.5 turns between locks added to its ease of handling, and only fingertip pressures are ever needed.

The Imperial really took to San Francisco's steep hills. It wasn't bothered by the cable-car tracks, and its powerful 340-hp V-8 let it zip up the Bay City's steep hills like a sprinter. Yet the car has plenty of stopability in its huge, 11-inch, flared-drum brakes. A parking pawl locked the Imperial's transmission

and was quite capable of holding the car on San Francisco's steepest hills. The step-on parking brake would also hold the big hardtop on steep hills. We couldn't find a hill steep enough to bother our Imperial the slightest bit in starting.

Heading back toward Los Angeles, we took the Coast Highway — 90 miles of twisting, turning, climbing and descending, narrow, two-lane roads. This meant a good test for the Imperial's handling, and we didn't find it wanting. For a big, soft-riding luxury car, our Imperial handled quite well indeed. It didn't seem to have so much lean or body roll as similar big sedans, and it took a very highly banked, tight curve to cause carburetor flooding. Our route required lots of braking, accelerating, and many turns of the steering wheel. All we can say is that driving comfort was all anyone could possibly ask of any automobile. For any less driving effort, you'd need a chauffeur. Driver fatigue was almost non-existent, and it took many miles behind the Crown coupe's wheel to find this out.

Many creature comforts helped make driving easier. The car has many interior lights that go on when the doors are opened, but once underway, a small switch located just above the driver's window would turn on only the back seat lights so the passenger could read a map without disturbing the driver.

Extra equipment on our test car included Chrysler's excellent single-unit air-conditioning and heating system. Any possible temperature was immediately available, from fresh, cool air to bushels of heat that poured out of the car's many outlets. All outlets are directional. Cool air blowing gently into our face helped a lot when we wanted to stay awake during a long drive. Early-morning starts were easy. In seconds, it seemed, the heater and defroster had the windshield cleared, and the car was warm as toast. The single unit adds $590.20 to the Imperial's cost, while a dual-unit outfit sells for $777.75.

An excellent AM-FM radio with rear-seat speaker added greatly to our traveling comfort. Tinted glass and safety belts (retractable seat belts are now standard in all Imperials), Auto-Pilot, the vinyl-covered roof, and a handy remote-control deck-lid opener that op-

---

(LEFT) *Getting all four wheels off the ground after sharp dips proved Imperial's rugged suspension could take hard jolts.*

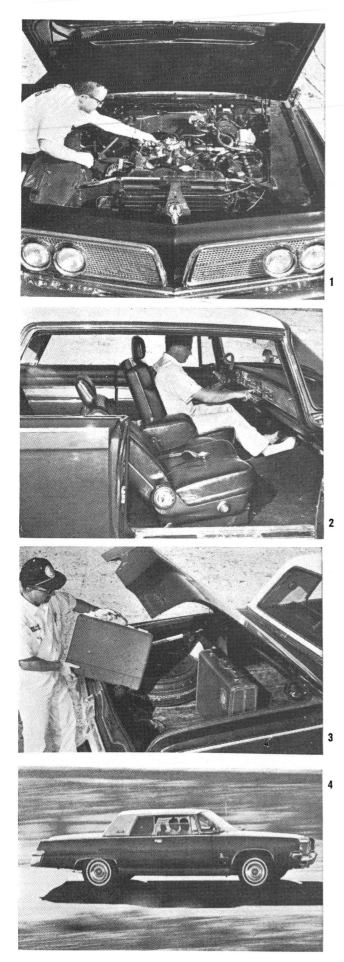

1) Beefy 413-inch V-8 is smooth, quiet, and packs very solid punch. It offers 340 hp and a whopping 470 pounds-feet of torque. Block and heads are cast-iron, with aluminum pistons.
2) Interior gives top-drawer comfort, immense leg room, and fine driving position. Reclining seat offers extra comfort.
3) Trunk capacity is huge by any standard. High lip makes heavy luggage a chore to load, spare a job to lift up and out.
4) Side view shows off new styling and car's good road manners.
5) Braking test found stopping distances shorter than last year's Imperial. We experienced some wheel lock-up and slight swerving. Two stops from over 100 mph faded the brakes badly.
(OPPOSITE) In addition to new styling, Imperials boast 154 significant engineering improvements that isolate or insulate road noises and make car even quieter and smoother than before. Personalized Imperials offer vinyl-covered roofs in black, white, or blue; plus convertible tops in black, white, blue, tan.

erated from a button inside the glove compartment completed the options on our test car and brought the price up to $7097.25.

Steady freeway cruising at legal 65-mph limits found our Crown coupe getting as high as 14.5 mpg — not bad for 5300 pounds of automobile with two people and their luggage added. San Francisco's steep hills and home-from-work traffic gave us a 10.2-mpg low. Our average for nearly 2000 miles of driving was a respectable 12.55.

Since Riverside Raceway was busy with movie-making, we used the facilities of Willow Springs Raceway for our performance testing. The '64 was a bit faster, a bit quicker than the LeBaron sedan tested last year, but not by any great margin. Our runs to 30, 45, and 60 mph took a quiet 4.1, 7.1, and 11.8 seconds respectively. The big hardtop lunged off the line with modest wheel-spin and whistled through our quarter-mile test strip in 18.4 seconds, recording 78 mph on our Weston electric speedometer. Pushing the shift buttons at 4800 rpm produced fractionally better results than when we let the automatic shift for itself, but no matter how it's done, this is no drag racer.

Performance is completely adequate for all normal driving, and highway passing was as good as any luxury sedan's — better than most. On our drive across the desert to Willow Springs, we found a long stretch of deserted road and wound the big Imperial up to an indicated 117 mph, which figured out to an actual 109 mph. At this speed, we were passing over some dips that allowed the ponderous Imperial to get all four tires completely off the ground. Yet we felt we always had control (anyway, as safe as anyone could feel at 109 mph). One rebound and the car was stable again — it didn't continue to jounce up and down as some cars will. Cruising along the wide-open spaces, we could set the Auto-Pilot at any speed from 100 mph on down. Crosswinds could be felt, but never bothered us much.

Imperial buyers have a wide choice of 17 solid exterior colors and 44 roof/body combinations. The vinyl-covered top goes for $91.20. And they can choose from 27 interior layouts. Top-grain leather or a combination of nylon Bedford cord and leather are offered as interior choices. The Crown line, consisting of a two- and a four-door hardtop, and a convertible, and the LeBaron four-door hardtop make up the Imperial four-model line-up.

Extensive rust-proofing goes into all Imperials. They're dipped seven times and sprayed six times before their nine-coat paint job is applied. The first eight coats are hand-rubbed; the last one's machine-buffed. /MT

IMPERIAL CROWN COUPE
2-door, 5-passenger hardtop

OPTIONS ON CAR TESTED: Air conditioning, AM-FM radio with rear speaker and power antenna, heater, Auto-Pilot, vinyl roof, remote-control deck lid, head rests, tinted glass, seat belts

BASIC PRICE: $5718
PRICE AS TESTED: $7097.25 (plus tax and license)
ODOMETER READING AT START OF TEST: 1732 miles
RECOMMENDED ENGINE RED LINE: 5200 rpm

PERFORMANCE

ACCELERATION (2 aboard)

0-30 mph	4.2 secs.
0-45 mph	7.3
0-60 mph	12.2

Standing start ¼-mile 19.0 secs. and 76 mph
Speeds in gears @ shift points
1st ......41 mph @ 3800 rpm   3rd .....109 mph @ 4200 rpm
2nd ......79 mph @ 4200 rpm

Speedometer Error on Test Car

Car's speedometer reading	31	45	50	61	72	84
Weston electric speedometer	30	45	50	60	70	80

Observed miles per hour per 1000 rpm in top gear ....26 mph
Stopping Distances — from 30 mph., 33 ft.; from 60 mph, 176 ft.

SPECIFICATIONS FROM MANUFACTURER

Engine
Ohv V-8
Bore: 4.19 ins.
Stroke: 3.75 ins.
Displacement: 413 cu. ins.
Compression ratio: 10.1:1
Horsepower: 340 @ 4600 rpm
Torque: 470 lbs.-ft. @ 2800 rpm
Horsepower per cubic inch: 0.82
Carburetion: 1 4-bbl.
Ignition: 12-volt coil

Gearbox
3-speed automatic (TorqueFlite); dash-mounted pushbutton controls

Driveshaft
2-piece, open tube

Differential
Hypoid, semi-floating
Standard ratio: 2.93:1

Suspension
Front: Independent, non-parallel control arms with torsion bars, tubular shocks, and link-type stabilizer
Rear: 6-leaf semi-elliptic springs, tubular shocks, and rear axle stabilizer struts

Steering
Rack and sector, with integral, full-time power assist
Turning diameter: 47.6 ft.
Turns lock to lock: 3.5

Wheels and Tires
5-lug, steel disc wheels
8.20 x 15 4-ply tubeless whitewalls

Brakes
Hydraulic, duo-servo, with vacuum power assist; self-adjusting; flared cast-iron drums
Front and rear: 11-in. dia. x 3.0 ins. wide
Effective lining area: 287.2 sq. ins.

Body and Frame
Welded, double-channel box-section frame with lateral crossmembers
Wheelbase: 129.0 ins.
Track: front, 61.8 ins.; rear, 61.7 ins.
Overall length: 227.8 ins.
Overall width: 79.9 ins.
Curb weight: 5285 lbs.

IMPERIAL Le BARON

Chrysler's Largest has a Stylish New Look

ONE OF THE BEST sellers of the current automotive model year, on a percentage-gained basis, of course, is the Imperial series built and marketed by the Chrysler Corporation. Riding the crest of the wave of returning enthusiasm for prestige/luxury cars, the drastically restyled 1964 Imperial is selling at a rate nearly double that of 1963.

There are several good reasons for the rebirth of interest in the Imperial, not the least of which is its changed body styling and its deserved reputation for mechanical excellence. Most important, *Car Life* feels, is the metamorphosis of the Imperial into a contemporarily-styled, top-quality automobile aimed exclusively for the moneyed, sophisticated carriage trade. We

don't mean to imply that Imperials of yore were not aimed at this market, because they were, but that the Imperial has never been better suited to the demands of this smallish segment of the automotive field.

In the past, the Imperial stylists have perforce created the car in the family image of the other corporate vehicles, particularly those of the Chrysler line. Thus it was possible to buy what looked like and performed at least as well as an Imperial, at a greatly reduced price, although it had not the Imperial's luxurious appointments. The Imperial effect was diluted. With the creation of a separate, new style for the Imperial, the car no longer looks "just like a bigger Chrysler." It looks distinctively like an Imperial.

In price structure, the Imperial takes over where the Chrysler line ends. The advertised delivered price of the most expensive Chrysler sedan is $5860 for the New Yorker Salon; the same for the least expensive Imperial sedan (Crown 4-door hardtop) is $5560. The base sticker price on the test Imperial LeBaron is $6434 and, as can be seen in the data panel, by the time a few non-standard items are included, the price climbs to well over $7600.

This is a lot of money, in anyone's league. So, what does the Imperial buyer get for this sizeable investment? He gets an exclusively styled (only about 25,000 copies per year), finely appointed, elegantly finished motor car. He gets as standard equipment such things as power steering, power

28.4 mph for each 1000 engine rpm. This, of course, returns effectively quiet cruising speeds (the engine is turning only 2460 rpm at 70 mph), at a fuel consumption rate of 10-13 mpg.

The transmission is identical to the TorqueFlites used throughout the Chrysler line. It has 2.45:1 and 1.45:1 geared ratios along with direct, and a 2.20:1 torque converter stall ratio. With a 15.8:1 "breakaway" ratio at the start, the transmission is admirably suited to a heavy car such as the Imperial. Push-button controlled, it can either "hold" each gear as the driver commands, or shift up through all three forward speeds automatically. The automatic shifts take place, under wide open throttle, at 3600-3800 rpm, first-second, and 3800-4000 rpm, second-third. Trial acceleration runs showed that manually holding the shift points until the engine had reached 4400 rpm produced the shortest elapsed times for the standing ¼-mile. Because of engine limitations imposed by the need of maximum "quiet" exhaust and intake muffling, use of rpm more than 4400 produced no gain in speed or reduction of e.t.

The engine is willing enough and in

some lighter chassis we have tested does extremely well. A Chrysler 300, similarly equipped but with a 3.23:1 axle, (February '62 issue) turned the ¼-mile at 83 mph in 16.7 sec.; it weighed 1100 lb. less! This ohv V-8 has been a workhorse around the Chrysler Corporation since its introduction back in 1958 as the replacement for the hemispherical cylinder head FirePower series. It currently is the standard unit for the New Yorker and Salon, as well as the Imperial, and belongs to the same design family as the 361, 383, 413 and 426 cu. in. engines offered elsewhere in the corporate line-up. Of wedge-chamber configuration, it requires premium fuel for its 10.1:1 compression ratio but in return gives very good torque and low-speed operating characteristics. It is very smooth, and in the Imperial, this counts for nearly as much as power.

The Imperial has a frame separate from its body—the only passenger car in the Chrysler line which is still so produced. A conventional ladder-type of frame, it is welded up from stamped steel double channel, box-section side rails and single channel cross-pieces. The Crown convertible coupe has an

MARVIN LYONS PHOTOS

brakes, power windows and automatic transmission which are extra-cost items on lesser-priced cars. He gets a choice between 4-door hardtop sedan (Crown or LeBaron) and 2-door Crown coupe or convertible.

If performance is not outstanding, it at least is satisfactory for a 2¾-ton automobile. Accelerating such mass takes a good deal of power and despite 470 lb.-ft. of torque, the Chrysler 413-cu. in./340 bhp V-8 has only just enough to do the job. Helped out by the 3-speed automatic transmission, the engine does move the Imperial along at adequate rates, once inertia is overcome, while the high peaking speed of the engine lends itself to a very good top speed potential. This is partially due to the 2.93:1 rear axle ratio specified for all Imperials (no optional ratios) and the use of 8.20-15 tires. These impart a vehicle speed of

TRUNK and spare tire are upholstered, as befits a car of this type. Upholstery and finish materials throughout are top quality.

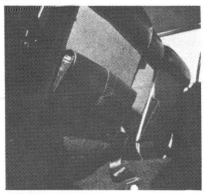

CLEVER touch is the huge map and miscellaneous pocket attached to the back of each front seat.

WINDOW lifts and door locks are all operated from this arm-rest console. Below, the reclining seat available as an option.

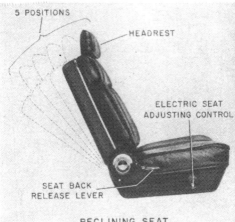

5 POSITIONS
HEADREST
ELECTRIC SEAT ADJUSTING CONTROL
SEAT BACK RELEASE LEVER
RECLINING SEAT

IMPERIAL Le BARON

X-member in addition, to provide more torsional stiffness. Suspension, engine, drive-train and body components are all bolted to this frame through complex insulative devices which damp out sound and vibration. Isolated and insulated from the road as it is, the Imperial passenger compartment thus becomes extremely quiet and comfortable. The back-seat passengers can hardly tell what the chauffeur is doing.

Suspension is typically Chrysler and comes from the Chrysler parts-bins. The front is independent, through long-and-short parallel arms and torsion bar springs. The bars run parallel to the frame and are 48.6 in. long by 1.04 in. in diameter. A 0.75 in. anti-roll bar is fitted across the front. The rear suspension is non-independent, through a live axle supporting the car on a pair of parallel longitudinal leaf springs. These produce a spring rate at the wheel of 125 lb./in.; the front rate is 115 lb./in. Some anti-dive for braking reaction is incorporated into the front suspension by the tilting toward the rear of the upper control arms.

As with acceleration, the weight of

such a large automobile figures mightily in its ability to stop within a reasonable length of time and space. The Imperial is equipped with a vacuum-operated power brake booster as standard equipment and this can provide as much as 1460 psi brake line pressure at 100 lb. pedal load. Brake drums are 11 in. in diameter, 3 in. wide, and have a flared "heat sink" lip to pull off heat from the actual rubbing surfaces of the drum. The brake swept area is 414.7 sq. in., which gives it nearly the largest brakes in the U.S. industry. But do they do the job? CL's testers tried their usual two crash stops from 80 mph and found that they do, but with no more than average effectiveness. The deceleration rates were 18 and 22 ft./sec./sec. with some locking of the rear wheels noted. The combination of power booster and the self-servo action of the shoes seemed overly sensitive and it took a delicate touch on the brake pedal to stop the car in the shortest distance, without swerving. A panic stop would produce more tail-wagging than a Hawaiian luau.

This particular test Imperial was finished with a formal black exterior and

a blue broadcloth-and-leather interior which combined to give the impression of quiet, but rich, good taste. There is a tendency toward over-decoration in the dash panel area, what with the use of vertically corrugated trim the full width of the panel; but, in all, it comes off far better than previous Imperials. The exterior paint was flawless (as well it should be for $7600!) but the chrome trim cap strip along the fender tops showed "daylight" gaps when viewed from the driver's seat.

Imperial styling will inevitably be compared to that of the Lincoln Continental and what is the harm in that? Hasn't the Continental achieved considerable acclaim as the best-styled car of the era? The crisp fender peaks, the squared-off roof and body lines and the formal good looks of the Lincoln have permeated the entire industry. Yet the Imperial has its own distinctive features which set it off from the Continental, notably its divided grille and spare tire-like protuberance from the smooth planes of the rear deck. The former we like, the latter we don't; spare tires went out as a design cliché back in 1956. And, as if to compound the homeliness, an airplane propeller-like trim device extends across this mis-shapen posterior, its hub containing an Imperial eagle medallion, its blade tips the various stop, turn and tail lights. We can only hope that amputation of this growth will take place for '65.

As can be imagined, seating in one of these vehicles is extremely comfortable while the combination of a power-assisted seat adjustment and a tilting steering wheel make it possible for the driver to select infinitely varied positioning. Yet the driver's seat does not go up quite high enough to let the driver easily see the right front fender tip, which would be a helpful adjunct when parking. We note, too, that vision out of the smaller rear window of the LeBaron sedan gives a blind spot at the right rear quarter.

The driver's (or chauffeur's) job is not made any easier by the ribbon-type of speedometer or low-set instruments (a full set of four, rather than the cheaper, more common warning lights). On the other hand, the quick power steering makes maneuvering this big car easier than might be expected.

In all, the Imperial is a rich-looking, large, distinctive car with adequate performance and brakes, but with a high level of quality and quiet. Although it resembles a Lincoln, the differences are obvious when the two are side by side in the parking lot and the Imperial (for the most part) has enough character of its own to stand out in any crowd. Then, too, it doesn't have any less-expensive junior versions, so the man who drives an Imperial is obviously a man of means. ■

CAR LIFE ROAD TEST

1964 IMPERIAL
LeBaron 4-door hardtop Sedan

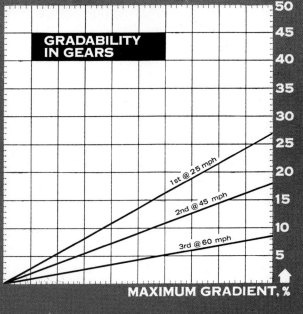

SPECIFICATIONS

List price	$6455
Price, as tested	7676
Curb weight, lb	5340
Test weight	5600
distribution, %	53/47
Tire size	8.20-15
Tire capacity, lb	5660
Brake swept area	415
Engine type	V-8, ohv
Bore & stroke	4.19 x 3.75
Displacement, cu. in.	413
Compression ratio	10.1
Carburetion	1 x 4
Bhp @ rpm	340 @ 4600
equivalent mph	131
Torque, lb-ft	470 @ 2800
equivalent mph	79.5

DIMENSIONS

Wheelbase, in.	129.0
Tread, f & r	61.8/61.7
Overall length, in.	227.8
width	80.0
height	56.8
equivalent vol. cu. ft.	599
Frontal area, sq. ft.	25.2
Ground clearance, in.	5.6
Steering ratio, o/a	19.4
turns, lock to lock	3.5
turning circle, ft.	47.6
Hip room, front	61.0
Hip room, rear	62.0
Pedal to seat back, max.	47.0
Floor to ground	13.5
Luggage vol, cu. ft.	17.8
Fuel tank capacity, gal.	23.0

CALCULATED DATA

Lb/bhp (test wt)	16.5
Cu. ft/ton mile	90.0
Mph/1000 rpm	28.4
Engine revs/mile	2110
Piston travel, ft/mile	1320
Car Life wear index	27.8

PERFORMANCE

Top speed (4250), mph	121
Shifts, @ mph (auto., forced)	
3rd ( )	
2nd (4400)	86
1st (4400)	51
Total drag at 60 mph, lb	175

ACCELERATION

0-30 mph, sec	4.0
0-40	6.0
0-50	8.8
0-60	10.4
0-70	16.1
0-80	20.8
0-100	38.5
Standing ¼ mile, sec	18.2
speed at end, mph	75

SPEEDOMETER ERROR

30 mph, actual	30.4
60 mph	57.6
90 mph	84.1

FUEL CONSUMPTION

Normal range, mpg	10-13

EXTRA-COST OPTIONS

Air cond., power door locks, AM/FM radio, tinted windows, limited slip diff., adjustable steering wheel, outside mirror.

GEAR RATIOS

3rd (1.00) overall	2.93
2nd (1.45)	4.25
1st (2.45)	7.18
1st (2.45 x 2.20)	15.8

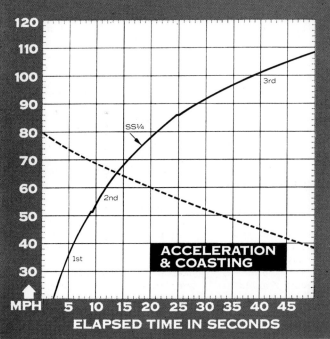

ACCELERATION & COASTING

ELAPSED TIME IN SECONDS

GRADABILITY IN GEARS

1st @ 25 mph
2nd @ 45 mph
3rd @ 60 mph

MAXIMUM GRADIENT, %

CHRYSLER

Chrysler's Imperial may well be the most luxurious car on the domestic market and is possibly the finest car in the world. This is my reaction to a test drive of the 1965, unchanged in engineering but given more styling and interior touches. It will do 120 mph and then stop without swerving. It is quiet, rides firmly without jounce and handles in a manner which belies its size. The 300L is a hot performer which noodles around town like a Six. The New Yorker has class to spare. If these cars don't sell, its because the public doesn't know what's good for it. End of report.

INSTANT SPECIFICATIONS

CHRYSLER:

ENGINES--330/365/400 hp V8s

WHEELBASE--124" L.O.A.--218"

WEIGHT-- 4050 lbs.

112

DISTINCTIVE RECTANGULAR grilles have headlamp pairs floating in the outer corners.

Imperial

A completely changed personality comes from crisp-edged new body replacing last year's flowing curves

SELDOM have such changes in appearance been made in a car without changing every piece of metal in the frame and structure as we see in the new Imperial. Still a body and frame car, it uses the same basic frame with torsion bar-ball joint independent front suspension and long leaf springs in the rear.

Nowhere outside the car nor in the interior will your eye spot a familiar object unless it be the air-conditioning grilles or perhaps a door handle. The windshield and frame are carried over from 1963 but every thing else is brand new.

The body mounts themselves being new results in not only a smooth and quiet car as before but one which is firmer feeling on rough gravel roads.

A number of hidden braces have been added inside the doors and in the rear quarter panel in addition to the normal inside panels of the door structure. An in-

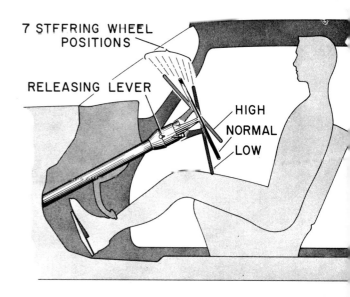

THE NEW CHRYSLER *Corporation five-position reclining seat is at its most comfortable in the Imperial.*

ADJUSTABLE WHEEL THAT *can safely switch position while under way is new to Imperial for '64.*

EVEN AS A CONVERTIBLE, *Imperial's tried and true body-frame combination seemed more firm this year.*

teresting sidelight is that these inner beams, which act as more solid anchorages for the window lift motors and mechanism, are fastened with new structural adhesives instead of welds or conventional fasteners. An innovation are the die cast frames which grip the window glass more firmly and provide a more accurate track for the nylon rollers. There's an additional glass-stabilizing channel in the rear doors which keep the glass vibration-free even when the windows are partly open. Since all Imperials are either two or four-door hardtops or a convertible with windows required to stand alone, such rattle-free operation is important.

Mechanically, the Imperial has a number of refinements such as the integral permanent filter in the automatic transmission and new, vacuum diaphragm-operated choke. However, the 413 cubic inch V-8 with single 4-barrel carburetor remains unchanged. It is fitted to a push-button controlled Torqueflite automatic as before. Wheelbase remains the same at 129 inches but over-all length has been increased three inches to 227.

NOVEL CONVERTIBLE top cover has rigid sides, flexible center.

Wheelbase	129
Over-all length	227.8
width	80
height	56.8
Weight	4930
Minimum road clearance	5.6
Wheel and tire size	8.20x15
Chassis:	
Front suspension	Independent; arms, ball joints, torsion bars
Rear suspension	Hotchkiss; solid axle, leaf springs
Hydraulic brakes	Duo-Servo
Power brakes	Standard
Drum diameter/lining area	11/287.2
Steering ratio (mech./power)	N.A./19.4
Wheel turns (mech./power)	N.A./3.5
Power steering	Standard
Turning circle	47.6
Gear type	Rack and sector
Interior:	
Headroom f/r	39.3/38.7
Seat height f/r	8.5/11.3
Steering wheel leg clearance	3.4
Legroom f/r	41.15/41.5
Hiproom f/r	61/62
Compartment room f/r	40.8/31
Trunk volume	17.8
Body types available:	
2-door hardtop	X
2-door convertible	X
4-door hardtop	X
Engine:	
Bore and stroke	4.19x3.75
Displacement	413
Compression ratio	10.1:1
Horsepower	340@4600
Torque	470@2800
Carburetor type	1 4-Bbl
Oil capacity	5 qts.
Water capacity	17 qts.
Fuel capacity	23 gal.
Grade recommended	Premium
Rear axle ratio, manual	N.A.
auto	2.93
overdrive	N.A.
Automatic trans. type	Torque Converter, planetary gears
Forward ratios, manual	N.A.
auto	2.45:1
	1.45:1
	1.00:1

Basic dimensions are for the 4-door hardtop unless otherwise noted.

Imperial

(ABOVE) *New Imperial V-8 has largest displacement mill ever offered by Chrysler, 440 cubic inches. It shows improved performance at passing speeds. New wider radiator core increases cooling capacity.*

(LEFT) *Spanish scroll design adds grace to upholstery of Imperial Crown. Split front seats adjust 6 ways with dual motors. Power seats are standard on LeBaron. Reclining passenger seat comes with headrest.*

(BELOW) *Crown hardtop options include a grained vinyl roof covering, tinted windshield, Search Tune AM-FM radio, and an improved headlight dimmer. Multi-position steering wheel is new Imperial option. It boasts both tilting and telescoping actions.*

PARTICULAR PEOPLE buy Imperials, and when they do, they usually shoot the works and buy every option and accessory offered. Thus, the real news is on the 1966 Imperial's interior. Yet the car does have a few exterior modifications worthy of note. The rear deck hump, that should've housed a spare wheel and tire but didn't, is reworked and, up front, there's a new grille.

The line-up is unchanged, with 2-door hardtop and convertible Crown series cars remaining personalized, individual vehicles. Crown and LeBaron 4-door hardtops are again offered.

One engine, a 440-cubic-inch V-8 with silenced air cleaner and dual exhausts (on convertibles, single on others) is standard, replacing last year's 413-inch V-8. TorqueFlite automatic transmission is also standard and uses a 2.45 axle ratio in 1966.

Some 63% of Imperial's buyers ordered full leather trim last year, while 93% had their cars equipped with air conditioning. Auto-Pilot is also on the best-seller list. It's only natural to assume that most 1966 Imperials will be fully equipped. A new Search Tune AM-FM radio with power antenna is bound to be a top seller.

Biggest news is in Imperial seating. Four-door sedans offer a special option called the 50/50 bench seat. It's a split-back seat with individual armrests and a 6-way control lever for both driver and passenger. In addition, the passenger side reclines and has its own optional headrest. No bucket option is offered on 4-door models, because the contoured bench is thought to be the best of 2 worlds and is wider to boot. This seat is a LeBaron standard feature that's optional on others. Buckets will be offered on 2-door models. These new "aircraft" buckets are individually adjustable and incorporate a built-in, adjustable headrest and reclining feature on the passenger's side. Buckets have a 6-way adjustment.

The new 440-inch V-8 is supposed to give 0-60-mph times of 10 seconds or less and cuts down passing in the 50-70-mph range by 10%. New engine mounts cut down vibrations.

Tilt-and-telescope steering wheel, full leather or high-quality wool broadcloth interiors, and a new grain-textured vinyl covering for the roof are other Imperial options. Blue-tinted glass, a smoother automatic transmission, improved automatic beam-changer that dims the lights when approaching cars come within 1200 feet, and a moisture-resistant deck-lid lock are among detail improvements on the new Imperial.

Luxury, comfort, and more of the same stand out as the main objectives for Imperial, currently enjoying its third best sales year. As usual, it's a very impressive motor car. /MT

IMPERIAL

Crown Convertible Coupé

ENGINE CAPACITY 440 cu in, 7,210.28 cu cm
FUEL CONSUMPTION 13.2 m/imp gal, 11 m/US gal, 21.3 l × 100 km
SEATS 6 **MAX SPEED** 116 mph, 186.8 km/h
PRICE IN USA $ 6,146

ENGINE front, 4 stroke; cylinders: 8, Vee-slanted at 90°; bore and stroke: 4.32 × 3.75 in, 109.7 × 95.2 mm; engine capacity: 440 cu in, 7,210.28 cu cm; compression ratio: 10.1; max power (SAE): 350 hp at 4,400 rpm; max torque (SAE): 480 lb ft, 66.2 kg m at 2,800 rpm; max engine rpm: 4,400; specific power: 48.5 hp/l; cylinder block: cast iron; cylinder head: cast iron; crankshaft bearings: 5; valves: 2 per cylinder, overhead, in line, push-rods and rockers, hydraulic tappets; camshafts: 1, at centre of Vee; lubrication: rotary pump, full flow filter; lubricating system capacity: 10.03 imp pt, 12 US pt, 5.7 l; carburation: 1 Carter AFB-4131 S downdraught 4-barrel carburettor; fuel feed: mechanical pump; cooling system: water; cooling system capacity: 29.92 imp pt, 36 US pt, 17 l.

TRANSMISSION driving wheels: rear; gearbox: Torqueflite 8 automatic, hydraulic torque convertor and planetary gears with 3 ratios + reverse, max ratio of convertor at stall 2, possible manual selection; gearbox ratios: I 2.450, II 1.410, III 1, rev 2.200; selector lever: steering column; final drive: hypoid bevel; axle ratio: 2.940.

CHASSIS box-type ladder frame, X reinforcements; front suspension: independent, wishbones, lower trailing links, longitudinal torsion bars, anti-roll bar, telescopic dampers; rear suspension: rigid axle, semi-elliptic leafsprings, torque arms, telescopic dampers.

STEERING screw and sector, adjustable steering wheel, servo; turns of steering wheel lock to lock: 3.20.

BRAKES drum, servo; area rubbed by linings: total 414.70 sq in, 2,674.81 sq cm.

ELECTRICAL EQUIPMENT voltage: 12 V; battery: 70 Ah; generator type: alternator, 35 Ah; ignition distributor: Chrysler; headlamps: 4.

DIMENSIONS AND WEIGHT wheel base: 129 in, 3,277 mm; front track: 61.80 in, 1,570 mm; rear track: 61.70 in, 1,567 mm; overall length: 227.80 in, 5,786 mm; overall width: 80 in, 2,032 mm; overall height: 56.60 in, 1,438 mm; ground clearance: 5.60 in, 142 mm; dry weight: 5,336 lb, 2,420 kg; distribution of weight: 52.2% front axle, 47.8% rear axle; turning circle (between walls): 50.8 ft, 15.5 m; width of rims: 6''; tyres: 9.15 × 15; fuel tank capacity: 19.1 imp gal, 23 US gal, 87 l.

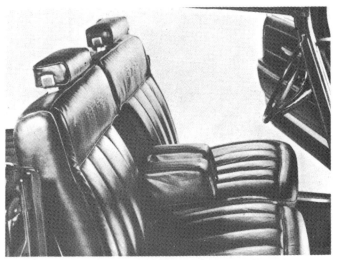

BODY convertible; doors: 2; seats: 6; front seats: bench.

PERFORMANCE max speeds: 51 mph, 82.1 km/h in 1st gear; 88 mph, 141.7 km/h in 2nd gear; 116 mph, 186.8 km/h in 3rd gear; power-weight ratio: 15.2 lb/hp, 6.9 kg/hp; carrying capacity: 1,058 lb, 480 kg; speed in direct drive at 1,000 rpm: 28.3 mph, 45.6 km/h.

PRACTICAL INSTRUCTIONS fuel: 100 oct petrol; engine sump oil: 8.27 imp pt, 10 US pt, 4.7 l, SAE 5W-20 (winter) 10W-30 (summer), change every 4,000 miles, 6,400 km; gearbox oil: 15.49 imp pt, 18.50 US pt, 8.8 l, ATF A Suffix A, change every 32,000 miles, 51,500 km; final drive oil: 3.34 imp pt, 4 US pt, 1.9 l, SAE 90, change every 32,000 miles, 51,500 km; greasing: every 32,000 miles, 51,500 km; valve timing: inlet opens 14° before tdc and closes 62° after bdc, exhaust opens 62° before bdc and closes 18° after tdc; normal tyre pressure: front 28 psi, 2 atm, rear 30 psi, 2.1 atm.

VARIATIONS AND OPTIONAL ACCESSORIES limited slip final drive; cleaner air system; air conditioning system; separate front seats.

CROWN

Comfort Competitor In the Luxury League

WHATEVER IMPERIAL is for 1967, it isn't a '66 . . . for this is one case in which the press agent-abused "all-new" comes very close to meaning exactly that. There's a new chassis that abandons the separate body and frame in favor of unit construction (in keeping with the way all other Chrysler Corp. automobiles are built) and new exterior sheet metal. The mechanicals are much the same as previously, which is not necessarily a bad thing. Though Imperial still is larger than any other Chrysler product, it retains strong corporate identity.

It is clear that Chrysler, after running a poor third to Cadillac and Continental for longer than Chrysler management cares to remember, is aiming for a larger slice of the booming luxury market. And it might just earn that bigger piece of the action, provided Imperial can overcome its rich-little-old-lady's-car image.

One comparison that came to mind during several days of living with the car was that it would be quite interesting to blindfold a series of subjects and drive them in one example each of the Luxury Three. Though it wasn't practical to conduct this experiment, there was little doubt that test subjects would have been unable to distinguish Imperial from Cadillac or Continental by virtue of shortcomings in any of the sensory areas—ride, noise level, seating comfort, acceleration or cornering sway.

The Imperial which is receiving the most play in the popular press this year is the Crown Coupe with the Cruiser Lounge option, which incorporates a revolving front passenger seat, folding table and reading lamp. Though the Cruiser Lounge is a big attention-getter, it is available only with the 2-door hardtop and is found in very limited quantities. What *CL*'s test crew received was a well-proportioned 4-door hardtop sedan that is bigger than it looks.

The Imperial's bigness doesn't show up during a casual walk-around inspection and there may be factors in the car's favor here: Styling is in unity with the remainder of the corporate fleet. Relatively clean lines weren't objectionable—or particularly exciting. The Imperial's size is far more apparent

from inside, where leg, hip and head room are in abundance. The driver learns size during the first tight parking maneuver. An overall 224.7 in. makes a very large amount of car to herd around and when its 44.9-ft. curb-to-curb turning circle—it seemed twice that—is applied to sharp, narrow driveways, there comes an immediate awareness of the vehicle's bulk.

As this car was one of the first of *CAR LIFE*'s '67s, with its attendant "safety package," each test driver was asked to determine whether or not he felt any safer in the Imperial over a comparable '66 model. To a man, they answered, "No," though they were perfectly aware that interior padding, energy-absorbing steering column, turning lights and the like have produced a car that is, on paper, safer.

Drivers were more inclined to rate driver convenience as a visible indication of safety: Comfortable driver equals safe (potentially) driver. To elaborate, the 6-way power seat, though nothing new, has a sufficient range of adjustment to please any size of human behind the wheel. Coupled with a steering wheel that was adjustable for column length and rake, there was no question that anyone could set up an optimum driving position. The next logical step is adjustable pedals.

What does one say about the interi-

THE IMPERIAL'S massive 440-cu. in. engine, with improved carburetion and redesigned intake ports to accommodate an increased fuel/air charge at higher rpm, is rated 350 bhp at 4400 rpm and 480 lb.-ft. of torque at 2800 rpm.

OVERALL LENGTH OF 224.7 in. and a curb-to-curb turning circle of 44.9 ft. make the Imperial Crown seem a very large automobile indeed in narrow streets and crowded parking lots. Clean lines tend to minimize the sedan's bulk, however.

or of a luxury car? It is luxurious, of course. Quality blends of leather, wood and fabric were tastefully applied. Comfortable seats offer good thigh and back support, and incorporate pull-down armrests. Fine instrumentation and an outstanding heating/cooling system were packaged with a mixture that said, "This is the best we can offer on all fronts."

A changed dash, presumably safety-oriented, invites some discussion. Aside from highly-readable gauges, a light warns the driver to "check gauges" (fuel low) while another light is designed to inform him that one-half of the 2-circuit hydraulic brake system has failed. The dash itself is recessed under a padded brow. Control switches (except for recessed ignition) are primarily toggles and rolling wheels. Arrangement of controls was such that night adjustments could be made easily without breaking road concentration.

The Imperial carried a pair of options—air conditioning and Auto Pilot—which were applauded, not so much because they are new or unique, but for their function as applied to the luxury car. The air conditioner operates thermostatically to blend dehumidified warmed air with cold to maintain a chosen temperature, though the Imperial had no direct reading temperature gauge, such as Cadillac offers. The air conditioner proved its effectiveness in an unseasonal rainstorm, keeping all windows free of condensation, which was noted to be a condition that plagued almost every other car on that day.

AS FOR THE Auto Pilot, it proved to have several advantages, not the least of which was fuel economy. During one 250-mile test leg, mainly in medium-traffic on an interstate highway, the unit was set on the 65-mph legal maximum. Because it wasn't necessary to alter speed more than a dozen times (a light tap on the brake disengages the control) fuel mileage improved to just over 14 mpg. On a subjective level, few drivers realize how fatiguing it is to hold a car exactly at the speed limit, especially a car that is just as comfortable at 90 as at 65. Constant jockeying of the throttle, watching the speedometer and minding the road are old-fashioned. The faithful Auto Pilot minds the throttle, permits relaxation which can be transformed into better road alertness. On hills, the unit maintains the set speed within 2-3 mph, up or down. Test crewmen regarded the Auto Pilot as an accessory which could be used to advantage anywhere traffic flows at a constant rate.

LUXURY-SAFETY interior was marred by highly reflective chromium plated mouldings at windshield perimeter.

ABUNDANT PASSENGER space is a strong point of the Crown. Rear seat hip, head and leg room are more than adequate.

SPACIOUSNESS MARKS the Imperial's cargo compartment, but spare location makes wheel change operation difficult.

IMPERIAL eagle graces distinctive hood ornament.

ARMREST toggle switches control window lifts.

Interior comfort on the road was rated in keeping with the car's luxury image. Theoretically, it is a great deal more difficult to damp noise and vibration out of unit construction than out of separate frame/separate body cars, but Chrysler engineers have done a very creditable job with the Imperial.

A ride that is soft and pleasant, without being mushy, is what luxury car customers desire and the Imperial offers it, along with excellent handling for such a large car. It should be pointed out that any car with its weight in the Imperial's range—5230 lb. curb weight—generates a lot of inertial energy, especially in side forces while cornering. It's hardly the ideal car to bend through a road race circuit, though the 9.15-15 Goodyear Power Cushions, at normal 24/24 psi inflation, did a quite acceptable job of sticking to the turns. The tires are rated for 6720 lb. total capacity at that inflation pressure, which provides a wide safety margin. Actually, with the cavernous trunk stuffed with luggage, a family aboard and a full tank of fuel (25 gal.) the tires would still provide a 335-lb. safety factor. A summer vacation group, driving rapidly across a hot desert highway in this Imperial could do so without fear of tire failure.

Imperial's mammoth 440-cu. in. engine is said to be improved this year with a new carburetor which provides 25% more cross-sectional area in the intake manifold runners, and reshaped head intake ports that accommodate an increased fuel/air mixture at higher engine speeds. The seat-of-the-pants judgment is that 350 bhp at 4400 rpm and 480 lb.-ft. of torque at 2800 are plenty. Indeed, during acceleration tests it was no trick to hold the brake, wind the engine and leave great streaks of rear tire rubber despite the 2.94:1 rear axle. The trick was to feather off the line without breaking the tires loose.

WITH SMOG a point of concern nationally, CL became curious about the 440 engine's emissions. Though all new cars sold in California must have an exhaust control device (Chrysler's is the Cleaner Air Package), this Imperial turned out not to be so equipped, which wasn't illegal because the car was not officially registered, apparently destined for ultimate delivery out of the state. Subjecting the car to an official state of California air pollution control test, the engine (at 1100 miles and in good tune) emitted 444 parts per million of unburned

gasoline (containing the hydrocarbons that create photochemical smog) and 2.82% CO (carbon monoxide). California's standard for unburned gasoline is 275 ppm, and for CO, 1.5%. Big engine, big problem without some sort of exhaust control.

In analysis of the car's performance, CL arrived at only one significant point of exception to the Imperial's function. This was inefficient braking. With power discs in front, it would seem that Imperial should approach the ultimate. Certainly there was nothing wrong with deceleration at 19 ft./sec./sec. from 80 mph. However, it could have been much better, and would have been had not the rear end hopped upward, permitting the rear brakes to lock. With rear tires sliding, there was a moderate loss of directional stability. And, it was very difficult to prevent the rears from locking under panic-stop conditions. In the latter condition, the deceleration rate dropped to an unacceptable level. The 54/46 front/rear weight distribution offers a clue as to why; certainly a few heavy suitcases in the trunk would have helped. But what would truly be more effective would be some form of proportional braking, or an anti-locking device. It was disappointing to see this

---

1967 IMPERIAL
CROWN 4-DOOR HARDTOP

DIMENSIONS

Wheelbase, in.	127.0
Track, f/r, in.	62.4/61.1
Overall length, in.	224.7
width	79.6
height	56.2
Front seat hip room, in.	63.2
shoulder room	58.9
head room	39.0
pedal-seatback, max.	51.2
Rear seat hip room, in.	62.4
shoulder room	59.2
leg room	38.9
head room	37.3
Door opening width, in.	29.6/29.4
Floor to ground height, in.	11.9
Ground clearance, in.	5.5

PRICES

List, fob factory	$5836
Equipped as tested	7243

Options included: Air conditioning, automatic speed control, tilt/telescope steering wheel, tinted glass, whitewall tires, power door locks, seats and windows.

CAPACITIES

No. of passengers	6
Luggage space, cu. ft.	16.8
Fuel tank, gal.	25.0
Crankcase, qt.	4.0
Transmission/diff., pt.	18.5/4.0
Radiator coolant, qt.	19.0

CHASSIS/SUSPENSION

Frame type	unit
Front suspension type: Independent, non parallel control arms, torsion bars, telescopic shock absorbers.	
ride rate at wheel, lb./in.	118
anti-roll bar dia., in.	0.9
Rear suspension type: Live axle with longitudinal asymmetrical, semi-elliptic leaf springs, telescopic shock absorbers.	
ride rate at wheel, lb./in.	124
Steering system: Power assisted recirculating ball, parallelogram, trailing, parallel Pitman and idler arms, equal length tie rods.	
gear ratio	15.7
overall ratio	19.1
turns, lock to lock	3.5
turning circle, ft. curb-curb	44.9
Curb weight, lb.	5230
Test weight, lb.	5625
Weight distribution, % f/r	54/46

BRAKES

Type: Two circuit hydraulic, ventilated cast iron discs, fixed calipers, front; cast iron drums, duo-servo shoes, rear.

Front disc, dia., in.	11.76
Rear drum, dia. x width	11 x 2.5
total swept area, sq. in.	471.6
Power assist	integral vacuum
line psi @ 100 lb. pedal	1155

WHEELS/TIRES

Wheel size	15 x 6.0JK
optional size available	none
bolt no./circle dia., in.	5/5.5
Tires: Goodyear Power Cushion	
size	9.15-15
recommended inflation, psi.	24/24
capacity rating, total lb.	6720

ENGINE

Type, no. cyl.	ohv, 90° V-8
Bore x stroke, in.	4.32 x 3.75
Displacement, cu. in.	439.497
Compression ratio	10.1
Rated bhp @ rpm	350 @ 4400
equivalent mph	122
Rated torque @ rpm	480 @ 2800
equivalent mph	78
Carburetion	1x4
barrel dia., pri./sec.	1.44/1.69
Valve operation: Hydraulic lifters, pushrods and rocker arms.	
valve dia., int./exh.	2.08/1.60
lift, int./exh.	0.425/0.437
timing, deg.	18-60, 64-16
duration, int./exh.	256/260
opening overlap	34
Exhaust system: Single, reverse flow muffler, resonator.	
pipe dia., exh./tail	2.50/2.00
Lubrication pump type	rotary
normal press. @ rpm.	45 @ 2000
Electrical supply	alternator
ampere rating	46
Battery, plates/amp. rating	78/70

DRIVE-TRAIN

Transmission type: Automatic, with torque converter and 3-speed planetary gearset.

Gear ratio 4th ( ) overall	
3rd (1.00)	2.04
2nd (1.45)	4.65
1st (2.45)	7.20
1st x t.c. stall (2.00)	14.40
synchronous meshing?	planetary
Shift lever location	steering column
Differential type: Hypoid, limited slip	
axle ratio	2.94

kind of stopping performance from what is an outstanding automobile in other details.

Chrysler emphasizes that one of the Imperial's safety features is a set of non-reflective wipers. Great. The wipers didn't reflect. But the bright chromium plated molding on the inside perimeter of the windshield did. The reflection was noted while evaluating an annoying distortion in the glass near the extreme edge which, admittedly, is not an area of frequent use. At these prices it would have been nicer to have had better optics.

OTHER PETTY gripes center around small items. The turn signals' control lever is so sensitive that it tended to flick off with just a minor steering correction while approaching a turn. This simple lapse could buy a driver a traffic citation in some locales. The next problem is the signal indicator. To preclude a driver's having to glance at the dash to check the indicator flasher, rearward facing amber repeaters have been set in the front fender tips. This is a good idea, especially at night when they are fully visible, but in the sunlight, particularly with the sun behind the car, these tiny lamps were difficult to discern unless one was willing to di-

SMOOTH STYLING and the strength of the 440-cu. in. engine may soon destroy Imperial's image as a car for wealthy little old ladies.

vert his attention from the road and focus on the fender tip for three or four flashes. They should be brighter, perhaps larger, and an audible click in the driver's compartment would not be amiss.

One comment repeated by several new car tire-kickers was the apparent vulnerability of the cornering lights. They form the front blade edge of the fenders and thus would seem to offer little resistance to, say, the very firm tail-

gate of a carelessly backed pickup truck.

Taken as a package, and relating it to its two traditional luxury competitors, the Imperial is well worth the consideration of anyone ready to purchase in this price range. Does it have the indefinable quality of prestige which equates closely with the appeal inherent in Continental and Cadillac? Who can say? The sales figures a year from now will be the only positive indicator. ■

CAR LIFE ROAD TEST

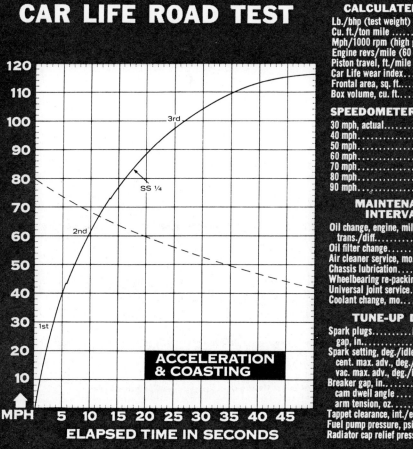

ACCELERATION & COASTING

ELAPSED TIME IN SECONDS

CALCULATED DATA

Lb./bhp (test weight)	16.1
Cu. ft./ton mile	102
Mph/1000 rpm (high gear)	275
Engine revs/mile (60 mph)	2180
Piston travel, ft./mile	1350
Car Life wear index	34.3
Frontal area, sq. ft.	24.9
Box volume, cu. ft.	583.5

SPEEDOMETER ERROR

30 mph, actual	29.3
40 mph	38.5
50 mph	48.0
60 mph	58.1
70 mph	67.1
80 mph	77.6
90 mph	89.1

MAINTENANCE INTERVALS

Oil change, engine, miles	4000
trans./diff.	12,000/6 mo.
Oil filter change	8000
Air cleaner service, mo.	6
Chassis lubrication	36,000
Wheelbearing re-packing	12,000
Universal joint service	36,000
Coolant change, mo.	12

TUNE-UP DATA

Spark plugs	MoPar P-3-5P
gap, in.	0.035
Spark setting, deg./idle rpm.	0/620
cent. max. adv., deg./rpm.	19/4600
vac. max. adv., deg./in. Hg.	21/16
Breaker gap, in.	0.014-0.019
cam dwell angle	28-32
arm tension, oz.	17-20
Tappet clearance, int./exh.	0/0
Fuel pump pressure, psi.	3-5
Radiator cap relief press., psi.	16

PERFORMANCE

Top speed (4200), mph	117
Shifts (rpm) @ mph	
2nd to 3rd (4200)	73
1st to 2nd (3900)	44

ACCELERATION

0-30 mph, sec.	3.4
0-40 mph	5.2
0-50 mph	7.3
0-60 mph	9.6
0-70 mph	12.7
0-80 mph	16.4
0-90 mph	20.6
0-100 mph	27.1
Standing ¼-mile, sec.	17.4
speed at end, mph	82.8
Passing, 30-70 mph, sec.	9.3

BRAKING

(Maximum deceleration rate achieved from 80 mph)

1st stop, ft./sec./sec.	19
fade evident?	no
2nd stop, ft./sec./sec.	19
fade evident?	moderate

FUEL CONSUMPTION

Test conditions, mpg	11.75
Est. normal range, mpg	9.8-14.1
Cruising range, miles	245-352

GRADABILITY

4th, % grade @ mph	
3rd	13 @ 60
2nd	19 @ 40
1st	34 @ 22

DRAG FACTOR

Total drag @ 60 mph, lb.	169

CHRYSLER CORP.

Crown 4-dr Hardtop Door

Imperial

The traditional **Imperial** emphasis on comfort, luxury and elegance is advanced even further in 1967. Slight touches to exterior styling highlight its smooth good looks. 1967 additions consist of parking lights in the front fender tips, and the headlights inserted in the grille. The 1966 **Imperial** has its headlights in square bezels, covered with glass. Model lineup is retained from 1966.

The **Imperial** line has all the standard safety features that are used in the other Chrysler models. ■

1968 report

IMPERIAL

It takes a close look to notice the changes in '68 Imperials. Externally, there are no changes with the exception of sidemarker lights and a new horizontal bar grille. Inside, however, there is a new deeply recessed instrument panel embossed with rich antique bronze overlays.

There will be five 1968 models: the four door sedan, Crown four-door hardtop, Crown two-door hardtop, convertible and the top-of-the-line LeBaron four-door hardtop.

Prestige is definitely the image portrayed by the Imperial. Its overall length is almost 19 feet and its weight is over 5,000 lbs. The interiors are soft and luxurious with nothing but top quality materials used. Options include the constant speed control, AM-FM or FM stereo radio with five speakers and automatic temperature control system.

The seating arrangement is varied among different models. There are divided front seats with individual arm rests for the LeBaron and Crown four-doors, with a reclining seat back for the passenger. Crown coupe two-and-four-door lines have the traditional bench seat, and the convertibles feature leather uphol-stery on individual seats (bucket seats) with a six-way adjustment and reclining back on the passenger side.

Of course, the Imperial is available with all the Chrysler Corp. power options, which will give its owner a car with the ultimate in luxury and comfort.

Imperial is top of line car in Chrysler Corp. It has powerful 440 TNT engine to power it, plus extensive interior styling for particular car owner. Twelve safety features are incorporated in Imperial, which comes in five models.

The Chrysler Crown Imperial

USING the "Mobile Director" to cover the Sebring 12 Hours.

AT present, the prestige American cars undoubtedly comprise Cadillac, Lincoln Continental and Imperial, with possibly the Buick Electra and Oldsmobile Luxury Sedan as runners-up. Despite the attractions (and status symbol) of owning imported European vehicles, the first three makes command a vitally important market in the USA, Canada and South America, and also have a high resale value. One must not forget that they are primarily designed to provide high performance, comfort and silence on the long thru'ways of the Americas, and to double up as luxurious town carriages.

Make no mistake, the engineering quality is very high indeed and, while their very vastness makes them odd-looking to European eyes, they possess a special appeal of their own. A few years ago they were ungainly, chrome-splashed, finned monsters, but today lines have been simplified and garish trimmings dropped; aesthetically a new approach to dignified automobiles has taken place—particularly in the case of the Crown Imperial coupé by Chrysler.

Now this is a large car by any standards, but the designers have produced a vehicle of such excellent proportions, and with such a commendable lack of unnecessary ornamentation, that it can lay claim to being the most attractive American closed car since the advent of Raymond Lowey's original Studebaker. Possibly Chrysler stylists learned a lot from recent association with the Italian Ghia concern, for, even in a country where automobiles are taken for granted, this particular example attracted an immense amount of attention, and highly favourable comment, from such hard-boiled folk as "gas-station" attendants.

I was lent a coupé for a trip from New York to Florida and back. This was complete with full "executive" fittings, and was magnificently finished throughout. It had a 7.2-litre V8 engine giving 350 bhp at 4400 rpm, and producing a torque figure of 480 lbs/ft at 2800 rpm on a compression ratio of 10 to 1. The car ran throughout its rpm range in complete and utter silence, and this engine must surely be one of the quietest power units on any passenger car.

Mind you, the car needs a powerful engine (a 375 bhp version is also available), for it weighs close on 2¼ tons. However, the immense torque, together with a faultless automatic transmission, provides really flashing acceleration all the way up to 100 mph, to the consternation of drivers of "hi-performance" fastbacks with all the available tuning equipment. Maximum speed is around 125 mph, which I reached several times on deserted highways where friends assured me that there was no radar activity, and that there was little chance of speed cops lurking behind trees. Nevertheless I always felt that I was taking a chance, and it was possibly more by luck than anything

else that the sirens did not sound, and no red spotlamps flashed. I could also have been nabbed from above, for more than a few state patrols operate from helicopters to catch unsuspecting speeders.

The absence of wind noise and the uncanny mechanical silence would have made listening to the stereo radio easy at any speed. Alas, this was the only component on the car which didn't work properly, so I had to forget it. With electrical control for seats, windows, doorlocks and every conceivable item of equipment that could be made to operate without effort, I *would* have to have a radio set which went on the blink!

The air conditioning plant was 100 per cent efficient and, with windows raised in the hottest and most humid weather imaginable, my wife and I kept delightfully cool. In point of fact, this equipment is not merely an extra on the Crown Imperial, but was designed specifically for the car to operate in such temperatures as are found in the deserts of Montana and elsewhere.

The brakes are most effective for an American car, possibly due to the adoption of 11 ins discs in front, and similar-diameter drums at the rear. Naturally they are servo-controlled and have dual master cylinders. The suspension is particularly good, with torsion bar, IFS and semi-elliptic rear and antiroll bars. The car is commendably free from any tendency to lean, and with the 9.15-15.4 four-ply Firestones adhesion

was fairly good, except when the roads had just become wet, when rather excessive wheelspin was apparent during rapid acceleration. As for the powered steering, it was difficult to realize that this was fitted as there was never any "dead" feeling, and it was most responsive. Anyway, it would have indeed been arm-busting to attempt to park 127 inches of wheelbase without powered steering.

A fitment which I did not altogether care for was the "electric eye" automatic dipping device. This is rather too efficient, for it is apt to operate from the illumination cast by distant signs (especially petrol pumps). Fortunately it is possible to revert to manual control, which I did after racing along a dark highway and then finding the lamps dipped automatically as a brightly lit train rounded a bend.

Immense care has been taken to provide really luxurious seating, and the front seats are provided with headrests. Both, of course, are fully reclining. Luggage space is indeed huge, and British friends suggested that the boot could quite easily be used to smuggle a couple of Minis. There is every possible instrument: the heating is as excellent as the air conditioning, and the wiper motor has three speeds.

Most two-door closed cars are difficult to enter and leave without a great deal of contortions. On the Crown coupé there is an electrical device which causes the front passenger seats to tilt to the most forward position, when the seat backs are canted forward. The car also had the "Mobile Director", which permits the owner to convert the interior into a travelling office, or to provide living accommodation on long trips. The front passenger seat rotates 180 deg to face the rear, and a folding table (normally the centre arm-rest) can be set up in three different positions, to be used as a writing desk, typewriter platform or card table. Extras such as an electric typewriter and transistor TV set can be supplied and fitted if so desired, and a radio telephone can be mounted close to the unit.

An efficient electrical system is essential, for this Crown coupé had, in addition to the starter, no fewer than 15 different electric motors. It says a lot for the equipment that the outsize alternator copes with everything, and even at the end of some 3000 miles of motoring it was unnecessary to top up the large-capacity battery. Only ¼ pint of oil was consumed, and petrol consumption (on premium fuel) worked out at just over 15 mp(US)g. Possibly a 2.94 to 1 axle helped!

Altogether this is a magnificent automobile, and one that was always a pleasure to drive; not exactly ideal for crowded British roads, but a most restful vehicle on motorways capable of putting in a remarkable number of miles in 8 or 10 hours of driving.

Luxury: The great American dream

Can the lowly family sedan attain the stature of the majestic marques?

By Bill Sanders

Her head tilted back on the seat. A tenacious vitality glowed in the opacity of her stare. Electric blue eyes, laser beams of concentration, penetrated the off-white headliner. Outside, the tepid February afternoon hovered in sultry fever over the Southern California beach. Incarnadine salmon sun cauterized tinted windows with merciless pyromania. Inside, the velvet soft coolness of air conditioning insulated the plush, soft world of sensuality. She looked relaxed, yet somehow mechanically tense. The imperturbable, perfectly composed features showed no trace of emotion. The sentient, beautiful face was a mask, hiding a veil of consciousness.

"Relax . . . enjoy yourself, sweetheart. After all, you don't ride in a Coupe de Ville everyday," I suggested.

Voice, the new sound, startled her. The straight, blonde hair was brushed aside as her hand swept instinctively upward. She moved slightly, an angry frown marred the soft lips.

"What is it with you? Can't you see I'm listening to the stereo? Man, what a drag. Wow!"

"Oh."

. . . That's right, baby. Stereo. This is the year of stereo. It don't mean a thing if it ain't got that zing. Stereo. FM multiplex or tape deck. Take your choice or take both. Speakers in the front, speakers in the back, speakers in the doors: surround yourself with sound. Electric seats and windows are passe. Stereo makes a luxury car in 1968 . . . or does it?

What constitutes a true luxury car? How much luxury do you get for your dollar? Will the addition of luxury options make a Chevy, Ford or Plymouth a luxury car? Luxury is as luxury does. It can be a state of mind, but ultimately becomes much more than that out of physical necessity. It is not only a material judgement, but is psychological as well. Concerning the latter, "image" is a prime luxury prerequisite. "Image" is half the battle.

Chevrolet tried valiantly with Caprice, but it doesn't come close to the Coupe de Ville, even with vinyl roof and flashy wheel covers. Ford's LTD is relatively close to the Continental

— you know they are from the same maker — but Continental still has its own mystique. With the VIP, Plymouth has produced a car of nondescript, movie-type elegance. It looks like a limousine, but what is it? It comes closest to its big car counterpart in "image," but, rather than elevating the VIP in stature, the close resemblance only impairs the prestige of the Imperial. And the difference in price between the VIP and Imperial LeBaron is substantial: $3648.35 in our test cars.

Body styling seems to be inseparable from "image." Coupe de Ville still reigns champ with massive, but well contoured lines. Chevrolet has endowed Caprice with style features similar to the Coupe de Ville's, but they don't project the massive quality. Continental styling remains aquiline, but with individuality, while Ford body contours are more fluid and less angular. Both Chrysler subjects seem to be several years behind in styling, with a stark, boxy appearance.

Comfort is dominant in the big cars, but only in degree. Coupe de Ville seats are massive and luxuriously comfortable. Six-way electric adjustment puts the front seat in any desired driving position, but, with a bench-type seat, front passenger must accept the same arrangement, like it or not. Our test Caprice had front bucket seats with center console. These seats were no different from any Chevy's and were manually operated: you only moved forward or backward. Seating comfort in the Coupe de Ville was excellent; in the Caprice it was ordinary. For plush, luxurious seating our test Ford LTD was the paragon of comfort in the intermediate group and came closest to the big cars in this

area. In fact, the LTD seemed every bit as comfortable as the Continental. Continental power seats also have excellent positioning. Plymouth seats, like the Caprice's, were ordinary, but did have power adjustment and fair positioning on the driver's side.

Chrysler Imperial may not turn many heads with its Dowager Queen Mother styling, but the Chrysler men certainly know how to please one's tired old body with fastidious creature comforts. Seating is superior, especially in the rear. Split front seats on our LeBaron 4-door sedan test car had individual electric controls, allowing driver *and* passenger to adjust his seat to any desired position. Front seats also had individual fold-down armrests, as did the front seats on the VIP. Even the other two big cars don't have this feature. One staffer summed up the LeBaron succinctly: "It's like driving your living room down the highway."

All three big cars had leather seats, a priceless luxury touch. Our Caprice had "leather-like" vinyl that was obviously vinyl and not too leather-like. Both LTD and VIP were upholstered in black nylon, which, when tufted, as in the LTD, gives a more eye appealing, luxury look in the lower priced car at much less cost.

Entering the rear seat compartment on all the coupes was a difficult project, especially in the Coupe de Ville and Continental with their massive front seatbacks. The Caprice, with bucket seats, was the easiest to enter. Both VIP and Imperial were 4-door sedans and rear seat entry and exit was relatively simple, especially in the Imperial, which had plenty of rear seat legroom.

The two groups come closest in convenience. You can add most of the electric and vacuum gadgets, power accessories, and stereo to the intermediate cars and still get a car for $2000 to $3000 less. Of course the question, "What constitutes a luxury car?" still remains, but if the options alone turn you on, you're better off buying the loaded intermediate.

Electric window and door lock operation differs immensely from car to car. Our LeBaron Imperial had the best arrangement. Window buttons are toggle switches and are by far the easiest to operate. The panel is slanted in the forward part of the door armrest at an angle that makes all the buttons visible — a feature that greatly facilitates their use. Both Cadillac and Lincoln have window buttons flat on the door armrest and can be operated by feel only, a situation that often results in the wrong window going up or down. Ford had the worst location, flat on the door panel, which required an elbow that would bend in a different direction from that achievable by most humans. Unfortunately, the Caprice had roll-up windows, so we couldn't judge the placement of controls in the car.

Chrysler and Plymouth have the best dashboard arrangements and design. They are similar but distinctive. Both feature a high, wide padded top, allowing the dash to be recessed beneath. Because of this arrangement, toggle switches are used and are much more convenient than sliding handles or padded knobs. In place of the wood veneer used on both the Cadillac and Lincoln dash panels, our Imperial had antiqued bronze paneling inlaid across the dash and doors. Cadillac and Chevrolet seem to have too much padding on the dash, which is disconcerting. Cadillac has a good dash layout, but some of the instruments are difficult to reach around the steering wheel. To reach the glovebox from the driver's seat, you have to move far to the right, an impossibility when you are wearing a seat belt. Dash on the Caprice is simple, but far from elegant. It's not much different from the ordinary Chevrolet's. Lights, wipers and lighter are all difficult to get your fingers around, as they are recessed for safety. Stereo system in the Caprice was one of the best, even in comparison to the higher-priced cars! Dash on the Continental was well laid out and more convenient than the Caddy when it came to reaching radio and heater. Lower instruments on the Ford and Lincoln, such as vents and lighter, are down and under and almost impossible to find or reach.

Cadillac has a unique, but complicated speed control system mounted on the dash that allows you to set a pre-determined speed. We liked the system used on the Caprice much better as it involves only a button on the turn indicator lever and is far simpler

Chrysler Imperial

LeBaron had no trouble negotiating San Francisco's famous hills and bridges, handling and ride are excellent. Low windshield line gives good visibility. Dashboard is well laid out with easy-to-grasp-and-use toggle switches. Interior comfort is outstanding, but boxy, angular styling and lack of distinction give car a mediocre look. Luggage space is good.

to operate. The Cad system keeps you from going faster than the speed set, which could be dangerous when passing. The Caprice just takes a tap on the accelerator and the speed control is over-ridden. Both cancel automatically when braking. Also well known and offered only on the Cad is the time-delay light switch, which turns the lights off automatically after you leave the car.

Both Chrysler cars have a convenient ignition light that operates on a time delay, it comes on when you open the driver's door and goes off after a brief interval. Rear seat reading lights are offered in each of the big three, and are located in the rear roof quarter panel. Imperial has the best design with lights directed down at an angle. They don't flood the car with light, to the distraction of the driver, as do the others. All three top cars have individual rear seat cigarette lighters, items not found on the lower priced models. And, Imperial goes one better with individual lighters on all four doors.

Chrysler leads the way with steering wheels too. Theirs are by far the easiest to operate with thin center bars that don't hinder grasp or turning. Lincoln, Ford and Cadillac have cumbersome, thick center bars that get in the way when trying to find a good grip and when steering. The Caprice wheel is better, but not as good as either the VIP or LeBaron's.

Luggage space varies considerably. Obviously you're going to get more room in a bigger car. Smallest space is in the LTD, although it is rather deep. Lowest liftover of *all* cars was on the VIP, with trunk floor even with the bumper. Spare tire in all six cars is placed in the forward-most part of the trunk, making it necessary to physically enter the trunk to remove the spare. It's interesting to speculate what a 95-pound woman will do on a deserted road with a flat.

When it comes to ride, we really start to separate the men from the boys. Slice it down the middle. The generation gap is there — wide and impassable. Weight differences range between 1000-1300 pounds (give or take a few) and you know it as soon as the cars start rolling. Ford probably comes closest to a comparable ride with its big brother. The Lincoln is smoother and heavier, but the LTD still gives a solid, heavy feeling in its ride. VIP may look like a limousine,

but when you compare riding qualities with the Imperial, you know it's still a Plymouth. While it has a substantial feel, the Caprice is probably further from the Coupe de Ville than the other two. Our Imperial was the quietest under all conditions, with the Cadillac running a close second. Wind noise around the Continental, with windows up, was unaccountably bad, whistling and howling at any annoying decibel level. On the other hand, LTD showed the least tendency to interrupt conversation among the lower-priced three.

Emotions also run the gamut when it comes to handling. Imperial maneuvers relatively easy for a big car, and we had a 4-door. That is partly due to the higher seats and lower dash and windshield design than in the Cad and Continental, in which you appear to sit much lower. Imperial goes through moderate corners without much roll or sway, while the VIP, in reality a small car, handles atrociously. Cad and Caprice are both nimble and responsive, with the Caprice probably best among the smaller cars. An unusual phenomenon was the deceptive size of the Coupe de Ville, which psychologically aided handling. Outside it looked monstrously long; inside it seemed not much bigger than the Caprice. Continental handling was bad news too, with an unusual amount of correcting necessary to maintain a good road track. While not as responsive or agile as the Caprice, the LTD handles well, much better than the Lincoln. A tilting steering wheel is an absolute must. Our only car without that appendage was the LTD, and the wheel was positioned at such a crazy angle you almost seemed to be steering with arms over your head, a feat that doesn't go far toward aiding handling qualities.

Power steering on all is effortless and is most convenient on the bigger cars. Sometimes it was a little too fast on the lighter cars. Weight added to a more solid feel in the steering.

Braking was rather similar in response and effect, except on the Chrysler boats. Their brakes can be summed up in one word: pathetic. When braking from 60 to 0 mph, our VIP locked up and swerved all over the place. And that was with front discs. Braking had seemed better on the Imperial during a long weekend trip, but at the test track, front disc brakes started

smoking after only a few high-speed stops, and those without full panic pressure. Caprice brakes are good with front discs, but a considerable and frightening amount of nose dip accompanies high-speed stops. Some deviation from the straight was noticed. Cadillac has some mighty smooth brakes on the Coupe de Ville. The big car pulled down straight and even, without any feeling of swerving, either way. Continental and Ford both exhibited the same qualities, and stopped evenly without veering in either direction on a side bias. No fade was noticed in Ford, Continental, Cadillac or Chevrolet after repeated stops.

Big engines are used in all the cars we tested. And, big engines are a vital necessity to power all the accessory equipment running off the mill. Tremendous torque output is synonymous with the engines on the bigger cars, and this favorable power-to-weight torque ratio gives them good acceleration and passing speed. Surprisingly, there was little difference in acceleration times, on all cars we tested, when running with and without air conditioners on. In other cars we have tested, especially the big bombs, we noticed a considerable drain on power with air conditioning in operation. Perhaps that fact is taken into consideration on the luxury models and compensated for.

In the final analysis, after testing and comparing these six cars, one overwhelming conclusion is evident. The cars themselves repeatedly and belligerently make you aware of it: there is no compromise with luxury; it has to be a total concept. You can't dress-up a lesser car and get the comfort, feel, ride and "image" of a luxury car. A line from an Aesop fable, *The Fox and the Mask*, states it simply: "Outside show is a poor substitute for inner worth." As with anything you buy, you don't get "something for nothing." With luxury cars, you pay for what you get, and you don't get true luxury unless you are willing to pay for it. There's no other way.

"...Tune that stereo a little, will you, baby, I hear some static. And the left rear speaker is too loud."

There was no movement on the huge, white leather seat next to me. In the opulence of the cool twilight I could see: she was asleep.

Turn page for specs.

	CHEVROLET CAPRICE	CADILLAC COUPE DE VILLE	PLYMOUTH VIP	CHRYSLER IMPERIAL LeBARON	FORD LTD	LINCOLN CONTINENTAL
PERFORMANCE						
(Performance figures computed in "D" range, without air conditioning working) Acceleration (2 aboard)						
0-30	3.4 secs.	3.6 secs.	3.5 secs.	4.2 secs.	3.9 secs.	4.0 secs.
0-45	5.4 secs.	5.7 secs.	5.5 secs.	7.4 secs.	6.6 secs.	6.6 secs.
0-60	8.0 secs.	9.1 secs.	8.5 secs.	12.4 secs.	9.3 secs.	10.6 secs.
0-75	12.0 secs.	13.1 secs.	12.1 secs.	17.4 secs.	13.5 secs.	15.8 secs.
Passing Speeds:						
40-60	4.2 secs., 307.4 ft.	5.0 secs., 366.0 ft.	4.0 secs., 292.8 ft.	6.8 secs., 497.7 ft.	5.0 secs., 366.0 ft.	5.4 secs., 395.2 ft.
50-70	5.0 secs., 440.0 ft.	5.5 secs., 484.0 ft.	5.0 secs., 440.0 ft.	8.0 secs., 704.0 ft.	5.4 secs., 475.2 ft.	6.9 secs., 597.2 ft.
Standing Start ¼-mile:	89 mph, 16.2 secs.	86 mph, 17.0 secs.	86 mph, 17.0 secs.	77 mph, 18.4 secs.	84.1 mph, 16.8 secs.	80 mph, 18.2 secs.
Speeds in Gears:						
1st . . . mph @ rpm	55 @ 5200	48 @ 4400	48 @ 4500	47 @ 4400	52 @ 4000	48 @ 4500
2nd . . . mph @ rpm	85 @ 5200	82 @ 4400	75 @ 4500	79 @ 4400	88 @ 4000	85 @ 4500
3rd . . . mph @ rpm	102 @ 4000	94 @ 4200	106 @ 4500	90 @ 4000	96 @ 3000	98 @ 4000
MPH Per 1000 RPM	18.2 mph	19 mph	15.6 mph	18.9 mph	20.1	19.3
Stopping Distances:						
From 30 mph	24 ft.	27 ft.	35 ft.	46 ft.	32 ft.	33 ft.
From 60 mph	107 ft.	149 ft.	138 ft.	158 ft.	131 ft.	136 ft.
Mileage Range	20.2 – 25.4	9.1-13.2	10.4-11.8	9.2-14.5	12.2-13.8	9.4-15.2
SPECIFICATIONS						
Engine	90° V-8 OHV	90° V-8 OHV	90° V-8 OHV	90° V-8 OHV	90° V-8 OHV	90° V-8 OHV
Bore & Stroke — Ins.	4.25 x 3.76	4.30 x 4.06	4.25 x 3.38	4.32 x 3.75	4.13 x 3.98	4.38 x 3.83
Displacement — Cu. In.	427	472	383	440	428	462
HP at RPM	385 @ 5200	375 @ 4400	330 @ 5000	350 @ 4400	340 @ 4600	340 @ 4600
Torque: lbs.-ft. @ rpm	460 @ 3400	525 @ 3000	425 @ 3200	480 @ 2800	462 @ 2800	485 @ 2800
Compression Ratio	10.25:1	10.5:1	10.0:1	10.0:1	10.5:1	10.25:1
Carburetion	1 4-bbl.	1 4-bbl.	1 4-bbl.	1 4-bbl.	1 4-bbl.	1 4-bbl.
Transmission	automatic	automatic	automatic	automatic	automatic	automatic
Final Drive Ratio — Std.	3.07:1	2.94:1	3.23:1	2.94:1	2.80:1	2.80:1
Steering & Ratio	Power, recirculating ball nut. 21.2:1	Variable ratio power. 16.6:1	Power, recirculating ball nut. 19.12:1	Power, recirculating ball nut. 19.1:1	Power, recirculating ball nut. 21.9:1	Integral gear and power cylinder, recirculating ball. 20.5:1
Turning Dia. — Curb-to-Curb — ft.	41	47.5	42.8	44.9	41	47.4
Wheel Turns — Lock-to-Lock	4.0	2.6	3.5	3.5	3.7	3.8
Tires — Std.	8.25 x 14	9.00 x 15	8.25 x 14	9.15 x 15	8.45 x 15/4	9.15 x 15
Brakes	Front disc, rear drum	Front disc, rear drum	Front disc, rear drum	Front disc, rear drum	Front disc, rear drum	Front disc, rear drum
Suspension	4-wheel coil spring, independent front	4-wheel coil spring, independent front	Independent front torsion bar semi-elliptical leaf rear	Independent front torsion bar semi-elliptical leaf rear	4-wheel coil spring, independent front	Independent coil spring front semi-elliptical leaf rear
Body/Frame Construction	Body/Frame	Body/Frame	Unit	Unit	Unitized	Unitized
Overall Length — Ins.	214.7	224.7	213.3	224.5	213.9	221
Width — Ins.	79.6	79.9	77.7	79.6	78	79.7
Height — Ins.	54.3	54.3	56.3	57.0	53.9	54.2
Wheelbase — Ins.	119.0	129.5	119	127.0	119	126
Front Track — Ins.	62.5	62.5	62.0	62.4	62	62.1
Rear Track — Ins.	62.4	62.5	60.7	61.1	62	61.0
Fuel Capacity — Gals.	24	26	24	25	25	25.5
Curb Weight — Lbs.	3840	4900	4000	5284	3863	5244

LUXURY OPTIONS AND PRICES

CHEVROLET CAPRICE

Retail price as tested: $5056.25

OPTIONS

Power windows	$100.10
6-way power seats	94.80
4-way bucket power seat	69.55
Light monitor system	26.35
Tinted glass	39.50
Vinyl roof	89.55
Strato bucket seats	158.00
AM/FM radio with multiplex stereo	238.15
Air conditioning	368.65
Power disc brakes	121.15
Tilting steering wheel	42.15
Speed & cruise control	52.70
Rallye wheel covers	10.55
Power steering	94.80
427-cu.-in. engine	263.30
Automatic transmission	237.00

PLYMOUTH VIP

Retail price as tested: $4728.75

OPTIONS

Vinyl roof	$ 86.75
Split bench seat w/cloth & vinyl, passenger recline	104.20
383-cu.-in. engine	137.60
Basic group: AM radio, power steering, power brakes, 3-speed windshield wipers, remote control mirror	212.75
Automatic transmission	216.20
Air conditioning	350.25
Rear seat speaker	14.05
Left power seat	90.30
Power windows	100.25
Tinted glass	39.50

FORD LTD

Retail price as tested: $4860.80

OPTIONS

Vinyl roof	$ 84.99
Luxury interior trim	112.69
Automatic transmission	233.17
Power windows	99.94
Power steering	94.95
Tilt steering wheel	42.76
Power disc brakes	64.77
Air conditioning	368.72
Stereo tape deck	133.86
AM radio	61.40
Tinted glass	42.12
Deluxe wheel covers	56.98

CADILLAC COUPE DE VILLE

Retail price as tested: $7467.40
(Price differential $2411.15)

OPTIONS

Padded roof	$131.60
Leather upholstery	137.90
AM/FM radio with multiplex stereo	288.40
Tinted glass	50.55
6-way power seats	83.15
Automatic climate control heater/air conditioner	515.75
Power door locks (2 doors)	47.40
Tilt/telescope steering wheel	89.50
Automatic headlights	31.60
Interior deck lid release	52.65
Front disc brakes	105.25
Rear window defogger	26.35
Speed & cruise control	94.75
Automatic headlight dimmer	50.55
Power front vent windows	71.60
Automatic level control	78.95

CHRYSLER IMPERIAL LeBARON

Retail price as tested: $8377.10
(Price differential 3648.35)

OPTIONS

Vinyl roof	$136.15
Leather interior	124.55
Sure grip differential	56.35
Air conditioning	493.45
AM/FM radio with multiplex stereo	294.85
Power door locks, electric	70.70
Interior deck lid release	29.60
Tinted glass	52.70
Tilt/telescope steering wheel	92.45

LINCOLN CONTINENTAL

Retail price as tested: $7351.28
(Price differential 2490.48)

OPTIONS

Vinyl roof	$136.85
Leather w/vinyl trim interior	137.26
Power front vent windows	71.64
6-way power seats	83.28
Spare tire cover	10.95
Tilt steering wheel	66.95
Interior deck lid release and speed, cruise control	134.56
Rear window defogger	42.20
Air conditioning	503.90
AM radio, stereo tape deck	244.54
Automatic headlight dimmer	50.05
Tinted glass	52.53
Power door locks	47.45

COMMENTS

CHEVROLET CAPRICE

WE LIKE:

Multiplex stereo radio and speaker system . . . good performance . . . hidden ash tray design and placement on console . . . easy rear seat entry . . . solid body and good ride.

WE DON'T LIKE:

Bucket seats in luxury car . . . horizontal sliding levers for heater, air conditioner . . . difficult to grasp, padded switches . . . recessed ignition . . . center console with horseshoe shift lever.

PLYMOUTH VIP

WE LIKE:

Dash layout . . . easy to operate toggle switches . . . thin bar steering wheel . . . fender mounted turn indicators . . . time delay ignition light . . . rear seat leg room . . . low liftover in trunk . . . big car feeling . . . twin armrests for front seats . . . front visibility over hood.

WE DON'T LIKE:

Brakes . . . quality control . . . recessed ignition . . . radio too far from driver . . small glove compartment . . . not quite comfortable seating positions . . . difficult front seat exit . . . handling.

FORD LTD

WE LIKE:

Seating comfort . . . styling . . . ride . . . thickly padded upholstery and simulated tortise leather trim . . . performance . . . attention to detail . . . quiet operation . . . handling.

WE DON'T LIKE:

Steering wheel position . . . location of power window buttons . . . thick steering wheel bar . . . padding around dash makes reading instruments difficult . . . poor location of emergency brake warning light . . . lower switches difficult to reach . . . radio system.

CADILLAC COUPE DE VILLE

WE LIKE:

Automatic headlights . . . styling . . . ride . . . solid body . . . extremely soft woven carpet . . . good acceleration and performance in big car . . . soft leather . . . stereo radio and dial . . . lighter, ash tray in one unit . . . excellent steering and handling . . . seating comfort . . . thermostat climate control.

WE DON'T LIKE:

Complicated cruise/speed control . . . narrow rear entry in coupe . . . excessive padding on windshield posts and dash . . . wide, padded center bar on steering wheel.

CHRYSLER IMPERIAL LeBARON

WE LIKE:

Bronze finish panels on dash and doors . . . individual lighter in each door . . . slanted power toggle switches on door armrest for easy visibility . . . rear compartment reading lights . . . time delay ignition light . . . seating comfort and ride . . . maneuverability . . . stereo system . . . lift-up metal door pulls . . . quietness . . . individually operated front power seats . . . door glove compartments . . . thermostat air temperature.

WE DON'T LIKE:

Styling . . . brakes . . . quality control . . . overload cutoff when power front seats are operated simultaneously . . . small front glove compartment . . . non-solid feeling of body . . . rear fender bumper projection.

LINCOLN CONTINENTAL

WE LIKE:

Good instrumentation . . . wooden steering wheel . . . thermostat temperature control . . . solid body . . . dash layout . . . seating comfort . . . clean lines.

WE DON'T LIKE:

Wind noise . . . foot tiring position of accelerator pedal . . . handling . . . awkward position of cruise/speed control on-off buttons . . . steering wheel center bar . . . narrow rear seat entry-way.

OPULENCE WITHOUT OSTENTATION

Chrysler's luxury package for the secure set

The term 'royal' has to do with kings and such, and generally means a pretty high ranking. But even kings are ranked by emperors, and the term covering the affairs of emperors is 'imperial.'

Spell that word with a capital letter, 'Imperial,' and you have a pretty high-ranking car, too.

Americans have never gone for the traditional trappings of royalty. The aristocracy of this country is not necessarily hereditary. Instead, it is based on money.

The Imperial is definitely a money car, and as the prestige wagon of the Chrysler line, it has a heritage that goes back to the early days of this country's automotive history, and actually pre-dates the first appearance of a car bearing the Chrysler name.

Just the same, when a car sells in the $6,000 range, the buyer has a right to expect it to be good. He has a right, so far as most people are concerned, to expect to be very nearly perfect.

This is a rich man's car, there's no doubt about that. The man who buys one should be able to live on the scale of a man who owns and drives a $6,000 car. For the man who does live on such a level, however, the Imperial has a lot going for it — in some ways, perhaps it has a little too much going for it.

For instance, driving this car on the freeway can be a sort of reverse test of driver ability. California's 65 and 70 mph speed limits are not unreasonable, but our ROAD TESTers often found they were innocently exceeding these limits. This car rides so easily — and has so much power — that lest the driver beware, he'll soon glance at the dash and, to his horror learn he is cruising along at 85 mph or better. That is, if he is lucky he will find this out from a look at

The handle that closes the door is a quaint touch from the days of real horses. Door closes with an audible indication of solid coachwork.

THE IMPERIAL

The Imperial is listed as a 'six-passenger' vehicle, but the six have more room than a driver and three passengers in many other models.

the dash. If he isn't lucky, he'll learn the same thing when he glances in one of the rear-view mirrors and finds a pair of bright red lights.

Still and all, that's really faulting the driver, not the car. Equally unfair is the complaint this car drives so easily that, on a long trip, a driver might find it all too easy to doze off or, at least, pay less attention than he should to his driving.

All of which adds up to one thing — this car is luxurious in a dreamy kind of way.

This is a big car, a good-looking car, and a powerful car. The front-to-rear length is just a fraction less than 230 inches — more than 19 feet — and the dry weight is a pound more than 4,800. The 440 inches under the hood are big, too.

In both overall dimensions and under-the-hood power, the Imperial is in the boat class — but that is not meant as an insult. The lines, like those of a fine vessel, are clean. Parked next to most other American '69 models, it looks huge. Standing by itself, and seen from a little distance, empty, it could be much smaller. Thanks to the absence of to-the-roof doorposts, it can have an almost small hardtop affect. This, though, is lost if there is anyone sitting in the vehicle. Big guys look small, and small guys all but disappear.

You know it is big, too, when you try to park it. A $6,000 car has everything, and you can appreciate the power brakes that bring it to a smooth stop, and the power steering that make it possible to get next to the curb without putting in a daily stint on the bar bells.

As an experiment, we tried to park it in

Clean lines can make the Imperial seem smaller than it is, also insure it will still be good looking five years hence.

The Imperial leans in a tight turn, but the car was never designed to compete on a road racing course. As a freeway cruiser it offers armchair comfort.

next to the adjoining car as possible was it possible to open the driver's side door enough to squeeze out.

Which gives you some idea of what we mean by the style of living a man with a $6,000 car should have. He should, for instance, be able to afford also a home with a nice wide driveway and a roomy — even for a one-car family — very roomy garage.

Power and performance

On the drag strip, the Imperial turned the quarter in 16.58 seconds, and was travelling a true 86.36 when the quarter ran out. The acceleration — the ratio is 13.7 pounds per horse, with the maximum 350 horses at 4,500 rpm — is positive from a stoplight, from the freeway on-ramp, or from 60-plus mph

true). You also see smaller cars darting into spaces that look just too small.

More seriously, it might be a good idea, on a car of this size, to go back to the free-standing parking and stop lights atop the fenders, so that the driver will know exactly where the corners of his vehicle are located, though this knowledge comes with time.

Luckily, not all driving is in heavy traffic or in cramped quarters, and for the highway or freeway, the Imperial is hard to beat for ease and comfort. Bumps that would slow another car are hardly felt; smaller bumps, ones that might still give a little jolt, are only heard, not felt at all.

One very nice thing about the Imperial — you don't have to worry about going too slow. We handled our test vehicle in all kinds of traffic, including traffic that

the carport of a friend's apartment. The carport is reached through a narrow alleyway, its spaces are at 90 degree angles to the alleyway, and the spaces themselves are not too generous.

It was possible to park the Imperial — but not easy.

Lining up, with little more than the Imperial's 19-foot length to get turned halfway-to, involved many fillings and backings, with the power steering getting a dead-wheel workout.

But that wasn't the worst. The 79-plus inches of width all but filled the carport's available space. Only by pulling as close

as a shove on the gas puts the Torque-flight into passing gear.

What does 'positive' mean? In this case, it means that at any of the conditions cited, the driver is gently but firmly pressed back into the soft seats . . . and that is a nice feeling, indeed.

Roadability and handling

Driving the Imperial is a pleasure most of the time. In heavy traffic you have the feeling the world has become too small, and that every car is a distinct danger (which, come to think of it, is literally

Power disc brakes at the front bring the Imperial to a halt in good stopping distance for a car of its weight. Power assist is a bit touchy.

just wasn't moving for fair periods of time, and moving only slowly after that, and the temperature gauge didn't seem to notice the lack of air flow any more than it noticed an 80 mph slipstream.

On highways and freeways, the auto speed control makes driving almost too easy — but the control, on the turn signal stalk, could be in a better location. A button on the end of the arm takes over the right foot duties at any speed over 30 mph. To speed or slow, just use the gas or the brakes, as conditions warrant. After slowing, you can resume the speed established simply by twisting the knurled ring set a half-inch down the arm. After increasing speed for passing, the control takes over as soon as the foot is removed from the gas pedal.

The Imperial's ride is not 100 per cent perfect, however. Thanks to plenty of overhang fore and aft, and a fair amount on each side, plus concessions to a soft-as-can-be ride, this car can lean in several directions — at once.

Hitting a dip on the road sets up a gentle rocking that continues, *a la* ship in a gentle sea, for several seconds. A sharp turn taken at any speed, as in hitting the gas while turning onto a freeway on-ramp, induces a fair amount of sway, enough to make you happy you have your seat belt on and a firm grip on the steering wheel.

For most driving, the ride isn't bad — and the car does have front end telescopic dampers and a anti-roll bar restraining the longitudinal torsion bars on its wishbone independents.

Brakes and safety

Stopping, with power brakes, is positive — you feel the seat belt you'd better be wearing. In braking tests, the Imperial came to a complete stop from a true 60 mph in 160 feet and was still under control. Any faster stop — or attempt at a stop — is likely to leave car and contents sitting sideways. In handling during hard stops short of panic, the Imperial has a better score than many large cars on the road today.

If seat belts are a must, the shoulder belts presented a slight problem. Even with an adjustable steering wheel, there was no good compromise when faced with three different factors — fairly straight-arm steering position, a shoulder harness even with some play, and the position of the ash tray. Granted, it is most likely not wise to smoke while driving, but nicotine fiends are not likely to worry about this.

In any case, the ash tray was the only item on the dash that could not be reached easily, even with the shoulder belt, slightly slacked, on duty.

Comfort and convenience

So much of things the Imperial has in common with so many other cars. The word for this vehicle is "luxury," and you become aware of the luxury the minute you get behind the wheel — or even take a good look.

It is not at all difficult to become attached to the seats — neither bench nor bucket, but a cross between the two that approximates the ease and comfort of the huge leather chairs that belong in front of a roaring fire on a cold night. But a car on the highway is not a seat before the fire, and for the driver, at least, there could be a little more lateral support, even if this destroyed front seat symme-

Plenty of room under the Imperial's rear deck — but heaven help the man who has to unpack to get at the spare tire.

try. After all, there is plenty of room for three in the front seat, but seat belts for only two.

The front seat passenger has a lever below seat level next the door that turns the seat into a lounge, though the operator's manual suggests this not be done while wearing the seat belt, which makes sense.

The driver has an even better deal. In addition to being able to control fore-and-aft seat positioning, he has power-assisted seat height and angle control with three switches located just above the floor on the side of the street. Playing with these is one way to pass the time when held up in traffic, but look out — fiddling with them can, unconsciously, become a habit.

With a dashboard — plus window controls on the arm rest — giving an airliner cockpit air, the handle for closing the doors gives the Imperial an oddly quaint touch. Even though it is rectangular in shape, the handle is a good, old-fashioned door-knocker-type ring. Perhaps, though, this is intended as an 'imperial' touch. It gets the doors closed (with the 'thunk' of closing giving a constant reminder that this is a solidly built vehicle) and that is what counts, and the arrangement also eliminates potentially dangerous protuberances.

Instruments of immediate interest to the driver are centered around the easily-read (for that matter, they all are) speedometer, which measures off to the 120 mph mark. Since a claimed top speed is 119, Imperial deserves marks for honesty. The gear shift indicator is just below the speedometer and, as usual, the ignition starter will only start when the car is in 'park' or 'neutral.' An interesting dash signal has no meaning of its own — it is a red light that reads 'check gauges' and is called the 'sentry signal.' It comes on when the gas level drops below a quarter-tank, when oil pressure drops, or when the car overheats. Another light warns that part of the braking system has failed — which is most likely the best possible way of getting that bit of information. Two more signals in the near vicinity of the speedometer might well be done without. These are the 'lock doors' and 'fasten belts' warning lights, which come on as the ignition is engaged. Any driver who needs these is either not mentally equipped to drive any car, or, at least, is for the time being better off calling a cab.

All of our carping about 'idiot lights' and the lack of proper instrumentation may be beginning to pay off. The Imperial's dash has a proper complement of gauges to tell the thinking driver things he would like to know about conditions out there under the hood. There's an honest to Henry Ford oil pressure gauge and alternator charge dial as well as a real coolant thermometer. What bugs us still is the necessity of going to the top of the line to find these items.

Other switches on the dash control the lights, the windshield wipers, the windshield washer, the dash lights, the AM-FM radio-tape player console, and the air conditioning-heater combination.

Another big dashboard plus — a glove compartment' that has plenty of room for gloves, Kleenex, road maps, auto club folder, and quite a few other items as well.

Not that the Imperial is perfect, just, as today's cars go, very nearly so.

One literally jarring note is the headlights. They close with a loud 'clunk' that takes getting used to. In a car as well-finished as the Imperial, an inexpensive rubber cushion for the headlights is noticed by its absence.

The automatic temperature control, with variable force, is a definite asset to driver and passenger comfort — but for a few minutes every time it is turned on, the car's interior is filled with an unpleasant odor of . . . of what? Damp inner tubes is one odor that comes to mind and, even in memory, it is not pleasant.

And then there is the trunk, which is as spacious as could be desired, *except.* Except for those rare unfortunate mo-

ments when a tire has to be changed. The spare is positioned so that the entire trunk must be emptied in order to take out that spare tire, which can cut the dickens from a long-distance driving time average.

Another 'minus' item to be scored against the Imperial, is one that may apply only to the test car, the finish.

Chrysler prides itself on pre-delivery checks on all its cars, with pre-delivery centers performing some 100 checks before cars are delivered to the dealer (or so it is claimed) and with the dealer hitting another 20 or so items.

Not all dealers take advantage of this service, but someone really should make sure the chrome trim along the sides has been properly fitted, since this is something easily spotted.

Whoever should have checked the side trim on our test car just didn't. The leading edges of the trim strips were noticeably separated from the body.

Also detracting from otherwise beautiful looks of the car were packing fibers escaping from behind the trim strips . . . would you believe a shaggy Imperial?

Well, perhaps these are really minor items, but a purchaser who has shelled out $6,000 or more for his set of wheels has a right to expect that just such minor

items, as well as the major ones, would be taken care of before he takes delivery.

Economy

It goes without saying that this car takes the very best in go juice, but so do a lot of other cars that don't approach it in price. Manufacturer's claimed gas mileage is 11 to the gallon, but in several hundred miles of driving under widely varying conditions, our test car gave just a fraction better than that. With a tank that holds 24 gallons, there are less than four fuel stops for every 1,000 miles. Oil consumption? Unnoticed.

Summary

The Imperial is a luxury car, and it is intended for the owner who can afford luxurious ways, including a luxurious home. It isn't for the guy who parks his car on the street, nor is it for the driver with a heavy foot. This car is for the man who has it made and wants the world to know it without going quite so far as to travel with a chauffeur handling the driving chores.

A perfect car it isn't — but its faults, if indeed they can be called such, are minor.

It costs a lot, but for the money, it is a lot of car. ♠

In addition to 440 cubic inches of power, space under the hood contains a plumber's nightmare, all of it necessary.

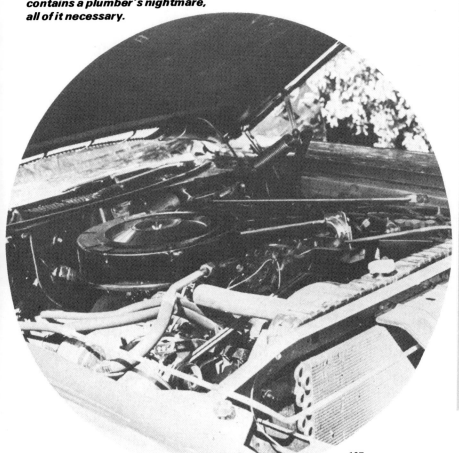

Imperial
Data in Brief

DIMENSIONS

Overall length (in.)	229.7
Wheelbase (in.)	127
Width (in.)	79.1
Height (in.)	55.7
Tread, front (in.)	62.4
Tread, rear (in.)	61.1
Turning diameter (ft.)	47.9
Fuel tank capacity (gal.)	24
Trunk capacity (cu. ft.)	n.a.

ENGINE

Type	ohv, V-8
Displacement (cu. in.)	440
Horsepower (at 4400 rpm)	350
Torque (lb./ft. at 2800 rpm)	480

WEIGHT, TIRES, BRAKES

Weight (lb. as tested)	5,365
Tires	9.15 × 15
Brakes, front	disc
Brakes, rear	drum

SUSPENSION

Front	independent, wishbones, longitudinal torsion bars, anti-roll bar
Rear	rigid axle, semi-elliptic leaf springs, transverse linkage bar, telescopic shocks

PERFORMANCE

Standing ¼ mile (sec.)	16.58
Speed at end of ¼ mile (mph)	86.36
Braking (from 60 mph ft.)	160

IMPERIAL

EXTERIOR STYLING CHANGES, IMPROVED INTERIOR TRIM FOR 1970.

New exterior and interior styling, new features and model relignment are included in Chrysler's Imperial for 1970.

Changes up front feature a new, more massive appearing grille with concealed headlights. Rear changes include new full-width taillights with backup lights relocated to the center. Individual Imperial name block letters have been added to the bumper.

Changes in side ornamentation include addition of a full length sill molding treatment, use of a double paint stripe in place of the upper body side molding, and a new rear side marker light. Available as an option is a vinyl body-side molding.

All-new, substantially improved interior trim designs enhance the interior appointment levels to a new high in luxury. The LeBaron 50/50 all-leather split bench seat with individual arm rests and passenger recliner is available in seven colors. New bench seats with bucket-contoured backs are available.

Among the other Imperial features for 1970 are: quieter interiors resulting from a new sound insulation package; new design single caliper full-floating power disc brakes; new wider rear track; long-wearing, high traction fiberglass belted tires as standard equipment; new windshield-concealed antenna with all radios; an AM/FM Multiplex-Stereo tape radio system

integrally designed into the instrument panel and featuring five speakers and the windshield-concealed antenna, and an optional rear seat heater.

Imperial is available in the Crown two and four-door hardtops and the LeBaron two and four-door hardtops. The Crown four-door sedan is discontinued for 1970.

Dimensions for the 1970 Imperial include: wheelbase, 127.0 inches; front tread, 62.4 inches; rear tread, 62.0 inches; length, 229.7 inches; height, 55.1 inches; width, 79.1 inches; effective head room front, 38.0 inches; head room rear, 37.5 inches; leg room front, 41.8 inches; leg room rear, 35.8 inches.

New full-width taillights with backup lights relocated to the center and Imperial name letters on bumper are among rear styling changes.

COLOSSAL COUPÉ

'Big is beautiful' is an expression often heard in relation to American cars. And to Dutchman Peter Sap, size really is important. That's why he is so fond of his 1969 Chrysler Imperial Coupé. **RON HERLAAR** *tries to figure out what else the owner of this magnificent specimen likes about the colossal coupé*

ABOVE: The lights are showing – it must be awake!
BELOW: Chrysler's truly massive (440cu.in.) V8
BELOW LEFT: Comfort and luxury can be found on board

EIGHT YEARS ago, Peter Sap left Holland and moved to the United States to try his luck on the other side of the Atlantic. In an attempt to earn a reasonable living, he started exporting classic European cars from the USA to the Netherlands and, in his search for Triumphs, MGs and Jaguars, he reckons he managed to see almost every square inch of the States. Nice work if you can get it ...

Peter remembers well the day he towed a Jaguar E-Type through the heavy traffic of downtown New York. Wandering around the underground parking facilities of the Empire State Building, he discovered an early twelve-cylinder Jaguar E-Type coupé, covered in dust and looking forelorn. With help from a security guard, Peter traced the owner of the vehicle and asked him if he was willing to sell his car.

At first the wealthy New Yorker didn't want to know about selling his Jaguar, but after a good night's sleep he reconsidered and was willing to negotiate. Evidently, the man did not have any idea about the value of the car, accepting an offer of just $5000. The fact that he had to hire a tow truck to 'drag' the Jaguar to the harbour did not bother Peter at all. He knew that he had just clinched the deal of a lifetime.

'Those days are over now', admits Peter. 'Prices have gone up and the quality of most of the cars is below average. Good European classic cars for a reasonable price are becoming scarce. To find one, you have to travel a lot more than you did a few years ago.'

As his scources began to dry up, Peter decided to move back to the Netherlands. Still, he does manage to spend a couple of weeks each year over in the United States, buying secondhand American pickup trucks, a species which is quite popular amongst certain enterprising groups of Dutchmen – such as contractors – due to their large tonnage and low road tax rate over in Holland.

> ## 'Whilst travelling round, Peter sometimes stumbles upon the odd classic American car that he cannot resist buying'

Whilst travelling round, Peter sometimes stumbles upon the odd classic American car that he cannot resist buying. Usually, these are for his own use, but when the collection becomes a little large he usually persuades himself to sell one or two. Oh, decisions, decisions.

Peter's preference is for American cars of the Sixties and Seventies. Not just any cars from those decades, but the truly BIG ones. As far as Peter's concerned, big IS beautiful. Indeed, that is the most important reason behind his purchase of this 1969 Chrysler Imperial Coupé.

'What I like most about the car is, I must admit, its size', explains the Dutchman. 'It is a coupé but it's almost six metres in length. Amazing!'

The owner of the big blue Chrysler bought the car at an auction in Texas. 'I was in the States when I read about the auction in a magazine. I figured that among the 500 or so cars being sold, there had to be at least one or two that would be of interest to me, so I took a plane to Texas.'

One of the things that immediately struck Peter when he arrived at the auction was the fact that none of the Americans who were bidding were checking the cars before buying them. 'They were buying cars, some of which were going for more than $50,000, without even looking under the bonnet.' No wonder people seemed a bit puzzled when they saw a certain Dutchman crawling underneath cars, testing suspension and listening to engines ...

The Chrysler Imperial Coupé, now demanding just about all the space there is around the small dykes and country roads of Betuwe, Holland, is one of the just over 16,000 such models which left the factory in 1969. The overall styling of the 300 series Chrysler was similar to that of the Newport; however, the former had a horizontal bar grille with a black insert surrounded by a heavily chromed bumper – one of the details that Peter Sap specifically likes about the Imperial Coupé. He also admires the car's hidden

COLOSSAL COUPÉ

headlights; with its 'shutters' closed, the Chrysler looks mighty impressive, almost mysterious.

The typical 'horizontal' styling of the Chrysler continues round the back. The long tail lights, separated by '300' lettering in the centre of the huge chrome bumper, give the car a very unusual and charismatic look.

Peter's auction bid of $3200 was obviously enough for him to become the new owner of what must be one of the longest coupés on this earth – 5.24 metres in total. And we reckon

'In many ways, Peter Sap couldn't have found himself a more ideal American auto. He loves big cars'

he had a bargain. The two-door Imperial is completely original apart from its colour, the car having been treated to a respray whilst in the States.

The engine was also overhauled some time ago by the previous owner, although it still looks as good as new even now. Highlighted in red on the shiny air filter unit are the letters TNT. They arouse great expectations about the performance of the 440cu.in. V8, fed through a four-barrel carburettor. And yet 350bhp (at 4400rpm) is not exactly astonishing from a 7.2-litre engine, I guess, particularly when its trying to propel 1868kg of good old American steel at a pace.

The factory price of the Imperial Coupé in 1969 was $4714 in standard form. Over and above the Newport model's specification, the 300 series came equipped with Torqueflite automatic transmission, a heavy duty battery and concealed headlamps.

Also as standard came indicator lights on the corner of each front wing, looking like the telescopic sight of a gun. A whole new experience, those flashing warning lights a couple of metres in front of you instead of merely on the dashboard ...

The interior trim of the 300 series was inevitably more luxurious than that of the Newport versions. Instead of all-vinyl bench seats, the Imperial Coupé featured buttoned foam seat cushions both front and rear. The front

bench seat with fold-down centre armrest in Peter's car is electrically adjustable six different ways, an extra which cost $103 back in '69.

That was not the only option on this particular blue Chrysler. In fact, its first owner invested in almost every extra available at the time, including power brakes and steering, a Tilt-A-Scope steering wheel, electric windows, air conditioning, central door locking, tinted windows and a vinyl roof covering. In all, these options increased the price of this high-spec Imperial Coupé by almost $1200 – adding around 25 per cent to the standard factory price.

In many ways, Peter Sap couldn't have found himself a more ideal American auto. He loves big cars; we discovered that earlier on. And he's also a fan of those that are packed full of original optional extras, anything which helps to make a car different from its identical looking counterparts. With his Imperial Coupe, Peter has the best of both worlds: sheer size and an upmarket, heavily 'optioned' specification. Even if Peter's collection needs 'thinning out' in the future, we have a feeling that his much loved Chrysler will be staying exactly where it is. Yes indeed. **CA**

COLOSSAL COUPÉ

Imperial - 1973

Imperial 2-Door Hardtop

Imperial 4-Door Hardtop Interior

In automotive design, engineering excellence, quality workmanship and attention to detail...this is Chrysler Corporation's top-of-the-line entry.

As befits a car in its class, the Imperial is a complete automobile. The biggest engine we make, a 440 cubic inch 4-barrel V-8, is standard. So are luxury features like: TorqueFlite automatic transmission with part-throttle kickdown. A vinyl roof in your choice of six colors. Smooth, silent Torsion-Quiet Ride. Power brakes with front discs and self-adjusting rear drums. Power steering and power windows. Air conditioning with automatic temperature control. Tinted glass. A "Rim-Blow" steering wheel. The Electronic Ignition System. And a new electronic digital clock.

Among options you may want to consider are an AM/FM multiplex radio with 8-track stereo tape...sun roof...and the new Security Alarm System with optional power door locks.

The 1973 Imperial model lineup consists of a 4-door and a 2-door hardtop.

Exterior Dimensions (Imperial 4-Door Hardtop)
Wheelbase ... 127 in.
Overall Length ... 235.3 in.
Overall Width ... 79.6 in.
Overall Height ... 56.2 in.
Front Track ... 62.4 in.
Rear Track ... 63.4 in.

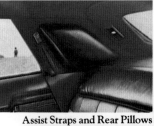

Assist Straps and Rear Pillows

Electronic Digital Clock

AM/FM Stereo Tape

Electronic Ignition

IMPERIAL
Le Baron

The only exterior change you'll find on the '71 Imperials is the addition of a couple of chrome escutcheon plates containing the eagle trademark to each of the headlight covers. The 4-door pillar sedan was dropped a year ago leaving only 2- and 4-door hardtops, and now the Crown series has been dropped, leaving these styles available only as LeBarons.

However, this seeming retrogression seems unimportant when you consider Imperial's new optional 4-wheel anti-skid system for its standard power-assisted, front-disc/rear-drum brake setup. This should certainly rate as the most important innovation in brakes since Duesenberg pioneered 4-wheel hydraulics back in 1920.

Experts have long known that the quickest way to stop is to keep all four wheels turning at a rate just short of locking up. With this technique the brakes are working at maximum efficiency and there is some contribution from the tire treads. And as long as the front wheels are moving, you have steering control.

Faced with an emergency, however, most drivers step on their brakes as hard as they can and the car slides uncontrollably to a stop. Here, the brakes are doing no work at all. Once the wheels are locked, they cease to contribute. All that's stopping you is the rapidly disappearing rubber at the points where the tires are rubbing against the pavement.

Obviously the stopping distance required will be greater and because the front wheels are locked, you can't steer around the obstacle that caused your panic. It's not a good technique, but few people function at their best in an emergency. Even experts, in stopping contests where there is no emergency, have a difficult time in consistently "feathering" the brakes to an ideal, controlled stop.

Two years ago Ford, in conjunction with Kelsey-Hayes, announced an optional electronic system that worked on the rear wheels only. This was an improvement but it still didn't and doesn't preclude the front wheels from locking, particularly on a wet or icy surface. In a car so equipped, you stop in a straighter line than before but you still can't steer around an obstacle in a panic stop.

Imperial's new system, developed in cooperation with the Bendix Corp., works on all four wheels. While it is functioning it is impossible to lock the wheels no matter how hard you try. If it should malfunction, it's "fail safe." This means that the system will automatically disconnect itself and you'll still have ordinary brakes.

The system consists of a logic controller which is essentially the brain, sensors at each wheel to signal impending lock-up, and three modulating devices, one for each front wheel and one for both rear wheels. Since even modern brakes are never perfectly equalized and the road surface might be slightly different under each tire, sensors are necessary at each wheel. If any wheel tends to lock, brake pressure at that wheel is electronically released and then applied at a frequency of about four times a second.

Ford presently charges $194 for its 2-wheel system as optional equipment on Thunderbirds and Lincolns (it's standard on the high-priced Mark III Continental). Imperial, however, will understandably have to charge more because the electronic system to four wheels is much more elaborate. Even $250, however, would be money well spent. For one, it might save your life. For another, tires for a car like the Imperial cost around $60 each and one panic stop can ruin a set of four

unless they are protected by an anti-skid system.

Other Imperial changes include a redesigned instrument panel and integral headrests for the bench seats. The new panel, however, still includes gauges for every engine function backed up by both individual and a master warning light. A power vent window for the 4-door hardtop is a rather odd option to the standard ventless glass which is also power operated. Standard power assists also are provided for brakes and steering.

The only engine choice is a 440-cubic-inch, 335-hp V-8 coupled to an automatic transmission. This one lost 30 hp in the process of being detuned for operation on low-octane fuels, but the average Imperial buyer is not likely to notice the difference in performance. He's also very likely to go on buying premium fuels.

Despite Lincoln's move to make it standard, automatic air conditioning will still cost extra on Imperials. The concealed headlights can be ordered

with an automatic washing system that consists of a small nylon brush with an attached nozzle. Whenever you actuate the windshield washer system, this brush cleans the low beam lights at the rate of 50 strokes a minute for a claimed 90% of clean lamp efficiency. All kinds of radios, 8-track stereo and the cassette system are optional, and it should be noted that Imperial is the only Corporation car to use a windshield with an imbedded antenna. •

LE BARON

ENGINE: 440 cu ins (335 hp).
TRANSMISSION: 3-spd auto std.
SUSPENSION: Torsion bar front, leaf rear.
STEERING: Power std; curb-to-curb 44.83 ft.
BRAKES: Front power discs, rear drums std.
FUEL CAPACITY: 23.0 gals.
DIMENSIONS: Wheelbase 127 ins. **Track** 62.4 ins front, 62.0 rear. **Width** 79-79.1 ins. **Length** 229.7 ins. **Height** 55.6-56.7 ins. **Weight** 5500 lbs. **Trunk** 17.2 cu ft.
BODY STYLES: 2-dr hdtp, 4-dr hdtp.

LeBaron

While automotive trends and industry statements have spelled out the decline of the annual model change, Chrysler's Imperial line, in direct contradiction, has fresh new styling for 1972. In addition, the car has a number of engineering innovations to improve safety, ecology and driver and passenger comfort to complement its overall luxury.

"Chrysler Corporation's objective for the 1972 Imperial LeBaron was to realize the maximum in quality, reliability, and maintainability and still retain the distinction of tasteful high style," says R. D. McLaughlin, general sales manager. How well they have done remains to be seen, but the number of changes in the Imperial line this year, in the face of the trend toward fewer changes, is impressive.

Imperial is Chrysler's biggest car, built on a 127-in. wheelbase with an overall length of more than 229 ins. The Imperial may be the largest unit-body car ever built. This type of body construction is usually limited to much smaller passenger cars because the smaller wheelbases require less metal structure to maintain body tolerances. Chrysler apparently has solved the strength problem to its satisfaction, and has no intention to revert to the traditional body and frame design of most other big cars.

Two models are offered in the Imperial line, a 2- and a 4-door hardtop. Stylists made a complete change in sheetmetal and included a new appearance. Bumpers were of paramount concern. The 1972 bumpers are built to protect the lights, exhaust system and heating and cooling systems during light-contact collisions. The fender skirts are made of fiberglas this year, a change in material that makes this body part more corrosion resistant.

Standard engine on the Imperial is the 440-cu.-in. V-8. This engine has a single snorkel air cleaner, and a new water pump with a rotating ceramic element that gives longer service life. A redesigned alternator has heavy-duty diodes and a lower operating temperature that gives improved performance at higher operating speeds. This year Chrysler is adding a synthetic lubricant to all its high power engines at the factory that provides anti-scuff protection during engine break-in.

A number of safety and quality features are new for 1972. A redesigned low-beam headlight that has a 5¾-in. sealed beam provides higher wattage and increased candlepower for improved night driving visibility. At the rear, brighter backup lamps have a higher candlepower and improved lighting direction for greater ease in seeing while backing up. Imperial's quality assurance program has been expanded. In addition to each Imperial being road tested prior

to shipment, new electronic test equipment has been designed for 1972. An ultrasonic system tests all aspects of metallurgical realiability of critical components. Brakes, steering components, axles, and suspension forgings are among the many parts that are checked. A new electronic ignition system is standard on all Imperials. This and all other systems are checked with another electronic tester while the car is on the assembly line. The machine is not only capable of testing reliability, but also has diagnostic abilities should there be a malfunction. Through electronic and computer equipment, all Imperials are checked for transmission wiring systems and instrument panel defects. Finally, an inspection is made through a road simulator chassis dynamometer. The new electronic ignition system eliminates the need for breaker points, a common cause for increased emissions due to engine misfirings, and except for the required changing of spark plugs, it is essentially maintenance free. The only wear areas in the distributor are simple bearings, previously proven reliable, which need a drop of oil for lubrication every 24,000 miles.

Greater driver and passenger comfort is provided by improvements in both heating and air conditioning. The Chrysler Air Temperature Control system makes automatic adjustment to the interior temperature by the driver merely setting the dial. An improved 3-speed windshield wiper washer system is standard. Wipers are now activated automatically whenever the washer button is depressed.

A new lap and shoulder belt system has been installed on the 1972 Imperial. Seat belt anchor locations have been changed on some models to provide more comfortable lap belt angles. Shoulder belt storage clips have also been relocated so the belts are easier to reach and remove from stored positions. Front seat lap belts and shoulder belts are a single-buckle, 3-point system whereby both belts are unfastened simultaneously. Automatic locking retractors are used at the driver's and right passenger's seating positions for lap-belt storage. The locking retractor ensures that sudden forward motion of a person wearing the lap belt is arrested while not requiring adjustment when the belt is initially fastened.

IMPERIAL

ENGINE: 440 cu. ins. (225 hp).
TRANSMISSION: 3-spd. auto.
SUSPENSION: Torsion bar front, leaf rear.
STEERING: Power std., curb-to-curb 44.7 ft.
BRAKES: Power front discs, rear drums std.
FUEL CAPACITY: 23 gals.
DIMENSIONS: Wheelbase 127 ins. **Track** 62.4 ins. front, 63.4 ins. rear. **Width** 79.6 ins. **Length** 229.5 ins. **Height** 56.0 ins. **Weight** 5085 lbs. **Trunk** 18.6 cu. ft.
BODY STYLES: 2-dr. hdtp., 4-dr. hdtp.

Simplified But Elegant

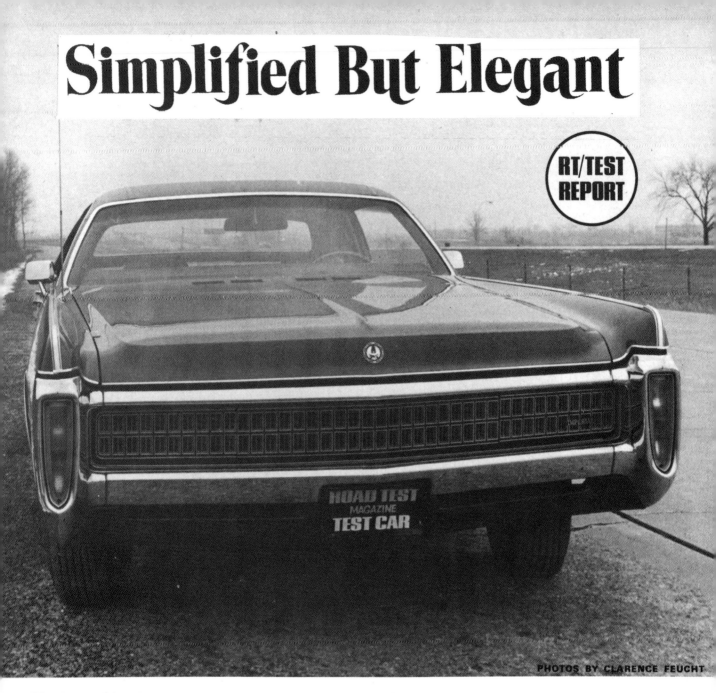

The Imperial LeBaron has been styled to withstand the acid test of time. And it suffers only from lack of exposure.

For a combination of reasons, the current model year produced very few "all new" car offerings. One of the handful which was considerably revised and thus rates this status is Chrysler Corp.'s prestige luxury auto, the Imperial LeBaron, subject of this ROAD TEST evaluation.

For 1972, the Imperial got a new body and, in the process, substantially changed styling. It now has what Chrysler calls "simplified but elegant" lines. To many critics of car design the Imperial comes off as one of the most tasteful renditions on the contemporary scene. In all basic ingredients, Imperial's appearance looks like it will be good for several years and also stand the acid test of time and trends — something

some earlier versions (and those of the competition) didn't.

As was the case last year, the Imperial LeBaron lineup is super simple, consisting of but two cars. These are the 2-door and 4-door hardtops, both on 229.5-in. bodies, each with the same 127-in. wheelbase — three inches more than Chrysler models. Variety, in the Imperial lineup — and individuality — are via the extensive option route, plus a wide choice of exterior finishes, interior colors, fabrics, other materials — and bucket seats, to name just a few items.

Standard equipment on all '72 Imperial cars makes a list so long we won't take up the large amount of space needed to name all of them. Highlights include vinyl top, air conditioning, tinted

glass, power windows, steering and brakes (with discs in front).

In addition, ROAD TEST's car had a group of options also too long to enumerate in this introduction, but covered later. Most important of these, and the only one we asked for on a "must" basis, was the Bendix Corp. 4-wheel anti-skid system, which costs a tidy $344 extra and, we feel, is worth every dime of that sum.

Chrysler calls the Bendix system "Sure-Brake." We tested it at the firm's proving grounds at Chelsea, Mich. in June of 1970, prior to introduction for the first time anywhere as an option only on the '71 Imperial. We had another turn with it on the Bendix skid pad at the firm's South Bend, Ind. proving ground last July. But for this report a few weeks of typical commuter and out of town trip driving, plus some brake

148

Arrow shaped knob protruding downward just below center section of steering wheel is release and lock for telescoping feature of tilt steering wheel. In and out movement of wheel is up to 3-in. Inside hood release is just above parking brake foot pedal.

tests of our own were wanted to get an unsupervised feel of this all-wheel package, which no other U.S. car offers.

A few other basic details about ROAD TEST's car: It was a four door LeBaron finished in a tastefully attractive exterior finish called gold leaf metallic. Interior had a luxurious gold cloth combined with leather and high quality vinyl. The car was nearly new — 04869 miles on the odometer. With the many options this car had you'd have to bring about $8000 to the showroom. And not expect much — if any — change back. The "bare" base price in Detroit, without taxes, tags, preparation charge (or even a radio, for that matter) is $6762. And worth it.

Unlike the case with most cars, the prospective purchaser of a 1972 Chrys-

ler Imperial doesn't have to contend with a long list of possible variables in the drive train category. There's but one engine, one transmission, one axle ratio and one suspension. Only driveline options are an anti-spin differential and a choice of tires — there are two extra types.

Powering the Imperial is the well-proven single 4-bbl. 440 cu in V8, one of the best balanced, smoothest running auto engines in the world. It produces 225 hp at 4400 rpm and 345 lb. ft. of torque at 3200 rpm (both SAE net) and runs very happily on regular grade fuel, having a compression ratio of 8.2 to 1.

Most important improvement in this engine for the '72 Imperial is use of Chrysler Corp.'s new transistorized electronic ignition system, which avoids design requiring breaker points and is therefore maintenance free except for a few drops of oil for the simple bearings every 24,000 miles. It's optional equipment and provides faster starts in all weather. Higher secondary (spark plug) voltage particularly at the higher rpm's helps keep the plugs clean for peak performance and at the same time extends their life. The alternator has also been revised for cooler running and thus longer life and for high speed driving output. Water pump design has been revised, again for longer service, now having a rotating ceramic element.

Imperial's automatic transmission, unchanged since last year, continues as one of the smoothest and quietest in the industry. It drives the wheels through a 3.23 to 1 differential. ROAD TEST's car had Chrysler's optional Sure-Grip rear, which costs an extra $56.80. It is well worth the price in better traction and reduced back tire wear. This is particularly true if the car will be operated much on ice, snow or other poor friction surfaces and if the driver often has a

In hard cornering Imperial's suspension gets a little strung out. Under power (in this pose) there's some understeer, plus a bit of tire wear.

tendency to push hard in starts from a standstill, as will be covered.

The typical buyer of a big U.S.-built luxury car isn't supposed to expect that a lot of engineering emphasis was placed on the auto's power-performance capabilities. These attributes are usually pretty far down on the priority list of those who buy this kind of vehicle. However, an increasing number of luxury car buyers want more than sheer comfort and a lot of conveniences in today's prestige cars. There's a growing need for get up and go in traffic. Like getting onto a high speed turnpike and in hard-nosed and moderately high speed commuter traffic. Result has been a trend to make the previously somewhat sluggish large "quality" cars much better performers. Peak torque developed and the consequent acceleration rates are much improved over a decade or so ago.

The '72 Imperial is a good example of this trend and even a little surprising for an auto which tips the scales (without driver or passengers) at over 4900 lbs. If the driver puts his foot into it, this car will move out with just about everything on the road except performance types. It will probably out-accelerate over half the late model cars on the road.

With transmission preloading, a problem with the Imperial, ROAD TEST found, involved initial rear wheel traction, even with the optional locking axle, which the car had. To avoid excessive tire spin on all but very abrasive surfaces anything close to maximum torque must be avoided until after the Imperial is

Power seats are individually controlled and have separate fold-down arm rests. In this view, driver's seat is fully back and right seat fully forward, showing maximum travel. With seats even and arm rests up, front will accommodate three adults.

underway a few feet. Otherwise elapsed times will suffer. So will the tires, from accelerated wear.

Interestingly, the 440 engine is sufficiently muscular that ROAD TEST got ET's which were almost as quick from idle, with a fast, smooth flooring of the accelerator as when the brakes were set and the transmission loaded under maximum rpm.

The Imperial was perhaps most impressive in runs from standstill to 30 mph. From idle, this required 4.8 sec. Transmission pre-loading cut it to 4.7 sec. Best zero to 45 mph times were 7.9 sec. from idle and 7.2 sec with pre-loading. From standstill to 60 mph required under 12 sec. with the best time from idle being 11.5 sec. Only 11.2 sec. was needed with the transmission loaded. With preloading 0 to 75 mph required 15.3 sec. and 15.7 sec. from idle. Best ¼-mile ET was 16.6 sec.

There was a significant variation between times for specific types of runs depending on tire spin. Some difficulty was encountered in getting minimum burn consistent with quickest acceleration. It's easy to get excessive slippage from a standstill if the accelerator is floored too quickly.

As might already have been guessed, Imperial performance in traffic doesn't leave anything to be desired unless the driver is of the confirmed hot rod type. Part throttle kickdown helps make the car almost nimble in operation at rapidly changing speeds and picking its way through the pack.

Roadability-wise, the 1972 Imperial is one of the best cars on the highway today. Very few autos come close to equalling it. One thing that makes it a great car for long trips at high cruising

speeds is solid mass — just a few pounds short of 2 ½ tons.

Chrysler engineers have brought the combination of torsion bar suspension in front, and long supple leaf springs in back, with modifications in shock absorber design and valving, to a very high state of refinement. Helping too is one of the most sophisticated rubber bushing isolation packages in production. It provides an abundance of harshness absorption while maintaining a comparatively firm feel to the car.

About the best way to sum up Imperial's overall roadability characteristics is to observe that the car gives a feeling of having been designed to run a lot faster than most state laws — and the general level of highway construction — permit. On an Autobahn in Germany, the auto could probably cruise rather effortlessly at 100 mph all day long without tiring the driver. We're assuming, of course, that he has the skills and experience to run a car at that kind of speed.

All this may not seem to have any bearing on today's U.S. highways and traffic conditions. It has. Point is that by producing a car with the high degree of roadability at top speeds, Chrysler engineers have put together an auto which is almost tame in the 65-75 mph range. In a single day's time an Imperial can eat up an impressive distance and still not leave a driver particulary tired.

In the handling category, of course, the Imperial can't be compared with autos which have the necessary suspension compromises (to ride quality) in order to excell in that respect. However, when subjected to rough treatment, the car does better than might be expected

Interesting feature of Imperial's headlight system is that for daytime driving only low beam lights will come on if car has optional automatic headlight dimmer. Its sensor, mounted behind grille, prevents inadvertent (or intentional) high beam use in daytime, there being sufficient incoming light to trigger it for low beam only.

of a large luxury auto. It's a fairly predictable vehicle and a forgiving one, with no bad handling personality traits. Purists, however, might fault the car for some understeer in hard direction changing, and perhaps for insufficient steering feed-back, but pushing the Imperial that far is really measuring it against the standards for another type vehicle.

For some drivers of big passenger cars, the Imperial may seem a bit massive, up front, particularly in overall broadness of the hood and fenders. But the car gets smaller the longer it is driven. It handles very well in traffic. But for maneuvering in parking lots and other tight places, some planning ahead and a bit more than average jockeying is required. These situations make the driver aware that this car has that 127-in. wheelbase, is 229.5 in. overall in length and requires over 44 ft (curb to curb) for a turn. Still, for what is offered on the open road, the less maneuverable characteristics of a big car can be tolerated.

More than any other way, it's in comfort and convenience that the '72 Imperial stands out most. The car provides a

Imperial trunk has 18.6 cu ft capacity, is carpeted. Spare tire has matching cover. Mechanism for opening trunk from inside car can be seen at top, center. Road Test's car had optional rear glass defroster and rear seat heater (upper right).

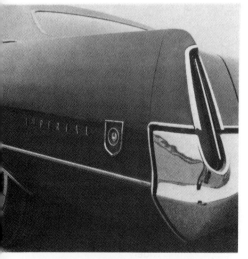

As is the case with the parking and turn signal lights up front, tail light lenses are recessed for better protection on '72 Imperial. Car is identified with much larger lettering on rear fenders than on front grille.

pile carpeting, automatic seat back release (2-door cars) rim blow steering wheel, four cigar lighters, inside hood release, 12-in. day/night inside mirror, remote control left outside mirror, remote trunk door release and under-coating.

All the above tends to insure a pretty high level of traveling comfort and convenience. Of other items available, at least one — a radio — is considered desirable. That item isn't standard on the Imperial, because there's a wide choice here and buyer's tastes vary so much it would be difficult to settle on a base model. The five currently available installations: AM/FM with search tuner and floor tuning control — $244.80; AM with 8-track stereo tape player — $271.50; AM/FM stereo — $301.60; AM/FM stereo with eight track tape player — $410.75 and AM/FM Stereo with cassette tape player — $436.40. All radios come with power antennas at no extra charge.

Other comfort and convenience-related options include automatic temperature control, which may be added to the standard air conditioner for a paltry $18.10. For hot weather areas, dual air conditioning with automatic control costs $250.80 additional. With it you must forego the otherwise available rear window defogger, which is priced at $31.15. ROAD TEST's car had the accessory group ($46.90 extra). It consists of a right outside mirror, color keyed floor mats, carpeted spare tire cover and door edge protectors.

Usually it's our practice to devote the immediately preceding portion of our evaluation to how a car rates in comfort and convenience, rather than take the space to cover what you get to contrib-

level of transportation which, to some tastes, is unequalled in a number of respects by any other U.S.-produced auto. Much that is standard equipment is of the comfort-convenience type so that little is left for the prospective owner to order in the way of options. If the approximate cost of all these otherwise extra-cost items is subtracted from the car's price, the theoretical sticker total for the basic Imperial, seen in that light, is reasonable indeed.

Miscellaneous standard items include an electric clock, courtesy map and glove box lights, rear seat reading lights, storage compartments with snap down lids in all doors, tripometer, 100% cut

On a moderately good, dry surface, Imperial will spin wheels more than a car length.

ute to these qualities, as we have done. Which leaves us no room to say much about our reactions to the car in this respect. Suffice it to say simply: It was great!

If there was an annual award for the safest car built in the U.S., Chrysler Corp.'s Imperial, equipped with the optional Bendix 4-wheel anti-skid system would surely be a top contender. Of all domestically produced passenger cars, only Imperial has a 4-wheel anti-wheel lockup package, to stress that point by repeating it.

Similar systems offered by Ford and General Motors are of the 2-wheel type, operating on the rear brakes only. The Imperial all-wheel approach isn't twice as good as these, because preventing back wheel lockup is recognized as doing over half the job. But the Bendix design offers one important plus. By making it impossible to lock the front wheels, steering control is retained with the Imperial installation even on very slippery surfaces.

There's no need to get into the philosophy behind the 2-wheel versus 4-wheel approaches, other than a few sentences to summarize each. It all comes down to a matter of dollars and cents, and customer acceptance. The Ford and GM 2-wheel systems cost around $200 while the Bendix-Imperial package runs $344.00. The latter sum has kept sales of the all-wheel system very low: Only 293 Imperial buyers out of 12,221 specified it during the 1971 model year — 2.4% of total sales. In the '72 model year, the figure is a bit higher: around 5% of 7803 Imperial sales through Feb. 29th. But Ford and GM have done much better in selling

optional 2-wheel anti-skid: Its cost is the apparent main reason.

Still, Imperial's anti-skid is an impressive system. In addition to planned checks of the option's performance, as part of brake evaluation, there was some routine driving on packed snow in which the option automatically came into play. A few other incidents involved stops in traffic on both wet and dry roadway which were sufficiently quick that there might have been wheel lockup. Here too the Sure-Brake installation operated — it is in a way a tire saver too, preventing flat spotting.

Aside from the anti-skid feature, Imperial's braking system, with power assist and front discs, is quite effective. In stops from high speed it might even be classed as impressive, considering the car's weight (4955 lb). On stops from 60 mph on dry but moderately worn pavement all were accomplished under 180 ft with the best measuring but 169 ft.

Imperial's brakes — considered apart from the Bendix package — exhibit very good resistance to premature wheel lockup. Unless excessive line pressures are induced by panic-type application, the anti-skid system didn't normally come into play on high friction road surfaces. However, if line pressure isn't dropped a little towards the end of a high speed stop (by easing pressure on the pedal) there will be a tendency for one or both rear wheels to stop turning. At that point anti-skid functions briefly.

Aside from Imperial's braking system, the car gets top marks in other safety-related aspects. Visibility is very good all around, with the rear glass providing a much better (broader) view than expected. It's actually more than the big (12-in.) inside day/night mirror covers. The remote-control left mirror adjusts easily and the matching optional right

mirror (part of the accessories group) is a safety plus.

Circuits (both standard) which lock all four doors from the driver's seat, and inactivate the power window mechanisms may also be considered safety features. (Window locking prevents children from playing with these switches.)

The windshield wiper-washer system on the '72 Imperial represents an improvement over prior models. When the washer button is depressed, the wipers automatically begin operation. Nice washer feature is that spray is produced only when the button is kept pressed down, permitting the driver to use as little — or as much — fluid as is needed, but no more. This arrangement conserves fluid since a fixed amount isn't used when less is required.

Adjustable headlight dimming, which may be varied for early or late switching to low beam is another safety feature. So is the time delay on headlights which permits illumination for a minute or so after leaving the car at night.

To tell it like it really is, the current Chrysler Imperial is a far better automobile than sales suggest, when compared to those of the General Motors Corp.'s Cadillac and Ford Motor Co.'s Lincoln Continental. It's a good question why so many buyers of top line cars buy other than Imperial. Two reasons, in particular, are rather widely accepted by auto industry observers.

One is image, which Imperial doesn't seem to have to the degree of the others. Then there's momentum developed over the years by the competing makes, particularly Cadillac. It is very hard to get a driver to switch from that

estimable auto after he has owned a few, several or many of them over a long period of time and has been generally happy with most — if not all — of them. This road tester happens to fall into this category.

Still, after a couple of weeks behind the wheel of a new Imperial, at least a few car owners — and maybe more than that — might well be tempted to switch to this car. It exhibits no defect in any respect, suffers only from lack of exposure. If and when a way is found to correct that situation, Chrysler Corp. will be selling a lot more Imperial cars; it deserves a greater following. ●

Imperial's under hood area has to be among the "busiest" of current model cars, especially if much optional equipment is ordered which has parts located here, and particularly with the Bendix anti-skid system, which adds a lot of large and small bits and pieces.

1972 IMPERIAL LeBARON 4-DOOR HARDTOP

SPECIFICATIONS AS TESTED

Engine. . . . . 440 cu in. OHV V8
Bore & stroke . . . . 4.32 x 3.75 ins.
Compression ratio . . . . 8.2 to one
Horsepower . . . . 225 (SAE net) at 4400 rpm
Torque. . . . . 345 lbs-ft at 3200 rpm
Transmission. . . . . 3-speed, Torque Flite automatic
**Steering . . . . 3.5 turns, lock to lock
44 ft, curb to curb
**Brakes . . . . disc front, drum rear
Suspension . . . . torsion bar front, leaf rear
Tires. . . . . L84 x 15, bias belted
Dimensions (ins.):

Wheelbase 127		Rear track 63.4	
Length. 229.5		Ground clearance . . 6.7	
Width 79.6		Height 56.0	
Front track 62.4		Weight . . . . 4955 lbs	

Capacities:

Fuel . . . . . . 23 gals   Oil . . . . 4 qts
Coolant. . . . 17.5 qts   Trunk. . . . . 18.6 cu ft

**Power assisted as tested

PERFORMANCE AND MAINTENANCE

Acceleration: Gears:
0-30 mph. . . . . 4.7 secs. 1st, 2nd
0-45 mph. . . . . 7.9 secs. 1st, 2nd
0-60 mph . . . . 11.5 secs. 1st, 2nd, 3rd
0-75 mph . . . . 15.3 secs. 1st, 2nd, 3rd
0-¼ mile . . . . 16.6 secs. at 83 mph
Ideal cruise . . . . 80 mph
Top speed (est). . . . . 122 mph
*Stop from 60 mph . . . . 169 ft
Average economy (city) . . . . 11 mpg
Average economy (country) . . . . 13 mpg
Fuel required . . . . Regular
Oil change (mos. / miles) 3/4000
Lubrication (mos. / miles) . . 3 years or 36,000 miles
Warranty (mos. / miles). 12/12,000
Type tools required . . . . SAE
U.S. dealers. . . . . 2949 total

*Anti-skid installed

BASE PRICE OF CAR

(Excludes state and local taxes, license, dealer preparation and domestic transportation): $6762.00 at Detroit
Plus desirable options:
$ 344.00 4-wheel Bendix anti-skid
$ 301.60 AM/FM stereo
$ 56.80 Anti-spin differential
$ 18.10 Automatic temp. control
$7482.50 TOTAL

ANTICIPATED DEPRECIATION

(Based on current Kelley Blue Book, previous equivalent model): $1592 1st yr. + $1141 2nd yr.

RATING	Excellent (91-100)	Good (81-90)	Fair (71-80)	Poor (61-70)
Brakes.	100			
Comfort.	98			
Cornering		85		
Details.	95			
Finish	93			
Instruments . . .		87		
Luggage		88		
Performance . .	92			
Quietness	96			
Ride	97			
Room	92			
Steering	91			
Visibility		90		
Overall	93			

IMPERIAL

Le Baron

Just what the cause or causes are that consistently relegate the Imperial to a poor 3rd place in the luxury car field have eluded Chrysler Corp. management ever since the line was first introduced in 1926. It has been a make in its own right since 1954 and for a brief period thereafter, it had its own D-series body shells and such exclusives as the industry's first standard power front disc brake system. Never, though, has it achieved an individual identity such as is accorded Cadillac and Lincoln.

It now uses a stretched version of the senior Dodge-Plymouth bodies that it shares with Chrysler, although the 127-inch wheelbase is 3 inches longer than Chrysler's. The key to spotting shared body shells is rear seat legroom, and the Imperial's 41.2 inches for the 4-door hardtop is the same as Chrysler and 3.2 inches more than Plymouth's. That in itself shouldn't deter buyers, as Cadillac Calais and DeVille body shells are also used on the Buick Electra and Olds Ninety-Eight.

Major efforts have always been expended on giving the Imperial specific front and rear styling but people, apparently, consider it just another, much more expensive Chrysler model. There was even a brief period when exclusive Imperial dealer franchises were available, but there was only one taker of record.

At another point in Imperial's history, advertising and promotion was concentrated in slick fashion magazines and in staging such galas as an annual Imperial Ball for New York, Chicago and Los Angeles society figures. All to no avail. Even funeral parlors have ignored the make as a base for coaches and limousines.

One probable reason is that while the car has been given specific styling, no one theme has been continued from year to year as has been the case with competition. Lincoln never really scored until five years after the present formal-looking design was first introduced. The one man who should understand that better than any other is Elwood P. Engel. He did the 1961 Lincoln in question and then moved over to Chrysler as vice-president of styling.

There is continuity of the economic kind for '73 in that engineers were able to adapt last year's front bumper to the new impact standards and thus avoided the expensive changes necessary for the lesser Chrysler models. The grille insert with a finer mesh is new but all else is a carryover from '72.

In addition to the top 440 4-barrel engine, automatic transmission, power steering and front disc brakes, standard features include air conditioning with manual temperature control, power seats and windows, and an automatic parking brake release. A vinyl roof cover is also included in the base price of both hardtop body styles. Major options are a dual air-conditioning system with automatic temperature control, steel-belted (but not radial) tires, and Imperial's still unique 4-wheel anti-skid control.

The value of this system, developed by Bendix Corp., over the 2-wheel variety used by GM and Ford is evident on slippery surfaces. Under these conditions the pedal pressure required to lock the front wheels is not very great and once locked, you lose steering control. Imperial's 4-wheel system prevents that and also possible damage to four tires worth $100 each instead of two.

No matter how hard you push on the pedal in a panic situation, an electronic sensor at each wheel signals the moment of imminent lock-up to a miniaturized computer which then causes the brakes in one or all of the wheels to be released and applied in rapid succession, much as a skilled driver "pumps" the brakes in a similar situation. The action isn't too noticeable inside the car until just before you come to a full stop. The other strange clunk you hear each time you start the engine is the sensors being deactivated by the ignition switch. When you last stopped to park, they couldn't tell whether you were skidding or standing still.

Interiors, as might be expected in a luxury car that strives to identify itself separately from the Chrysler New Yorker, are plush to an extreme. All-leather upholstery, though specified by a little over half of Imperial buyers, is an extra-cost option, with a combination of cloth and leather be-

ing standard. The electronic digital clock discussed elsewhere in this book is another feature standard on the Imperial, along with maintenance-free electronic ignition for the 440 4-barrel engine.

The Imperial dashboard should be a model for other luxury cars with its full set of engine instruments backed up by a warning light for every conceivable function. There is even a master warning light to let you know when one of the others really means business. Still another tells you to "check gauges," though this one can be annoying when you already know you're down to a quarter tank of gas. Periodic fills of leaded fuel, incidentally, are no longer needed because the exhaust valve seats in '73 engines are induction hardened.

Other options that should be mentioned include an electronic anti-theft and intrusion warning system, electric instead of vacuum operation of the trunk release, and a cassette tape player that can be combined with an AM/FM stereo radio. You can order a microphone with the cassette player that permits recording off the radio or dictating business memoranda. Many companies, in fact, now rely on in-car tape systems for sales messages. Their salesmen just can't escape.

IMPERIAL LE BARON
ENGINE: 440 cu. ins. (275 hp).
TRANSMISSION: 3-spd. auto.
SUSPENSION: Torsion bar front, leaf rear.
STEERING: Power std., curb-to-curb 44.8 ft.
BRAKES: Power front discs std., drums rear.
FUEL CAPACITY: 23.0 gals.
DIMENSIONS: Wheelbase 127.0 ins. Track 62.4 ins. front, 63.4 ins. rear. Overall length 235.3 ins., width 79.6 ins., height 56.2 ins. Weight 5150 lbs. Trunk 18.6 cu. ft.
BODY STYLES: 2-dr. hdtp., 4-dr. hdtp.

DETROIT'S BEST KEPT SECRET

Although the '74 Chrysler Imperial has been completely reworked and comes equipped with four-wheel discs, its potential to be a sales doubling winner is threatened by an old problem — lack of exposure.

Ambitious plans have been announced by Chrysler Corp. for the firm's flagship car, the 1974 Imperial LeBaron. For the new model year, Chrysler hopes to about double Imperial sales over those for the 1973 offering. For '74 the car is completely revised and provides a significantly higher level of luxurious transportation. In view of the many improvements, the company may reach the targeted goal.

In past years, Imperial has had its own wheelbase which at 127 in. was 3 in. greater than for the New Yorker and Newport models. For 1974 Imperial

goes to the 124 in. wheelbase and with that move there's some increase in the number of identical sheet metal parts. But within the ground rules of greater parts interchangeability Chrysler has made Imperial even more individualized and different looking than prior offerings, compared to the Chrysler models.

In the process of being completely reworked for '74, Imperial has been generally upgraded in many large and small ways. Some are visible, others are not. One small example of those easily seen is the carpeting in the trunk, plus the spare tire cover. These are now

identical in quality — are actually the same material — as that used in the passenger compartment — luxurious 25 oz. deep pile.

More important, on the not-so-visible mechanical side, Chrysler Imperial for 1974 introduces 4-wheel disc brakes — as standard equipment. The car thus becomes the first full size passenger vehicle built in this country to offer the many performance advantages of discs on all four wheels. Doing that on a regular production — rather than optional — basis was a somewhat bold move for the firm and one which clearly signals things to come in brake hardware for other domestic cars.

Imperial thus joins the Chevrolet Corvette as the only standard production autos built in the U.S. which offer what has for years been called the stopping system of the future. Although the technology for the all-disc system has been around for some time the added cost, plus parts production capability limitations, have kept this package from taking over from drum designs. (All the new machinery has been put to work handling the fast expanding front disc usage.) Chrysler's move, introducing the all-disc system on the comparatively low-volume Imperial, is seen as further boosting the firm's image for important engineering innovation which adds to overall car-building state-of-art.

Chrysler's plans to sell twice as many 1974 Imperial cars as were purchased of the 1973 edition isn't an unrealistic goal. The reason: Comparatively small numbers of vehicles are involved for an industry which for the most part thinks in terms of hundreds of thousands and millions of units. At this writing, it appears that about 16,000 copies of the '73 Imperial will have been produced, up from 14,900 of the '72's. So Chrysler has but to maintain a monthly selling rate of around something under 2,500 Imperial cars to double output in a 12-month period. Initial build schedules reflect this intent –– it isn't just a "paper" goal.

Imperial's all-new body reflects some fresh thinking which appears to further signal a major auto industry trend. The belt line has been dropped two inches with this space taken up by glass. Result is a thinner body, both physically and in appearance.

The single series of the car — LeBaron — is in two and four door models, both hardtops. All have halo vinyl roofs as standard, in a choice of seven colors. Overall length for both body styles is 231 in. — 4.3 in. less than last year's model. That's good news for motorists who have garages of marginal depth and also makes the 1974 model easier to get in and out of tight parking spaces.

The Imperial is a trace (0.7 in.) wider than the '73 edition at 79.7 in. and is significantly lower (by 1.3 in.) at 54.7 in. Base curb weight is expected to be down a little from last year's edition — about 55 lb. despite the fact that both front and rear bumper systems have again been beefed up. And there's also more insulation and sound deadening material in the car.

For 1974, Imperial's grille differs markedly from last year when it was nearly car wide. Now there's a strong central theme which to some viewers has a bit of the flavor of the British Rolls Royce. To others there's a little of the Continental Mark IV flavor. Although

individual reaction to specific design is highly subjective, it would seem that most luxury car owners will immediately like Imperial's grille and find it both tasteful and impressive.

The front bumper is a little on the massive side, but not obtrusively so, to meet the stiffer impact requirements for 1974 cars. Chrysler calls it "highly configured" and that's a fair description. Hidden headlights are continued, but unlike last year they don't continue the grille pattern. The covers are unadorned, except for the word "Imperial" in script on the left unit.

In back, Imperial styling is uncomplicated and very tastefully brought off. Here too the bumper is heftier than before, but is very well tucked in to smoothly continue body lines. The back window area has formal treatment and the deck lid is countoured. Rear lamps are tear-drop shaped and recessed for added protection.

Interior of the Imperial is a bit more lush than in the past. Standard interior trim is ribbed velour which is available in six colors. Optional is leather which Chrysler describes as "super soft" and is just that, to an impressive degree.

The test car Imperial was upholstered in this leather, which seems to equal flexibility of the type used in the manufacture of high quality dress gloves. That softness is the result of a unique tanning process, the company reports.

Both 2-door and 4-door model Imperial LeBaron cars have 50/50 front seats. In addition, the 4-door model has an individually adjustable reclining passenger seat.

In the main, Chrysler Imperial's drive train is unchanged from last year. Notable exceptions involve revision to the power plant to meet the somewhat stricter Federal (and California) emissions standards for the new model year. Engine (there are no optional powerplants) is Chrysler's largest — the 4 bbl. 440 cu in. 8.2 to 1 compression ratio V8 with electronic ignition (made standard with the '73 model). Since certification for emissions hasn't been completed at this writing, the exact output figures for this powerplant in 1974 remain to be released. They should be quite close or the same as tentative figures: peak torque of 350 lbs. ft. at 3200 rpm and 230 hp at 4000 rpm (SAE net figures). Unchanged from 1973 is the Imperial transmission — the 3-speed Torque Flite. The rear axle continues with a 3.23 to 1 ratio. A locking type rear is optionally available.

Big luxury car that it is, the '74 Imperial was found to be a very adequate performer under all normal driving conditions. The car is also somewhat livelier then the '73 edition. Reason for that, mainly, is that Chrysler engineers have learned a great deal in the last two years

or so concerning how to improve overall driveability while meeting increasingly more severe emissions standards.

If you had to pick the year in which emission standards took the biggest bite out of driveability and performance (industry-wide) it might well be 1971 or '72 depending upon make and model vehicle and whether it was built early or late in the model year. A comparison of elapsed times between the 1972 Imperial (see June 1972 issue) and the '74 offering, with the same ROAD TESTer at the wheel, are of interest. They indicate significant low-end improvements in acceleration (that's where it is by far the most important) even though emission limits have become stricter. Here are the figures — those for the '72 Imperial given first: (with both cars there was moderate transmission preloading) — 0 to 30 mph 4.7 sec.; 4.4 sec.; 0 to 45 mph 7.9 sec. — 7.1 sec.; 0 to 60 mph: 11.5 — 11.3; 0 to 75 mph: 15.3 sec. — 16.0 sec. The quarter mile required 16.6 sec. for the 1972 and 18.3 sec. for the 1974 model with the terminal speed for the former 83 mph and for the latter 82 mph.

While the 1972 Imperial posted better times for the 0 to 75 mph run and the quarter mile, the 1974 model might have at least equaled those if it weren't for one small impediment. That was an additional 175 lb. of payload in the latest test — a Chrysler engineer was along to run the clock. Still, from 0 to 60 mph and all points in between, the new Imperial is clearly the quicker car.

There are also other areas where improvements were noted over last year's Imperial. One of these: a little crisper handling, due in large part to the steel belted radial ply tires which the car now gets as standard (they are whitewalls). This is another example of increased value — previously steel belted bias ply tires were (in whitewall) an option costing an extra $25. (Radials were not available on prior models of Imperial.)

The rolling smoothness of radials at the higher speed levels is well established and the '74 Imperial gains a little here in the glide-like feel provided on good roadway. Testing the car at Chrysler Corp.'s huge proving ground at Chelsea, Mich., 60 miles west of Detroit, provided an opportunity to try the Imperial at speeds in excess of 100 mph to check for wind noise, vibration and turnpike roadability in general. Here the characteristics of radials were appreciated.

Chrysler engineers report the '74 model "is quieter" than the '73 offering, attributing the improvement to the completely redesigned (or revised) sound package parts. This package has also been expanded somewhat over the one used last year. In addition, everything was given a retuning, in part to match

In tight cornering, new Chrysler Imperial leans more than slightly, as expected from a soft luxury car suspension. But vehicle is highly controllable, with handling a shade crisper than previously, thanks to steel belted radial tires which are now standard equipment.

Super-accurate digital-readout, quartz-controlled clock in Imperial — an industry first for the car as a 1973 model — continues as standard. Here (upper left of dash) it shows time in afternoon photo was taken — 4:53:50 (the latter figures are seconds). Imperial instrument panel design is for maximum serviceability, with all instruments and controls, plus the radio, accessible without detaching the steering column.

Among the luxury features which are standard on the 1974 Imperial are automatic temperature control air conditioning, power windows and automatic parking brake release, plus power assisted steering and brakes. Chrysler describes the optional leather upholstery as having "the wrinkled look of an overstuffed chair." On the 4-door model, power front vent windows are an option. So is a package consisting of a right hand remote control outside mirror, floor mats and door edge protectors ($35.15).

the car to the specific qualities of radial ply tires. And all moving components were brought into a trace sharper balance.

All this contributes another small increment in the direction of further dropping the already very low noise-harshness-vibration (NHV) level. The payoff here is perhaps best noted on inferior roads and in cross country cruising at maximum legal speeds. High speed runs pointed up how impressively quiet the car is at top rates of travel.

High speed driving also suggested something else. The very low NHV level makes actual rate of travel deceptive, even in the daytime. This is far more true at night on a good but unlighted turnpike, because there's little exterior reference of how fast the vehicle is moving. Thus it would be possible for a driver who's not attentive to the speedometer to easily — and greatly — exceed posted limits.

In the brakes and safety department, a big step forward has been taken by Imperial with introduction of standard 4-wheel disc brakes. This system won't stop a specific car any faster than a high quality drum system. But it does everything else in superior fashion. All the well known advantages of discs are now at all four corners, rather than just in front, as with preceeding models.

Most important, overall, the system is better balanced. There's no need to make a lot of system compensations for the quite different operating characteristics of drum brakes compared to those of the disc type. One apparent result here is seemingly greater resistance of the rear wheels to lock up prematurely in high deceleration stops from speed.

There seems to be no need to get into detail about the plusses disc brakes offer over drums. All that is general knowledge by now. So we'll just list the points, by way of reporting why Imperial's brake package is better than the disc-drum setup it replaced.

Main disc virtues are far higher resistance to heat-induced fade, much less sensitivity to dampness and no possibility of temporary brake failure after complete saturation in water (as can happen in road flash flooding). In addition, discs have superior self adjusting design, expel dirt and water faster and more completely, are relatively immune to sticking and freeze-up. Further, the system is easier to maintain. Replacement of parts, including the friction pads, is a simpler and faster operation. There are other advantages to the design.

A few nuts-bolts details on the new Chrysler Imperial stopping package: In front there are one-piece 3.9 in. hubrotor assemblies, with the rotor having a diameter of 11.62 in. A new slider-type

caliper assembly is used. In the rear the rotor is of the same diameter as in the front and the slider type caliper assemblies have a 2.6 in. diameter. A 10 in. tandem power booster is a standard part of the system. It provides just the right amount of assist to provide good pedal feel and low effort, easily modulated braking.

This is quite important, for if discs in general may be faulted in any respect, it is that in some less-than-thoroughgoing past designs there have been some complaints that pedal feel was too hard with a consequent resistance to desired brake modulation. That was with discs in front only — putting them in back too would only tend to compound the problem. But Chrysler has apparently engineered around these problems very neatly.

A considerable number of stops were made from 60 mph, both to get distance data and to check for fade after the system got quite hot. Prior to that series, the car had been worked very hard by other auto writers. Some had insisted on trying panic stops from high speed. There was some evidence of friction pad glazing and considerable wear from all this abuse.

Still, with a cool system, stops from 60 mph were all well under 190 ft. with the best 178 ft. After a series of stops with brief cooldown driving in between, (ambient air temperature stood

Chrysler Imperial's new 4-wheel disc brake system is impressively well balanced, provides straight line stops one after the other with no significant evidence of fade and resists premature wheel lockup in high deceleration checks from cruising speed. Best stop from 60 mph was 178 ft with comparatively cool system which had received some very hard use before test runs were made. There was expected moderate front end dive and rear end rise during stops, as this view shows.

at 92 degrees F.) one run went to 206. There was the feeling here that the pads had already received the equivalent of perhaps 30,000 miles of driving and were getting on the thin side. System overhaul that night confirmed that suspicion.

Two further points on Imperial's all-wheel disc system: Perhaps the largest impression related to the balance of the system, and that each wheel's brake mechanism was doing a correct share of the stopping work. Result of that, of course, was unusually straight line braking right down to zero mph.

The parking brake system has long been an obstacle from a design standpoint to putting discs in back. Chrysler has here gone the more costly route used by the Chevrolet Corvette — a separate drum and regular brake shoes for parking only. This approach will, in a few years, probably be replaced by a less expensive parking brake. That design puts mechanical pressure directly on the friction pads for positive parking, thus avoids the need for a drum.

Several 1974 Imperial features may be classed both under brakes and safety and comfort-convenience. First is a new electronic gauge alert system which backs up dash instruments — ammeter, coolant temperature gauge and fuel supply gauge. If there's a problem in the battery charging circuit, if coolant temperature becomes excessive or fuel supply drops too low, the appropriate light emitting diode will glow to alert the driver.

Also standard equipment is a windshield wiper fluid level indicator, which is activated when fluid supply drops below one-third full. Another standard Imperial feature is a door ajar indicator, which operates both when a door is open or in the secondary latch position.

The Chrysler Imperial in 1974 continues with one of the highest levels of comfort and convenience available in any passenger car built in the world. It is in this category, for one, that the car is a cut above the regular Chrysler, at least in respect to standard equipment. Space limitations do not permit detailing here all the comfort-convenience features in view of the greater than usual coverage given the brake system. Suffice it to say that the '74 edition of the Imperial car offers an ultimate in over-the-road transportation.

Above the high standard equipment level, Imperial offers one of the most extensive lists of options in the industry. One exclusive item — 4-wheel anti skid — has, lamentably, been dropped. Unfortunately there wasn't sufficient demand for this $344 package to continue offering it. But all-wheel anti-skid will be back in due time, most automotive observers are confident. In the case of the Imperial it seems to have been an option for which the time had not yet arrived.

Testing the 1974 Imperial recalled some impressions acquired while evaluating the '72 model. Chrysler's prestige offering continues the tradition of a very well engineered vehicle which is quite easy to drive and is extremely quiet and comfortable in every respect.

Imperial needs — and deserves — increased exposure to those new car buyers who seek the best the U.S. auto industry has to offer in a standard size vehicle. Chrysler plans to give the car strong support by way of possibly doubling sales of the '74 edition over those for the '73 model. The company has the vehicle with the potential to do that. Whether or not the goal is reached will depend mainly upon dealers whose job is to sell the product. The '74 Imperial deserves to be a sales doubling winner.
Tony Grey

IMPERIAL LEBARON

SPECIFICATIONS AS TESTED

Engine	440 cu in OHV V8
Bore & Stroke	4.32 x 3.75 ins.
Compression ratio	8.2 to 1
Horsepower	230 (SAE net) at 4000 rpm
Torque	350 lbs-ft at 3200 rpm
Transmission	3-speed Torque Flite automatic
Steering	3.5 turns lock-to-lock
	44.69 ft curb-to-curb
Brakes	disc front, disc rear
Suspension	torsion bar front, leaf rear
Tires	WSW Steel belted radial, LR 78 x 15

Dimensions (ins.):

Wheelbase	124	Rear track	63.7
Length	231.1	Ground clearance	5.8
Width	79.7	Height	54.7
Front track	64.0	Weight (as equipped)	5184 lbs

Capacities:

Fuel	25 gals	Oil	4 qts
Coolant	18 qts	Trunk	20.0 cu ft

PERFORMANCE AND MAINTENANCE

Acceleration:

0-30 mph	4.4 secs, 1st
0-45 mph	6.9 secs, 1st, 2nd
0-60 mph	11.3 secs, 1st, 2nd
0-75 mph	16.0 secs, 1st—3rd
0-¼ mile	18.3 secs at 82 mph
Top speed (est)	120 mph
Stop from 60 mph	178 ft
Average economy (city)	10 mpg
Average economy (country)	13 mpg
Fuel required	Regular
Oil change (mos./miles)	3/4000
Lubrication (mos./miles)	3 years or 36,000 miles
Warranty (mos./miles)	12/12,000
Type tools required	SAE
U.S. dealers	3500

BASE PRICE OF CAR

(Prices given are for *1973* model with comparable equipment. Excludes state and local taxes, license, dealer preparation and domestic transportation):

4-door hardtop $7057.00 at Detroit

Plus desirable options:

$ 155.90	Leather upholstery
$ 247.80	AM/FM Search Tuner radio
$ 94.20	Automatic temp control
$ 95.80	Tilt/telescope steering wheel
$ 121.30	Power bench seat-6-way
$ 73.55	Power door locks
$ 33.15	Power trunk release

$7878.70 TOTAL

NOTE: Automatic control air conditioning and power windows are standard on 1974 Imperial.

Chrysler Imperial

Cadillac Fleetwood

Lincoln Town Car

By Jim Brokaw

The Cadillac isn't dead, it's embodied by the Fleetwood, but Lincoln's Town Car and Chrysler's Imperial look and act a lot like it.

When I was 15 years old, in the summer of '48, there weren't that many ways to earn some summer bread. A few of the stronger kids worked farmers' fields, while some of the strange, silent ones harvested sea moss in smelly dories from the off-shore kelp beds. "Mossin' " paid very well, but you had to be the son of a mosser, or the best buddy of a son to crack that cloistered clan. Since I was neither, and a relatively new kid in the very small and very tight New England seacoast town of Scituate, Mass., I joined the band of scavengers who carried golf clubs for the moneyed sportsmen at the brand-new-solid-concrete-on-top-of-a-hill Hatherly Country Club. Scituate was a vacation haven for the wealthy and wish-they-were of Boston. Hatherly was the social center for the Summer People.

I made some pretty good money that first peaceful and uncluttered year, picking up a few regular customers along the way. I had a good set-up, but my buddy Scott had the world by the wallet pocket. He was the personal, private caddy for MR. BARNES, who drove a Cadillac. Many club members had personal caddies, some club members had Cadillacs, but *Mr. Barnes* had *two* Cadillacs. To have one Cadillac was to be the butt of many jokes and humorous remarks, but it also meant being first through the clubhouse door. To have *two* Cadillacs meant being first through the clubhouse door, without the jokes.

I didn't really envy Scott on the days when he met Mr. Barnes at his house and rode to the country club in one of the Cadillacs—I died. One day when all the members were at the bar celebrating something, Scott let me get close enough to actually see inside. I was very careful not to touch it or Mr. Barnes would have discovered my fingerprints, Scott would have gotten in trouble and I would have been thrown off the grounds.

The following summer, everything changed. Along with my driver's license, I got a job at the Ford garage. Suddenly the new kid was a member of the Establishment. A steady job (paying 75¢ an hour), cars to park and deliver, and I worked every night until 10 o'clock right on Front Street. God, what a deal. The mechanics cussed right in front of me, some of the customers learned my name, and one day I actually drove the town police car out of the garage. I didn't even mind cleaning the restrooms.

Around the 4th of July, I was surveying my asphalt kingdom, waiting for a good-looking Summer Girl to come in for gas—they always charged it and if you stood just right, you could look down the front of their blouse while they signed the ticket. Suddenly I saw a brand new maroon Cadillac with a canvas roof cover oozing down the street. As it floated by, the driver gave me a big grin and lifted his left hand from the wheel just enough to be noticed. It was Scott, and he was *driving* Mr. Barnes' Cadillac.

Nancy Gilly pulled up to the pumps in her old man's Hudson convertible. I didn't even look down when she signed the ticket.

After awhile, Scott got real brave and gave me a ride. I don't know if he was supposed to or not, but we drove out of town and took the state road where we weren't likely to see anyone who knew us. All I remember about the car was that it felt like that time in the seventh grade when Roberta Hopkins leaned up against me from behind, right in the classroom. Scott got the Cad up to 100 miles an hour before we headed back to Front Street.

Later on, it didn't bother me anymore when Scott drove by in the Cad. Scoop neck blouses were getting popular, and the boss let me take a vacuum shift '46 Chevy home on rainy nights.

It was more than 20 years before I actually drove a Cad. I think it was a Calais or maybe a Coupe de Ville, I forget which. After I adjusted the seat to my taste and figured out where everything was, I slid out onto the street, waiting for Roberta Hopkins to press up against my back again. She never showed up. It was just a car. A little bigger than most, a little smoother than most, but just another car.

I had relegated Mr. Barnes' Caddy and Roberta to the figment file until the day

I had to return a Fleetwood, borrowed by some visiting brass. Lord a'mighty, what a car! Roberta wasn't leaning, but she was sitting in the back seat. I whipped the Fleetwood around the corner at the bottom of the La Cienega hill and that big blue sedan stayed flat as a Ferrari. I couldn't believe it. The Cadillac isn't dead, it is simply restricted to the Fleetwood.

We rounded up a Lincoln Town Car, an Imperial LeBaron, and a Fleetwood Brougham just to see what they were all about. Most cars are combinations of mundane concepts, functional execution, plus a little nylon and gingerbread to help the illusion. An occasional flourish of power, styling, or handling raises a given model out of the herd, but seldom does any make a complete statement. Not so with the big rolling palaces.

These crown jewels more than make a statement. They are the embodiment of a way of life. A very well-paid way of life. They are very expensive, starting out at eight grand for the basics. They are very big, almost 20 feet long and over 6½ feet wide. They are heavy. The Caddy, the lightest of the three, tips the scales at 2½ tons. Materials used are of the finest quality, construction is as solid as an anvil, and the attention to detail rivals that of an over-age lecher putting the hustle

CADILLAC

LINCOLN

IMPERIAL

CADILLAC   LINCOLN   IMPERIAL

SPECIFICATIONS:

	CADILLAC FLEETWOOD	LINCOLN TOWN CAR	IMPERIAL LE BARON
Engine:	OHV V-8	OHV V-8	OHV V-8
Bore & Stroke—ins.	4.3 x 4.06	4.36 x 3.85	4.32 x 3.75
Displacement—cu. in.	472	460	440
HP @ RPM	220 @ 4000	219 @ 4400	215 @ 3600
Torque: lbs.-ft. @ rpm	365 @ 2400	360 @ 2800	345 @ 2000
Compression Ratio	8.5:1	8.0:1	8.2:1
Carburetion	4-bbl	4-bbl	4-bbl
Transmission	3-speed automatic	3-speed automatic	3-speed automatic
Final Drive Ratio	2.93:1	2.75:1	3.23:1
Steering Type	Variable ratio power	Power	Power
Steering Ratio	17.8-9.0:1	21.6:1	19.1:1
Turning Diameter			
(curb-to-curb-ft.)	46.03	46.7	44.78
Wheel Turns			
(lock-to-lock)	3.25	3.99	3.5
Tire Size	LR78-15	230-15	L84-15
Brakes	Non-skid power disc drum	Power disc/drum	Non-skid power disc/drum
Front Suspension	Coils/shocks	Coils/shocks	Torsion bar
	stabilizer	stabilizer	shocks, stabilizer
Rear Suspension	4-link coils	3-link coils	leaf springs
	shocks	shocks	shocks
	auto level control		
Body/Frame Construction	Perimeter frame	Perimeter frame	Unitized w/sub frame
Wheelbase—ins.	133.0	127.0	127.0
Overall Length—ins.	231.5	229.5	235.3
Width—ins.	79.8	79.6	79.6
Height—ins.	55.5	55.5	50.2
Front Track—ins.	63.3	64.3	62.4
Rear Track—ins.	63.3	64.3	63.4
Curb Weight—lbs.	5.025	5.260	5.255
Fuel Capacity—gals.	27	22	23
Oil Capacity—qts.	4 (1)	4 (1)	4 (1)
Trunk Capacity	19.27	18.1	18.6
PERFORMANCE			
Acceleration			
0-30 mph	3.8	3.9	3.9
0-60 mph	10.2	10.4	11.8
0-75	15.1	16.1	17.2
Standing Start ¼-mile			
Mph	80	80.2	77.3
Elapsed time	17.6	17.6	18.1
Passing speeds			
40-60 mph	5.7	5.2	6.8
50-70 mph	6.5	5.9	7.4
Speeds in gears*			
1st ... mph @ rpm	51 @ 4.500	46 @ 4.000	42 @ 4.000
2nd ... mph @ rpm	84 @ 4.500	78 @ 4.000	70 @ 4.000
3rd ... mph @ rpm	94 @ 3.500	83 @ 3.000	80 @ 3.000
Mph per 1000 rpm			
(in top gear)	26.8	27.66	26.66
Stopping distances			
From 30 mph	32.1	28.1	29.8
From 60 mph	143.0	136.2	151.6
Speedometer error			
Car speedometer	30 45 50 60 70 80	30 45 50 60 70 80	30 45 50
True speedometer	30 45 50 60 70 80	29.4 43.1 47 55.9 68.6	29.8 44.1 48.5

*Speeds in gears are at shift points (limited by the length of track) and do not represent maximum mph.

on an 18 year old.

Driving these velvet tanks is an emotional experience. The seats aren't soft, they're firm, with full support from the back of the knee to the back of the neck. The seats are fully adjustable in every direction except sideways. All three machines aim to please. Tilt-telescope steering wheels fit all arm sizes from John Wayne to the Gallo brothers. Even the finger ridges on the back of the steering wheels are deep and vee-shaped for a firmer grip.

Visibility is virtually unlimited. Large inside mirrors are augmented by dual outside mirrors, both of which are remote controlled in all but the Imperial.

Steering response is amazingly quick and firm, far better than their less expensive cousins down at the "economy" end of the full-sized sedan list. While they could hardly be described as nimble, all three are very positive. They can all take an emergency lane change without undue upset to either vehicle or driver.

Picking the best of these is a task equal to the keenest judgment of Solomon. While we lay no claim to excess wisdom, there are differences which cater to the differing tastes of the wealthy who possess these rubber-tired symbols of distinction.

Cadillac treats its size as a natural adjunct to highway dominance by subtle employment of sharpened corners to emphasize the massive dimensions of the side view. A sense of special accommodation is achieved by utilizing a small individual drivers seat with a complete adjustment spectrum. Functional vehicle controls are isolated at various positions about the dash and left hand door panel. Everywhere the eye falls, there is either informational input, or a control device within easy reach.

The Brougham d'Elegance option includes velour upholstery as close to velvet as a durable synthetic can get. Liberal use of this "Medici" cloth extends to the front seat backs, door trim pads, door pull straps and the new retractable rearseat assist straps. Deep pile carpeting creates an almost irresistable urge to remove your shoes and run your toes through it—or perhaps someone else's toes through it.

The AM-FM stereo radio now includes a signal seeker as well as the tape deck option. In the Fleetwood 75, known as the "Limo" to the proles, there is a remote radio control panel for the rear seat.

The ultimate statement is the vanity mirror on the back of the passenger visor. Many cars have visor vanity mirrors, but the Brougham d'Elegance has one with a cover and six side lights.

The big 472-cubic-inch engine starts easily and stays alive even when cold. Power is more than adequate for normal operation, including use of all power options, and sufficient for most abnormal requirements.

Driving the Fleetwood is remarkably easy. You are aware of the great size, but it becomes a problem only when you forget that a Fleetwood must be driven with grace and dignity. The superb suspension will support rough handling, but a deft hand on the wheel produces a very stable ride. In fact, the only real fault is the amount of lateral displacement under brisk cornering. There is no sway at all, thanks to the automatic level control, but it does move a large amount of metal through a sizeable arc. Recovery is smooth without hunting and seeking.

I have long been of the opinion that VW drivers are oblivious to traffic and Cadillac drivers just don't give a damn. I was wrong. Cadillac drivers expect to be given priority, whereas VW drivers take pointed delight in *not* giving so much as an inch to a Cadillac. When one operates a Fleetwood, one must be tolerant of the less fortunate.

The Lincoln Town Car is a subtly, but distinctly, different approach to the same end. Where Cadillac strikes a balance between ride and handling, Lincoln goes for a glass smooth ride, with a penalty paid in rebound control. Cadillac emphasizes its monolithic dimensions, Lincoln tends to reduce the visual impact by subtly rounding off the corners, gently contouring the side flares, and discreetly placing the few pieces of chrome the marketing department deems necessary.

Each manufacturer creates unique names for its decor artifacts, such as corduroy velour bodycloth, simulated rosewood applique, flocked nylon, and long-shear cut-pile carpeting. However, there is only one word that describes Lincoln's interior; *silent,* dead silent. With the windows closed and the AM/FM/MPX stereo radio and tape deck turned off, you can hear yourself breathe.

Our Town Car had a blue/grey corduroy velour upholstery, which is crushed corduroy to those of you who still don't know what velour is.

It looked a bit flat in the daytime, but at night the light from the instrument panel casts a pervasive glow over the front interior giving the car a silver tint.

While Cadillac disperses its information and control sources, Lincoln neatly clusters everything in a balanced display directly in front of the driver with a full set of engine monitor gauges.

Visibility is equal to that of Cadillac with dual remote controlled outside mirrors.

Steering is precise and accurate, requiring very little wheel movement to control the two and a half tons of silence. The 460 cu. in. engine cuts a full share of mustard to the point where it actually broke the rear end loose under full acceleration at the drag strip. This was surprising since the torque peaks at a higher rpm than either the Cadillac or the Imperial.

Lincoln's ride is smoother than that of the Cadillac, with minor defects in road texture gliding past undetected. Rebound control is not what it could be, causing an extra cycle or two after encountering large changes in road contour.

The Imperial LeBaron is a unique blend of the treasured old and the ultra functional new. Both the 440 cu in engine and the torsion bar front and leaf spring rear suspension are old, but the electronic ignition and the digital clock are new.

It is more of a driver's car than the other two, with the best handling of all three, thereby paying the price of having the harshest ride of the three. Harsh is only in reference to the Cadillac and Lincoln. Compared to any other domestic it is very smooth.

The instrument panel follows Chrysler tradition by presenting a complete and easily readable display of information. Imperial uses indirect lighting for the panel, which accomplishes the design function of instrument illumination, but seems to lack the sense of dignity created by the rest of the black leather interior. Imperial takes two approaches to the statement of size. The rear end is well rounded, tending to diminish the impact of sheer mass, while the massive hood is flared upward at the outboard edges, giving one the sensation of riding along on a huge manta ray. This tends to generate a sense of security in the knowledge that nothing made by man could penetrate all the way from the distant front bumper to your driving compartment.

The AM-FM stereo radio and tape system is the equal of both Cadillac and Lincoln, all three can best be described as magnificent. One side benefit of the mutual, liberal use of fibrous finished interior materials is the superb acoustical efficiency.

The one notable deficiency we found in the stately machine was the absence of a remote control toggle for the right hand outside mirror. It is really an unforgiveable omission for any car in this category.

Another minor Imperial deficiency is the wind and tire noise. Although not excessive, it is detectable. With all of the attention to comfort and environment lavished on these gliding palaces, perfection becomes the standard. If a flaw is detectable, what may be perfectly acceptable in a lesser machine becomes a fault in these final statements of the domestic carriage art.

Driving any of the three generates a state of mind not found in other cars. The imagination, unbeleaguered by outside input, runs wild as you glide down the freeway in aloof silence. Stately while cruising, they are refreshingly agile in traffic. Great hordes of useable torque slip you very nicely into the available break in traffic. For a few delicious moments you can almost convince yourself that you really own one of these enduring symbols of wealth and power. ∎

THE LUXURY CARS

Imperial Palace
Fortress Fleetwood
Castle Continental

Crippled by the fuel flap and sniggered at lewdly by those smug Mercedes owners, today it seems that these great mastadons are dismissed as symbols of an ancient aristocracy whose strata was marked by expanse of wheelbase, and the heavenly quantity of gross cubic mass able to be shouldered by four beleagured tires. As the sole surviving heirs of princely Packards, dynosaurean Duesenbergs and the Brobdingnagian Bugattis, these marvels of grand proportion should be headed for the Smithsonian Institute by way of the mucky La Brea tar pits.

But are they?

Are these behemoths simply vestiges of a defunct class of affluence and influence, or are they firmly entrenched — perhaps now more than ever — in their positions atop the very peak of slippery Mount Status, whose crags we scale daily, whether we wish to acknowledge that fact or not?

Ah, but welcome to the current state of American affairs: beef prices manipulated by withholding the animals from market; endless rounds of strikes by unions whose members are engaged in serving the public; gasoline supplies that rise and fall in mysterious coincidence with rising prices; dry rot, manipulation and partisan hatcheteering in government. They leave us little to believe in, and less to trust.

The very qualities that appear to condemn these sail-less luxury liners will very likely ensure their perpetuation. In days past, the block-long Cadillac and shiny Lincoln with paint jobs three feet deep flaunted a socio-economic position we could never hope to achieve. They did, however, constantly remind us that such positions, such wealth, such power, did, in fact, exist. The gliding specter of the shiny Imperial eagle stirred within a few heretical souls the bold idea that if such positions of power and wealth existed, there must be some means of attainment. More than a few of the haughty, distant drivers of the velvet tanks clawed their way up from the very pavement they now whisper over to

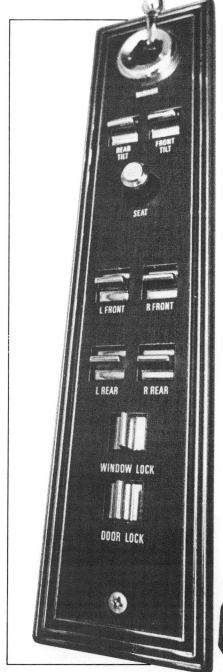

Lincoln's placement of seat controls on arm rest panel is less desireable than lower side-of-seat location of Cad and Imperial.

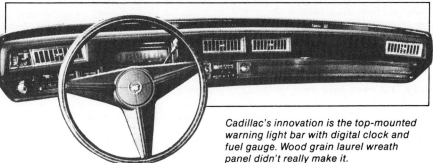

Imperial's seats featured amazingly soft kid-glove leather, but lacked support.

Cadillac's innovation is the top-mounted warning light bar with digital clock and fuel gauge. Wood grain laurel wreath panel didn't really make it.

165

finally purchase, with calculated disdain for the sticker price, the symbol of success.

The gasoline shortage won't affect them. By now, all of you are aware of the many little ploys used to acquire a sufficient quantity of fuel. Rest assured that those who languish on crushed velour seats know even a few methods we do not.

Parking is no problem. The spaces are either assigned, by name, or a convenient attendant takes care of such things.

The energy crunch is hurting the lesser pretenders of massive girth. Some say there will be no survivors, others of equal knowledge and awareness say there will always be full-sized sedans. Whomever is right, there is going to be a swarm of small, common-sense cars on the roads, interspersed with a few very large, very quiet, oversized wallet-wagons.

What is there about the LeBaron, Fleetwood, Town Car mystique that draws out that slender thread of ostentation that lies curled inside our ego? I'm not really sure, but when we acquired the test vehicles, nearly everyone on the staff, including those usually of a more sporty bent, absolutely had to use one of the tanks over the weekend. No one wanted it for himself, but he was taking good old Belschnitzen Veebelfetzer to either dinner, the airport, or the drive-in; and *he'd* really get a kick out of riding in class.

I must confess that my own reaction to closing out the rest of the world was a bit more base and vicarious. It gave me a sense of aloofness, a sense of power.

Nobody out there in the noisy world knew that I couldn't afford a tuneup for the big boat.

"Out there in the noisy world" is the key phrase for all three. Isolation from outside noise and climate, cushioned and pampered in every possible way is what the chariots of the gods are all about. All three cater to comfort and luxury, Cadillac casually informs that a legend has become a lifestyle; Lincoln quietly congratulates you for your prudence in having consideration for your passengers and Lincoln's luxury; Chrysler, however, appeals directly to the driver, pointing out his comfort and Imperial's engineering excellence.

Imperial, which is completely redesigned for '74, is very likely the best of the long line of Imperials. The instrument panel and dash is a superior combination of the elegant old and the functional new. Controls are small, easily distinguished by shape or location. In addition to the Chrysler-pioneered digital clock for automobiles, there are direct reading dials for temperature, alternator, and fuel, with built-in light emitting diodes to give you a back-up idiot light

right in the gauge. *There is even a light to inform you when the windshield washer fluid is low.*

The AM/FM stereo radio has a signal seeker function with three controls. Local, long range, and a foot pedal if your hands are busy elsewhere.

Our LeBaron had the optional sun roof. Both Chrysler and American Sunroof have done a thorough job of design and installation. There is no wind noise when the panel is closed, however, the airflow with the panel open is nothing more than a gentle tug at the top of your head. No great blast of air.

Cruise control is excellent. The center panel glove compartment even has little coin slots for toll money. The kid-glove leather, yes, *leather upholstery* is the best of class. The seats are very soft, but possibly too soft for support.

Chrysler's electronic ignition system, two-stage electric assist choke, the excellent TorqueFlite transmission, all combine to give consistent starts, smooth idling, and positive, smooth power under all but full throttle conditions. They also produce a phenomenal 14.7 mpg in fuel economy.

Four-wheel disc brakes—the first on any full-sized car in the domestic market—give sure, positive stops. We managed 27 feet from 30 mph and 130 feet from 60 mph. There was no rear-wheel lock-up, which is a function of the non-skid system, and weight transfer. The stops were dead straight.

Handling from the torsion-bar front suspension and the (leaf spring) rear suspension is the best of the three. Han-

Imperial's dash combines an excellent wood-grain surround with maximum function and best layout in a luxury car.

Cadillac subtly offers padded foot rests for rear seat guests. Rich leather upholstery.

Lincoln Town Car seats were most comfortable of the three big palaces. Velour mohair upholstery lends air of timeless dignity.

PERFORMANCE	CADILLAC	LINCOLN	IMPERIAL
Acceleration			
0-30 mph	4.30	3.97	4.2
0-50 mph	8.49	8.00	9.15
0-60 mph	12.00	9.50	12.1
Standing Start 1/4-mile			
Mph	77.05	77.65	80.28
Elapsed time	17.98	17.82	17.42
Passing speeds			
40-60 mph	6.58	5.9	7.1
50-70 mph	7.00	6.8	6.8
Stopping distance			
From 30 mph	32'1"	31'4"	27'5"
From 60 mph	182'7"	153'10"	129'3"
Gas mileage range	10.43	10.42	14.7
Width — in.	79.8	80.0	79.7
Front Track — in.	63.5	64.3	64
Rear Track — in.	63.3	64.3	63.7
Wheelbase — in	133.0	127.0	124.0
Overall length — in.	233.7	232.6	231.1
Height — in.	55.6	55.4	54.7
Curb Weight — lbs.	5,250	5,425	5,345
Fuel Capacity — gals.	27	22.5	25
Oil Capacity — qts.	4 (1)	4 (1)	4 (1)
Storage Capacity — cu. ft.	19.27	20.9	20+
Base Price	$9,312	$7,637	$7,062
Price as tested	$11,435	$9,452	$8,737
Engine:	OHV V-8	OHV V-8	OHV V-8
Bore & Stroke — ins.	4.3x4.06	4.36x3.85	4.32x3.75
Displacement — cu. in.	472	460	440
HP @ RPM	205 @ 3600	215 @ 4000	230 @ 4000
Torque: lbs.-ft. @ rpm	365 @ 2000	350 @ 2600	350 @ 3200
Compression Ratio	8.25:1	NA	8.2:1
Carburetion	4V	4V	4V
Transmission	Auto. Turbo Hydra-Matic	Auto. Select Shift	Auto. Torqueflite
Final Drive Ratio	2.93	3.00	3.23 (?)
Steering Type	Recirculating Ball & Nut Power	Recirculating Ball & Nut With Integral Power Unit	Recirculating Ball Power
Steering Ratio	17.8-9.0	21.6 To 1	18.9:1
Turning Diameter (curb-to-curb-ft.)	(Wall To Wall) 24.54'	46.7'	44.69'
Wheel Turns (lock-to-lock)	2.83	3.99	3.5
Tire Size	LR78X15 Steel Belted Radials	LR78X15 Steel Belted Radials	LR78X15 Steel Belted Radial Ply
Brakes	Power Disc/Drum	Power Disc/Drum	Power Disc/Disc
Front Suspension	Coils/Shocks Front Diagonal Tie Struts Stabilizer	Coils/Shocks Axial Strut Stabilizer	Torsion Bar Shocks Stabilizer
Rear Suspension	4 Link, Coils/ Shocks	Three Link, Rubber Cushioned Pivots Coils/Shocks	Leaf Springs Shocks
Body/Frame Construction	Perimeter Frame	Body On Perimeter Frame	Unitized Construction

dling is there, in the sense of getting all that mass here and there without discernable effort. As in all things, there are points where function comes a cropper. Handling has been achieved at the sacrifice of smooth ride. Surface reaction is greater in the Imperial than its two opponents, but a sizeable bump can be taken at speed without discomfort, or excessive damping time.

The seat belts are the one real irritant we found. The belt reels hang up when pulled out to buckle up. This could be laid off to accommodating the new interlock system, but belt reels have been the one area where Chrysler engineering doesn't have quite enough extra care. In their defense, Chrysler has rigged the shoulder harness so that it lays down across the rear entrance, almost eliminating an arrested landing on rear seat ingress.

Cadillac Fleetwood, long-time king of the luxury field, target of the pretenders, comes in three flavors: the Brougham, which is classy enough a title for most labelers; the Brougham d'Elegance, designed to induce maximum nasal elevation; and for those whose Wallabies come equipped with hydro-foils, and are smart enough to know what it means, the Fleetwood Talisman. Brougham features leather, Brougham d'Elegance emphasizes crushed velour, while Talisman languishes in crushed velour, which feels like velvet and is entitled Medici cloth. You have to be a history major to appreciate how much research went into the names. In addition to wall-to-wall Medici, Talisman offers multi-use consoles with illuminated writing pad; lockable storage compartment, vanity mirror and a storage bin.

Standard items on the Fleetwood encompass the normal luxury line. Power steering, brakes, windows, and seats. Multi-speed windshield wipers, carpeted footrests, visor vanity mirrors, multiple arm rests, reading lights, integrated litter box and an automatic parking brake release. The options range from sunroof to track master non-skid braking system.

Coil springs at all four corners with strut rods in front and four-link setup in back have rubber bushings everywhere one can fit. The automatic level-ride-control is the secret to Fleetwood's excellent road isolation. Road cracks and small bumps are totally ignored.

The non-skid braking system gives smooth, straight stops with no wheel lockup, performing equally well on minor brake applications as well as the knee-locking, white-knuckled type. We logged stops of 32 feet from 30 mph and 183 feet from 60 mph.

Variable ratio power steering, 17.1:1, makes maneuvering surprisingly easy. In spite of the massive dimensions, all three are easy to handle in traffic. Park-

continued on page 176

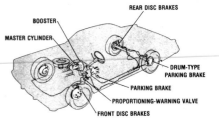

FOUR-WHEEL DISC BRAKES

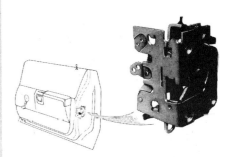

AIR CONDITIONING AND HEATING AIR DISTRIBUTION SYSTEM

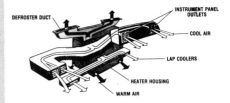

COMPACT DOOR LATCH

Chrysler Imperial
(Le Baron)

Luxurious New Look

Chrysler's Imperial is one of the few luxury cars to enter 1974 with extensive changes. It has an all-new design with lowered roof-line and the belt line dropped two-inches, providing additional glass area and a thinner body shape. The wheelbase is shorter than in previous years, 124-inches as compared to 127-inches last year.

A first in the luxury car market, four-wheel power disc brakes are standard on all Imperials.

There are two models offered, known as the Imperial LeBaron, and available in two-door hardtop or four-door hardtop. The overall length is 231-inches, width 79.7-inches and height 54.7-inches. Front track is 64-inches and rear 63.7-inches.

The only engine is the 440 CID V8 with 4.32-inches bore and 3.75-inches stroke. It is equipped with the four-barrel carburetor and produces 230 horsepower at 4000 rpm and 350 ft/lbs of net torque at 3200 rpm. The compression ratio is 8.2:1 so that regular fuel may be used.

Included with the standard features are power steering, TorqueFlite automatic transmission, power windows and air conditioning.

With a host of standard luxury items to please the typical buyer in this segment of the market, the Imperial LeBaron seeks to bolster its reputation in '74. It should do it.

(2-Dr)

A–Front leg room, max, +10″ 42.3	E–Rear head room, +4″ 37.0	Front shoulder room 60.5
B–Front head room, +4″ 38.1	F–Rear leg room, min, +10″ 39.5	Rear shoulder room 60.6
C–Front seat travel 4.6	G–Rear knee room, min, ... 5.9	Front hip room 61.0
D–Front heel to hip height 9.0	H–Rear heel to hip height 11.5	Rear hip room 60.6

GENERAL SPECIFICATIONS

Dimensions, Ins:

    Length 231.1
    Width 79.7
    Height 54.7
    Wheelbase 124.0
    Track, front/rear 64.0/63.7
Luggage capacity . . . . 20 cu ft
Engine . . . . 440 CID V-8 (4-bbl)
    Optional engine(s) . . . . none
Horsepower . . . . 230 at 4000 rpm
Torque . . . . 350 at 3200 rpm
Transmission . . . . . 3-speed automatic
    Optional transmission(s) . . . . . none
Brakes . . . . Power disc/drum
Fuel capacity . . . . 25 gal
Fuel economy . . . . 8.9 mpg
Base price (excludes state and local taxes, license, dealer preparation and domestic transportation): $7062

The King's Ransom Road Test

We look at big bucks from both sides now, and the intercontinental contenders are: BMW 3.0, Jaguar XJ-6, Mercedes-Benz 450 SE, Imperial LeBaron, Cadillac Eldorado and Continental Mark IV.

THE IMPORTS

By John Lamm

If you happen to be a fan of imported luxury cars and expect this to be a tirade against their American rivals, you will be disappointed in this portion of our road test. It's not because I secretly prefer the U.S. luxury cars (which I don't) or have been disappointed with the present offerings of BMW, Mercedes-Benz or Jaguar (which I am not), it is just that the domestic versus imported luxury car question makes an interesting discussion, but a terrible argument.

That is because the difference in luxury cars goes much deeper than "imported" or "domestic" labels. Any automobile is a direct reflection of its home environment. Everything from local laws, gasoline prices and national attitude to how history and geography dicate that any one automobile will somehow differ from its counterpart from another nation.

Let's use the obvious comparison of the U.S. and Germany. Right after World War II, we were able to get back to full automobile production relatively quickly; out went the bombers and in came the cars. Cadillac had a restyling in 1948 and introduced the overhead valve V-8 in 1949. BMW wasn't able to build their first post-war car in Munich until 1952. Even when the factories were humming, Europeans were selling to a public still grappling to rebuild their cities and their lives.

Out of these contrasts grew the divergent lines of luxury cars. American machines gobbled gas because it was cheap; the European cars had to nibble. Suspension engineers knew American luxury cars would be driven predominantly on wide smooth roads with gentle curves, while their overseas colleagues had to reckon with narrow village streets, Alpine roads and vision-blurring cobblestones. A more specific example: Mercedes-Benz went for years with less than adequate air conditioning, a problem aggravated,

THE DOMESTICS

By Jim Brokaw

Our annual King of the Hill road test has been a pleasant and entertaining little face-off for the last five years between the Cadillac Eldorado and the Lincoln Continental Mark IV.

The Eldo and the Mark IV symbolize more than any other vehicles sold in the U.S. the traditional Great American Dream of "making it," both financially and socially. The Imperial is, of course, a co-equal status symbol, however, the traditional image of the Imperial owner is that of the wealthy who "made it" a hell of a long time ago, and who prefer a little handling with their ride.

All three are big cars with high price tags and a design philosophy of luxurious isolation. Before you condemn them for sheer size (5000 pounds, 18 feet long) you should be aware of their evolution.

In the pre-WW II America, the Great Dream was to own your own home and a Cadillac. We had plenty of space for wide roads and big garages, but we also had some pretty rotten roads that broke up in the freezing winters. We had wide open countryside, but very noisy cities. We didn't have any smog, but an abundance of coal-soot and dust. We had no aristocracy, but a very stratified economic class structure. While we boasted of equal opportunity, we struggled for individuality. Proud of our "masses," we all strove to rise above them. While few people ventured into the "rich" section of town, the "rich" always managed to drive their long, sleek machines where the ordinary folk could see and envy.

The cars for plain folks; Ford, Chevy, and Plymouth, were small, noisy and rough riding. The only thing that could cope with frost heaves and pot holes was a combination of weight and a long wheelbase. Isolation from the road surface was obviously the first requirement of a luxury car.

THE IMPORTS

BMW—Ah, the smell of real leather permeates the 3.0 si. The seats they cover are the most comfortable of the group. The air conditioning didn't fare as well and was less than adequate. Entry and exit are simple, the seat belts among the best. The outside rear view mirror is motor-driven. Note the odds and ends tray on the dash.

JAGUAR—Coventry's redesign of the XJ dash (last year) is a vast improvement over the original. The burled walnut dash panel adds a warmth the German cars lack. Jag has an automatic temperature control and they were thoughtful enough to add a rear seat vent at the back of the center console. Unfortunately, though, the air conditioning broke.

MERCEDES—This is what the well researched interior is wearing. The shift lever knob is even designed so as not to penetrate the average eyeball socket. The seats are harder than many Americans are used to, but most could easily adapt to them. Note, as with the BMW, the complete lack of chrome. Everything has a non-reflective finish.

no doubt, because Stuttgart is at a coolish latitude equivalent to the western border between the U.S. and Canada.

There are a good many other qualifying factors, all meant as an explanation, not an excuse. They make it fruitless to point up how imported luxury cars may be better than the Americans . . . or vice versa. In fact, none is necessarily better, just different.

The very fact that I am writing the European half of this dual test makes it obvious I favor their sort of luxury car. That opinion begins with size. Despite the fact that we, as a country, have had the natural resources and the psychological rationale to build and buy large luxury automobiles, I never could enjoy those massive Cadillacs or Lincolns. I just don't believe you need a Lincoln Continental's 232 total inches and 2½ tons to make an automobile luxurious. The BMW 3.0 si's 195 inches or the Mercedes' 205 inches seem sufficient, particularly considering the interior room achieved within those dimensions.

Then there is interior design. We American's have always put a high price on an automobile's curves and chrome. Europeans, particularly the Germans, have stressed func-

BMW—Another neat display, though this one eliminates the oil pressure gauge. Those four levers to the right of the wheel are the rather confusing heater/vent controls. The a/c buttons are below, above the radio. It is all well thoughtout, but the complete lack of color in the interior gives the BMW a cold, almost unfriendly feeling.

JAGUAR—You certainly can't complain about a lack of instrumentation. The gauges are all simple to read, though the simple steering wheel through which you view them appears to have come out of an economy car. The wide center console cramps the footwell area. Other than that, we all enjoyed the rather American feel of the XJ-6 L.

MERCEDES—We found this instrument panel the easiest to live with, though some claim the one instrument grouping on the left to be confusing. The heating/ventilation/air conditioning system is superlative, once you master the four-lever two-dial controls on the center console. As with Jaguar, the power window controls are on the console.

THE DOMESTICS

ELDORADO—Quilted leather seats, six-way power adjustments for both occupants, reclining seatback for the passenger. Multiple air conditioning outlets ensure an even flow of automatically heated or cooled air to the entire interior. In spite of loops and keepers, the shoulder strap is an obstacle to rear seat entry.

MARK IV—Cut pile carpeting and quilted leather seats are similar to Eldo, but Lincoln shields the dash with a padded cover while Eldo recesses it away from the passenger. Mark IV seat and window controls are both located on the armrest. Stereo speakers are located in bottom door section.

IMPERIAL—If you want to see a seat, that's a seat. Individual compliant seat and back cushions covered with delightfully wrinkled kid glove leather. Imperial places shoulder restraint to the rear of the door opening to fold back out of the rear seat passenger's path. It still gets in the way somewhat.

As roads improved, so did the base cars, bringing Ford, Chevrolet and Plymouth size, isolation and comfort. The mechanics of luxury were available to everyone. Only size, price tag and the mystique of the magic names remained to serve as public notice of "success."

Eldorado, Mark IV, and Imperial; the personal luxury cars, still got the job done to the tune of 40,412, 57,316, and 14,426, units respectively, in 1974, one of the worse sales years in memory.

Approached from the outside, all three domestics present a formidable image of protective mass that invites you to view from a distance rather than saunter up and peer into the window, which is precisely the evolutionary statement our luxury cars have been seeking. Look, but don't touch.

Eldorado is distinctly Cadillac, bearing a strong family resemblance to the de Ville line. Mark IV is longer and sleeker in image. Imperial projects a quite different aspect of being very wide and very strong. Eldo is protective, Mark IV is swift and Imperial is solid, formidably solid. You just don't race an Imperial across an intersection if there is any chance at all of losing.

ELDORADO—Horizontal control display places frequently used auxiliary devices, air conditioning, radio, to the outside, infrequently used devices, cruise control, rear window defog, to the inside. Minimal instrumentation is augmented by top-mounted warning light bar.

MARK IV—Clustered instrument pod is closer to aircraft philosophy. Light colored wood grain veneer is very well executed, forming good background to emphasize control clusters. Steering wheel spokes are cleverly curled away from pod. Wheel mounted speed control is easiest of all to use.

IMPERIAL—Balance of engine instrument gauges, stacked at the left, and warning lights, behind speedometer, is best of the domestics. Push button climate control is easier to use at night than traditional lever control. Tilt-telescope steering wheel is added comfort feature. Vent location could be improved.

171

THE IMPORTS

JAGUAR—Our test car was an XJ-6 L, the last letter signifying the long, 112.8-inch wheelbase, four inches longer than standard. The car has a very graceful look, especially for its size. With the 4.2-liter six, it managed 18.4 secs in a quarter-mile, though its V-12 counterpart would have been the fastest of all. Fuel economy was disappointing—13.3 mpg.

BMW—The 3.0 si looks smaller because it is, with a 106-inch wheelbase. Like all BMWs, it is as much a sporting sedan as a luxury car. The only one of the group available with a manual transmission, it scored best at the track, with a 16.98 quarter-mile time. The three-liter six uses electronic fuel injection giving the car excellent driveability.

MERCEDES—They tell us even the taillight corrugations have a purpose, that being to prevent dirt build-up. The 450SE matches the XJ-6 L's 112-inch wheelbase, though the 450SE has a more purposeful look. The electronically injected V-8 got the car through a quarter-mile in 17.5 secs, but M-B will lower that next year with a 6.9-liter version.

BMW—How very German, the fitted drop-down tool tray in the BMW's trunk. That is standard along with electric windows, air conditioning, the alloy wheels, power steering, leather upholstery, power brakes and one of the first great Becker radios we've heard. Only the metallic paint ($308) and electric outside mirror ($65) were added options.

tion in their designs. There isn't one crease or piece of chrome on the exterior of a 450SE that isn't there for some proven reason. The BMW's design is a little less, shall we say, scientific, but is still meant more to envelope an interior package than just provide visual satisfaction. The XJ-6 L follows that same thinking, if a bit more stylish. It is the refinement of several Jaguar sedan designs from the genius behind all Jaguars, Sir William Lyons.

To the staunch Caddy fan, the imports are plain and lacking in pizzazz, but I happen to prefer their purposeful design. It was architect Louis Sullivan who helped argue that "form follows function" and, for many eyes, that can also mean beauty. It's an old argument. One man finds the egg a package of beauty; the other would rather chrome it. I find the lean, taut concept of the imports preferable to the bulginess of the domestics.

American luxury cars exist, of course, as a display of wealth. In that direction, they do quite well with their interiors. Cadillac, Lincoln and Chrysler tend to utilize soft seats, thick carpets and gadgets by the dozen. All three of our imported luxury test cars are more restrained and have the same basic interior configuration—bucket seats up front separated by a center console with a bench seat in back. They lack the variety of materials and colors offered in American luxury cars, though they offer benefits such as leather seats that are completely covered with leather instead of the more common American mixture of leather and vinyl.

It is obvious that the dashboards of the imports were laid out by experts more concerned with ergonomics than economics. All three have sufficient instrumentation placed straight ahead on very readable dials. The same accessibility applies to all switches and knobs, though both German cars have heating, air conditioning and ventilation controls that take some getting used to. Jaguar's version of automatic temperature control does it quite simply with two dials.

However, the heating and ventilation systems offer another interesting contrast between the domestics and imports. The center of the point is gadgets, one area in which Mercedes, BMW and Jaguar don't match the American cars. The Cad, Lincoln and Imperial all have full automatic

MERCEDES—Our test 450SE included the corporate alloy wheels, though at a premium of $597 per set. That about runs the list of exterior options offered for the car. There is an identical-looking model, the 280S, which shares all the features of the V-8 models, but is powered by a carbureted dual overhead cam six. It is slow, but economical.

THE DOMESTICS

ELDORADO—Blunt front fender caps give the Eldo a fierce countenance at speed. Falling mid-way between the two domestics, Eldo had second best acceleration, second best fuel economy, 14.39 mpg, which isn't bad for 5000 pounds and second best stopping distance. Price, $11,744 was also between the two competitors from Detroit.

MARK IV—Lower belt line profile softens the Mark IV dimensions somewhat. Best in quarter mile acceleration, the Mark was third in fuel economy, 13.27 mpg, and best stop from 30 mph. Price as tested, which includes a moonroof the other two did not have installed, was the highest, $13,631, but less than all three imports.

IMPERIAL—Outwardly flaring side panels impart solid, durable, impregnable image to the Imperial. Lowest priced of the test, $10,530, Imperial achieved best domestic fuel economy, 14.89 mpg, and the shortest stop from 60 mph and best stop from 30 mph. Full sail panel limits rear quarter visibility.

MARK IV—A common option for all three domestic vehicles is a sunroof.

All three curve around their occupants shielding them from the outside. There is no attempt at any image other than isolation. Genuine leather isolation.

All three are replete with illumination front, side and rear. The turn signals light up the side street for 50 feet. Here again, the emphasis is on subtly announcing the arrival of the occupants. You do not have to sneak a peek at the window sticker to be aware that the bottom line is well out of reach of the non-achievers.

Not so with the imports. Unless you happen to know that the BMW is a 3.0 si and what that means, the sight of a near $14,000 price tag on that little car is enough to induce cardiac arrest. All Mercedes look alike, from the outside and they do have a very distinct luxury image so you are already tensed up when you see the big numbers on the Stuttgart greeting card. A Jag is a Jag and if you don't recognize the car on sight, you do know that they are generally parked in wide sweeping driveways near the old man's Cad, somewhere on the other side of town.

Inside our domestics, the name of the game is isolation and environment control. Much of the 5000 pound test weight is used up in sound deadening material to isolate the outside noise. The U.S. is well ahead of the imports in this area, though the Jag does a very good job of keeping the sound out and the silence in.

Although we do not use a decibel meter to measure precisely the sound level, the collective staff ear gives the nod to the Mark IV as the silent one.

All three; Eldorado, Mark IV and Imperial, have leather covered, six-way power seats. The power controls all work with equal facility, but the Mark IV has a power lumbar control that really works. All three have a reclining feature on the passenger seat.

Seats on all are much firmer than in years past, but still yielding and very comfortable. They tend to get a bit squirmy on long trips, but Mercedes has the opposite problem. Their quite firm therapeutic seats are very comfortable on trips in excess of 100 miles, but a little hard on the buns for those short 30-mile commutes.

Instrumentation is sparse on all three with Mark IV having the least and Imperial having the most. All have a full array of warning lights.

Eldo's top mounted digital clock and fuel gauge on either end of the warning light bar is an excellent touch, as are the fender mounted light monitors.

Imperial's instrument and warning cluster is the most conveniently arrayed and gives the most information. Their push button climate control is easiest to use at night.

Imperial's seat leather is "kid glove soft," being superior in the pure sense of elegance to the competition. Eldorado uses the same type of "aged" leather appearance on their door trim.

Mark IV has a very light colored wood grain veneer

ELDORADO—Clever bit of one-ups-manship by Cadillac. They place an additional door handle to the rear of the passenger door, providing a means for the rear seat passenger to exit the vehicle without assistance from the front.

SPECIFICATIONS	BMW 3.0 si	JAGUAR XJ-6 L	MERCEDES-BENZ 450SE
Engine	SOHC in-line six-cylinder	DOHC in-line six-cylinder	SOHC V-8
Bore & Stroke-ins.	3.50 x 3.15	3.62 x 4.17	3.62 x 3.35
Displacement-cu.in./c.c.	182/2980	258/4235	275.8/4520
HP @ RPM	176 @ 5500	162 @ 4750	180 @ 4750
Torque-(lbs.-Ft. @ RPM	185 @ 4500	225 @ 2500	220 @ 3000
Compression Ratio	8.1:1	7.5:1	8:1
Carburetion	electronic fuel injection	Two Zenith-Stromberg carbs	electronic fuel injection
Transmission	four-speed manual manual	three-speed automatic	three-speed automatic
Rear Axle Ratio	3.64:1	3.31:1	3.07:1
Steering Type	ZF power-assisted with ball nut, three-piece track rod	Power-assisted rack and pinion	Power, recirculating ball
Steering Ratio	18.4:1	16.4:1	13.92-14.02
Turning Circle-ft.	35.2	36	38
Wheel Turns (lock-to-lock)	3.5	3.3	2.7
Tires	195/70 HR 14 radials	E70VR 15 radials	205/70-14 radials
Brakes	Disc/Disc	Disc/Disc	Disc/Disc
Front Suspension	Independent—Mac Pherson strut and lower wishbone	Independent—Upper and lower A-arms, coil springs, tube shocks, anti-roll bar.	Independent—upper and lower A-arms, coil springs, tube shocks, anti-roll bar
Rear Suspension	Independent—semi-trailings arm, coil springs, tube shock absorbers	Independent—lower wishbone, fixed length halfshaft, trailing arm, two shock/coil spring units per side	Independent—diagonal trailing arms, coil springs, tube shocks, anti-roll bar
Body/Frame Construction	Unit	Unit	Unit
Wheelbase-in/mm	106/2692.4	112.8/2865.1	112.8/2865.1
Overall Length-in/mm	195/4953.0	194.7/4945.3	205.5/5219.7
Width-in/mm	68.9/1750.0	69.7/1771.6	70.5/1790.7
Front Track-in/mm	58.3/1480.8	58/1473.2	60.0/1524
Rear Track-in/mm	57.9/1470.6	58.6/1488.4	59.3/1506.2
Height-in/mm	57.1/1450.3	54.1/1374.1	56.1/1424.9
Weight as Tested-lbs.	3395	4130	4100 (advertised weight)
Storage Capacity cu.ft/cm3	22.8	17.0	17.7
Fuel Capacity-gals/liters	20.8/87.9	24/100.8	28.8/121.7
Oil Capacity-qts/liters	6.6/6.9	8.75/9.1	7.9/8.3
Base Price (West Coast)	$13,831	$13,100	$17,863
Price as Tested $	$14,347	$13,100	$19,166

PERFORMANCE			
Acceleration			
0-30 mph	3.8	4.5	4.5
0-40 mph	5.5	6.5	6.6
0-50 mph	8.1	9.6	8.8
0-60 mph	10.9	12.9	11.1
Standing Start ¼-mile Elapsed Time (sec.)	16.98	18.41	17.55
Speed (mph)	83.2	76.5	79.9
Passing Speeds 40-60 mph	4.0	7.4	5.8
50-70 mph	5.6	8.5	7.2
Stopping Distance (ft) 30-0 mph	25.9	29.7	29.7
60-0 mph	147.2	140.2	131.2
Fuel Mileage	18.4	15.3	18.7

Speedometer Error Indicated Speed	40	50	60	40	50	60	40	50	60
True Speed	37.8	47.1	56.4	40.1	50.3	60.0	35.7	46.3	56.3

temperature control . . . just set and forget, if you will. Now I personally find it more impressive that you can cool the driver while warming the passenger in a 450SE, but as a buying country we love the complete climate control. Jaguar has now followed the American lead with "Automatic Temperature Sensing and Control" and Mercedes is working on it.

Our love of gimmickry shows up throughout the cars. There are "Moonroofs," six-way power seats (you can achieve the same variety of adjustment in the imports, but must do it manually), lights that shut off automatically, theft alarms and the tilt steering wheel. One reason for the lack of such "fun" in the imports can be seen in the angry answer of a Mercedes engineer when asked when they would have a tilt steering wheel, "We spend years to determine the perfect steering wheel position and now you want to change it?"

Apparently, the same attitude that keeps the cars lean and practical makes such options seem, well, frivolous. That same feeling puts less importance on such American necessities as total sound isolation and you would find all three imported luxury cars have a somewhat higher interior noise level than the domestics.

While the American luxury cars have sophisticated "luxury systems," the imports put the same emphasis on their mechanical features. Cadillac, Lincoln and Chrysler use overhead valve V-8s bolted to automatic transmissions for their luxury cars. The basic suspensions are no more sophisticated than those under an intermediate sedan. The imports, on the other hand, are a veritable festival of engineering. All have four-wheel independent suspension, though each shows a slightly different approach to the subject. The Jaguar has a dual overhead cam six (with an overhead cam V-12 in the identical-looking XJ-12), the BMW has a fuel-injected overhead cam six, while Mercedes uses the same sort of induction system on their 450SE's overhead cam V-8. Those refined mechanicals are one of the big selling points of this genre of car, though they do contribute to the car's prices and, in the case of Mercedes and Jaguar, add to the company's service headaches.

Again, it is a difference in need leading to a difference in philosophy. The Europeans need long range, high speed cruising ability, while the Americans prefer the brute torque to satisfy our love of acceleration and a wide variety of power-draining accessories.

The direction of their respective sophistication is most obvious when driving the cars—the Americans are best for luxuriating, the Europeans for driving. The Mercedes has the hardest feel of three, both in the seat and the suspension. It is only after at least 100 miles of driving that the firm support of the 450SE's seat softens and you begin to understand why it is there. The BMW is a much softer riding car that handles almost as well as the 450SE, but takes on a disconcerting lean in doing so. The Jaguar is just the short of the BMW's handling potential (though still quite good) and the combination of its seat, ride, handling and such factors and the feel of the brakes and steering give one the feeling that the XJ-6 would feel the most familiar to the average American. In fact, in many ways the Jaguar feels as though it could have been designed and built in Detroit. What comes home in all three is a well defined statement of how they feel about the usual compromise of ride versus handling. I have to agree with their staying on the handling side.

While we preferred the Mercedes ($19,100) it is also

CONTINUED ON PAGE 176

which is very well executed, brightening the interior considerably.

Eldorado falls short of traditional Cadillac excellence in their obviously substitute wood paneling.

Imperial relies on darkness and shade to put you in mind of multi-roomed stately old mansions with well polished mahogany or repeatedly varnished dark oak. Again, Imperial's image of established wealth.

Eldorado takes the blue ribbon for the extra touch with their dual handled doors. The rear mounted door handle to permit the rear seat passenger to exit without assistance from the front.

All three have optional sunroof or moonroof ceiling panels. All three have optional crushed velour velvet interiors whose elegance and sheer opulence can be exceeded only by something that moves and breathes by itself.

Interior appointments are two-thirds of what these cars are all about. Since this is not the market for nickel nursing and budget checking, the only decision that has to be made is, are you a leather person, a leather and cloth person, or a crushed velour person. You select your environment and how much of it you want to control.

Mechanically, there are more similarities than contrasts in the three domestics. All have large displacement, high torque, overhead valve engines. All have three-speed automatic transmissions. Imperial and Mark IV have conventional front engine rear drive configuration, the Eldo has a front engine front drive arrangment. Eldorado has front wheel disc rear wheel drum brakes, both Mark IV and Imperial have four-wheel disc brakes. All have an anti-skid feature. Eldo and Imperial utilize front torsion bar suspension, Mark IV employs front coil springs. Eldo and Mark IV have coils in the rear, Imperial uses leaf springs.

Ride and handling is the area where the diverging philosophies of the imports and domestics are most starkly contrasted. The Europeans place a priority on handling. The imports are closer to sports sedans utilized for long trips at high speeds on motorways and autobahns, on winding mountain roads and hedge-lined country lanes. The domestics emphasize ride. The prime difference is that the size of Germany and Britain (U.K.) are considerably smaller with much less contrast in terrain. Conversely every car built in the U.S. has to be saleable in every part of the U.S. from the narrow cramped roads of New England to the frost ravaged secondary streets of the upper Midwest, to the Rocky Mountains, through the Southwestern desert to the eternal dampness of the Northwest. If you expect to sell the same car in all areas, it has to be a compromise.

The choice was an isolated ride. It doesn't matter what condition the road is in, you won't be disturbed by it. Smooth they are, handle they don't, except in the strictest interpretation of the term.

All three can negotiate any curve, taken at a sane speed with plenty of lead time. All three can make an emergency lane change at freeway speeds without losing control.

On the handling course it becomes obvious that Eldorado's front drive set up is to eliminate the drivetrain tunnel. There isn't enough power to really pull the car out of a turn with the front drive.

Eldo exhibits pronounced understeer in an extreme turn and the isolation the produces the smooth ride also diminished road feel.

Mark IV, being a bit lighter up front, has less understeer in a corner, but not much less. It did have a bit more roll stability in the extreme, and a bit more exiting power.

Imperial was the best handling of the three with the most roll stability.

Braking is a testimonial to the engineers of all three manufacturers. Bringing 5000 pounds of anything to a smooth stop from 60 mph is a chore. All three do it well, but the brakes on the Imperial are a masterpiece. We made

CONTINUED ON PAGE 176

SPECIFICATIONS	ELDORADO	MARK IV	IMPERIAL
Engine	OHV V-8	OHV V-8	OHV V-8
Bore & Stroke-ins.	4.30x4.304	4.36x3.85	4.32x3.75
Displacement-cu. in./c.c.	500/8000	460/7360	440/7040
HP @ RPM	190@3600	223@4000	215@4000
Torque-(lbs.-ft@RPM	360@2000	366@2600	330@3200
Compression Ratio	8.5:1	8.0:1	8.2:1
Carburetion	4v	4v	4v
Transmission	Three-Speed Automatic	Three-Speed Automatic	Three-Speed Automatic
Rear Axle Ratio	2.73:1	3.00:1	2.71:1
Steering Type	Recirculating Ball (power)	Recirculating Ball (power)	Recirculating Ball (power)
Steering Ratio	20.0:1 to 16.2:1	21.8:1	18.9:1
Turning Circle-ft.	NA	43.3	44.78
Wheel Turns (lock-to-lock)	3.5	3.99	3.5
Tires	Uniroyal Radials LR78-15	Michelin Radials 230-15	Goodyear Polysteel Radial LR78-15
Brakes	Disc/Drum power	Disc/Disc power	Disc/Disc power
Front Suspension	TORSION BAR/SHOCKS/STABILIZER	COILS/SHOCKS/STABILIZER	TORSION BAR/SHOCKS/STABILIZER
Rear Suspension	COILS/SHOCKS/STABILIZER automatic level control	4-LINK/COILS/SHOCKS/STABILIZER	LEAVES/SHOCKS
Body/Frame Construction	PERIMETER	SEPARATE FRAME	UNITIZED W/ ISOLATED SUB FRAME
Wheelbase-in./mm	126.3/3157.5	120.4/3010.0	124.0/3100.0
Overall Length-in./mm	224.1/5602.5	228.0/5700.0	231.0/5775.0
Width-in/mm	79.8/1995.0	79.8/1995.0	79.7/1992.5
Front Track-in./mm	63.7/1592.5	62.9/1572.5	64.0/1600.0
Rear Track-in./mm	63.6/1590.0	62.8/1570.0	63.7/1592.5
Height-in./mm	54.1/1352.5	53.3/1332.5	54.5/1362.5
Weight as Tested-lbs.	5290	5430	5185
Storage Capacity cu.ft/cm3	12.5/1296	14.4/1493	19.6/2032.1
Fuel Capacity-gals./liters	27/108	26.5/106	25.0/100
Oil Capacity-qts./liters	6.0/6.0/ (with filter)	4.0/4.0	4.0/4.0
Base Price	$9935	$11,082	$8698
Price as Tested	$11,744	$13,632	$10,531
PERFORMANCE			
Acceleration 0-30 mph	3.9	4.3	4.2
0-40 mph	5.8	6.3	6.2
0-50 mph	8.2	8.7	9.6
0-60 mph	10.9	11.2	12.7
Standing Start ¼-mile Elapsed Time (sec.)	17.60	17.56	17.77
Speed (mph)	78.19	80.50	79.92
Passing Speeds 40-60 mph	5.8	6.5	6.0
50-70 mph	7.6	7.4	7.5
Stopping Distance (ft.) 30-0 mph	34'1	29'8	35'11
60-0 mph	159'8	160'3	134'2
Fuel Mileage	14.39	13.27	14.89
Speedometer Error Indicated Speed	40 50 60	40 50 60	40 50 60
True Speed	40.12 49.86 59.84	40.55 50.87 60.97	38.39 46.92 57.39

THE IMPORTS

CONTINUED FROM PAGE 174

some $4500 more expensive than the BMW or Jaguar. Consider that fact and the 450SE and 3.0 si are on about the same level, with the XJ-6 L (at $1000 less than the BMW) a close third.

Of course that is still a lot of money compared to the American cars, even with all their options in place. So every time you see a BMW, Mercedes or Jaguar you are seeing another overt blow against American luxury cars.

There is the new option, Cadillac's Seville. While obviously a domestic, it doesn't really fit into either of the catagories we've worked up here. The Seville mixes the exterior and interior style of the domestics with the size of the imports. In fact, it is almost the dimensional twin of the 450SE both inside and out. The Seville stays more on the ride side of the inevitable ride-handling compromise, not achieving the precise handling of the imports. At that, it is still leagues ahead of its larger compatriots from Cadillac, Lincoln and Chrysler.

Add to this the larger-than-normal options list that Cadillac bestowed upon the Seville and you go a long way to honestly bridge the gap between the import and domestic luxury cars. There are still hard line advocates on both sides that will refuse to admit the qualities of the Seville, but they are playing a snob's game.

Any observer can see many of the economic conditions that caused Europe to build smaller luxury cars—expensive gasoline and precious resources—are now affecting us too. In the end, the more compact luxury car looms as the reasonable alternative. ■

THE DOMESTICS

CONTINUED FROM PAGE 175

straight, consistent smooth stops shorter than any of the six cars except the Mercedes, which is outweighed by the Imperial by a 1000 pounds. And they were close enough to cover with a blanket.

Imperial is the best handling domestic and has the firmest ride. Eldorado is beautifully engineered to be driven by a person with slow reflexes and a tendency to overcontrol in perfect safety. Mark IV lies in between. None of the three will lure you up into the mountain switchbacks, but they are smooth as silk on the flat.

The two totally divergent philosophies have clashed head to head in Cadillac's new Seville. I can only add my concurrence to John Lamm's observations. We did not have the opportunity to give the car a full test, but a driving impression clearly indicates that the jump toward handling has been a long one. The Seville is a truly phenomenal balance of ride and handling in the achievement of a very reassuring agility without harshness. The kind of a car that will be comfortable on both the short hauls and the long ones.

We shall reserve final judgment until the complete test, but every indication is that the new king has just been born. The king of both hills.

Imperial, which performed remarkably well in all areas, has become the first victim of economic uncertainty and changing tastes. It is slated to become an option of the Chrysler New Yorker line for 1976. Perhaps what is passing into the archives is not the car, but the way we say, ''I have made it!■

ROAD TEST
continued from page 167

ing is something else. Parallel parking should be used as a last resort.

Fleetwood's split-level instrument panel displays the idiot lights in a single line across the top of the dash. It stands as a statement of the times that the only two gauges Cadillac deems worthy of mounting on the top row are the fuel gauge and the digital clock, both of which glower like angry watchdogs at night, constantly reminding you how much of each remains.

The one sore spot that greets the eye is the plastic Laurel-wreath wood panel. It doesn't have the slightest resemblance to wood, and it's tacky.

The Lincoln Continental turned out to be the most comfortable of the lot by a consensus opinion of the staff. The largest single factor was the seats. They are the best combination of support and

comfort. The ride was also the smoothest, but not by very much. Handling is quite satisfactory for what is envisioned as normal use. We·un-monied folk can only speculate, but even under bold treatment, the roll moment was slow and steady.

Continental's phony mohair, which is another form of the very popular velour, lends an air of established wealth to the interior.

The excellent stereo radio requires a disconcerting reach to the knobs. The slender turn signal stalk serves as the tilt-wheel control rod. It is a chore to find the narrow slot, releasing the wheel lock. While the dash contains most everything, alternator, fuel, temperature, oil pressure, and clock by Tiffany, they are not clustered in any specific arrangement. In condolence to the dash, Lincoln's horizontal-rod speed indicator is much easier to read than the traditional dial.

We also found the seat controls in the arm-rest panel to be less satisfactory than Cadillac's and Imperial's side-of-seat location.

We suffered a couple of interlock failures with the Continental's passenger side, but thankfully, both competitor's interlocks functioned without difficulty.

The durability of the Big Three—and we do mean big is virtually guaranteed as living reminders to us all that the good life is still out there somewhere, and if J. Dividend Residual can make it, so can I.

Not that it really matters to you and I, but the best of class really has to be the Lincoln. Imperial handles best and has the best dash panel, Cadillac is the best compromise for ride and handling with good ergonomics, but Lincoln is the most comfortable, and comfort is the name of the game. Don't be chagrined, you can be seen riding in any of them. ■